Advance

Student Involvement ...es

D0732799

"This book is an important contribution ... ... :nt and outcomes. Student participant responses in my research indic: :d that men and women of color, felt apart from the student life into which they were being socialized—at best, they felt as though they were guests in someone else's house. The editors and authors of *Student Involvement & Academic Outcomes: Implications for Diverse College Student Populations* provide much-needed insights from multiple perspectives to further the reader's understanding of this phenomenon and to promote actions to address it."

Caroline Sotello Viernes Turner, Professor, California State University, Sacramento and Past President, Association for the Study of Higher Education

"*Student Involvement & Academic Outcomes: Implications for Diverse College Student Populations* makes a valuable contribution that is substantive, extends knowledge, and has the potential to significantly influence policy and practice in higher education. This book offers a compelling combination of theoretical keystones and researched-based practices to help faculty and practitioners understand the effect and consequences of particular engagement activities and the diverse populations we serve. The practical strategies offered are exceedingly helpful as are the cautions that identify practices that may hinder the academic achievement of diverse student groups."

Raechele L. Pope, Associate Professor, University of Buffalo

"If you care deeply about student success, especially among students from historically marginalized communities, this is an essential book. Donald Mitchell, Jr. and his colleagues paint a clear picture of what we need to know about creating and sustaining environments where students will flourish. Supporting and advancing the latest research, these pages are full of practical counsel for strengthening colleges and universities and unearthing the greatest potential of our communities of diverse students. What makes this book especially important is the way it challenges previously held, sometimes inaccurate, assumptions about the best educational practices for students from a wide variety of backgrounds. The authors guide readers to better pathways for influencing and advancing student success and learning. This is the ideal book to read and discuss with colleagues and your students, who will no doubt be the beneficiaries."

Frank Shushok Jr., Executive Editor, *About Campus* and Senior Associate Vice President for Student Affairs and Associate Professor of Higher Education, Virginia Tech

Student Involvement
& Academic Outcomes

Virginia Stead, H.B.A., B.Ed., M.Ed., Ed.D.
GENERAL EDITOR

VOL. 2

———————

The Equity in Higher Education Theory, Policy, & Praxis series
is part of the Peter Lang Education list.
Every volume is peer reviewed and meets
the highest quality standards for content and production.

———————

PETER LANG
New York • Bern • Frankfurt • Berlin
Brussels • Vienna • Oxford • Warsaw

Student Involvement & Academic Outcomes

IMPLICATIONS FOR DIVERSE COLLEGE STUDENT POPULATIONS

Donald Mitchell Jr., Krista M. Soria, Elizabeth A. Daniele, John A. Gipson
EDITORS

Foreword by Robert D. Reason | Afterword by D. Jason DeSousa

PETER LANG
New York • Bern • Frankfurt • Berlin
Brussels • Vienna • Oxford • Warsaw

Library of Congress Cataloging-in-Publication Data

Student involvement & academic outcomes:
implications for diverse college student populations /
edited by Donald Mitchell, Jr., Krista M. Soria, Elizabeth A. Daniele, John A. Gipson.
pages cm. — (Equity in higher education theory, policy, & praxis; vol. 2)
Includes bibliographical references.
1. Minority college students—United States.
2. Minority college students—Research—United States.
3. Education, Higher—Social aspects—United States.
4. Cultural pluralism—United States. I. Mitchell, Donald, Jr., editor of compilation.
II. Title: Student involvement and academic outcomes.
LC3727.S78   378.1'9820973—dc23   2014040429
ISBN 978-1-4331-2620-8 (hardcover)
ISBN 978-1-4331-2619-2 (paperback)
ISBN 978-1-4539-1467-0 (e-book)
ISSN 2330-4502

Bibliographic information published by **Die Deutsche Nationalbibliothek**.
Die Deutsche Nationalbibliothek lists this publication in the "Deutsche
Nationalbibliografie"; detailed bibliographic data are available
on the Internet at http://dnb.d-nb.de/.

The paper in this book meets the guidelines for permanence and durability
of the Committee on Production Guidelines for Book Longevity
of the Council of Library Resources.

© 2015 Peter Lang Publishing, Inc., New York
29 Broadway, 18th floor, New York, NY 10006
www.peterlang.com

Printed in the United States of America

Table of Contents

Illustrations

Foreword

ROBERT D. REASON

It is an easy critique of higher education student success research and theory to simply state that certain populations of students were excluded from the sample upon which the research was conducted or the theory was normed. Certainly, researchers and theorists who created the foundation of our understanding of student success studied the students to whom they had access, often White, middle- to upper-class, and primarily male students. The tendency to only study this majority population (at the time) led to several pernicious results, including the tendency to normalize the experiences of the majority, the exclusion of or dismissal of experiences of nonmajority students, and the unexamined assumption that all students do—or at least should—have the same experiences as these students.

Tinto's (1987, 1993) model of student departure illustrates this point. By the time Tierney (1999) and Rendon, Jalomo, and Nora (2000) offered their critiques of Tinto's model, the model had already achieved "near paradigmatic status" (Berger & Braxton, 1998, p. 104). It is important to note that the process of model critique, reexamination, and re-articulation demonstrated by the scholarly interactions of Tinto and his critics offers an example of the power of uncovering the unexamined assumptions of our work. Tierney, as well as Rendon and her colleagues, identified a limited attention to the experiences of nontraditional students, the assumption that students needed to sever ties with home communities in order to successfully join their new college community, and what they viewed as a deficit perspective in Tinto's original theory as problems with Tinto's original model. Tinto revised his original model in substantive ways to emphasize the importance of classroom communities for nontraditional college students (Tinto, 1998) and the influence of students' home cultures in their success in higher education (Tinto, 1998, 2000).

Pascarella and Terenzini (1998), while preparing for the second volume of *How College Affects Students* (2005), offered higher education researchers some advice about studying college students in the twenty-first century. Of particular importance to these two preeminent scholars of college student success were the necessary changes to scholarship brought about by "the changing undergraduate student population" (1998, p. 151). Pascarella and Terenzini called on researchers to explore the conditional effects of college, that is, to ask the question: How might students from different social groups [race, ethnicity, socioeconomic or generational status] be affected differently by the educational interventions currently employed? Certainly, researchers have heeded the call to explore more deeply the different ways that college programs, interventions, and environments affect students differently, adding nuance to our understanding of college student success.

Although Pascarella and Terenzini (1998) approached their recommendation from a quantitative paradigm, suggesting the inclusion of social group–based interaction terms in statistical analysis that included a diverse student sample, other researchers have pushed our understanding of student success through focus on previously understudied populations, often using qualitative techniques. Harper's (2009) work on high-achieving African American male college students is a powerful example of the understanding that can be achieved through in-depth, qualitative analysis of the experiences of a single population of students.

Harper's (2009) work has spurred other researchers to explore student success as defined and achieved by diverse college students, but it has also changed the manner in which many of us approach the study of college-student success. Harper's work builds upon the perspective of community cultural wealth, as defined by Yosso (2005), and challenges the deficit perspective of much early student-success research. Yosso's work, as well as Harper's, requires higher education scholars to think differently about the strengths found in communities from which traditionally underrepresented and underserved students come and to recognize the capital found in family units, the acquired knowledge and skills necessary to resist constant microaggressions and maintain aspirations for success, and the ability to use existing knowledge to navigate an unfamiliar system.

The editors and authors of this volume, *Student Involvement and Academic Outcomes: Implications for Diverse College Student Populations*, add to this important conversation and push it further. The various chapters in this book reexamine the foundational understandings of student success in higher education, asking questions about "near-paradigmatic" understandings such as the effects of engagement on students' success and how those effects might be different for different groups of students. The authors push readers to look more closely at the unique effects of educational interventions, campus environments, and non-college-related activities (such as off-campus work) for different groups of students. And, finally, and perhaps most important, the authors challenge higher education researchers and practitioners to reconsider the strengths inherent in all students, regardless of (or more appropriately because of) the community from which they come.

The authors in this volume remind us that attracting diverse students to higher education institutions is not enough, but we also must focus attention on retention and success of all our students. They remind us that involvement in the interventions we have designed to facilitate student success may not be enough, but the quality of that involvement is essential and very likely different for different groups of students. Building upon the work of the foundational scholars in our field, the authors in this volume remind us of the need to continually reevaluate our unexamined assumptions so that we can best serve the students currently on our campuses.

Robert D. Reason
Iowa State University
Ames, Iowa

REFERENCES

Berger, J. B., & Braxton, J. M. (1998). Revising Tinto's interactionalist theory of student departure through theory elaboration: Examining the role of organizational attributes in the persistence process. *Research in Higher Education, 39*(2), 103–119.

Harper, S. R. (2009). Niggers no more: A critical race counternarrative on Black male student achievement at predominantly White colleges and universities. *International Journal of Qualitative Studies in Education, 22*(6), 697–712.

Pascarella, E. T., & Terenzini, P. T. (1998). Studying college students in the 21st century: Meeting new challenges. *The Review of Higher Education, 21*, 151–165.

Pascarella, E. T., & Terenzini, P. T. (2005). *How college affects students: A third decade of research* (Vol. 2). San Francisco, CA: Jossey-Bass.

Rendón, L., Jalomo, R., & Nora, A. (2000). Theoretical considerations in the study of minority student retention in higher education. In J. M. Braxton (Ed.), *Rethinking the departure puzzle: New theory and research on college student retention* (pp. 127–156). Nashville, TN: Vanderbilt University Press.

Tierney, W. G. (1999). Models of minority college-going and retention: Cultural integrity versus cultural suicide. *Journal of Negro Education, 68*(1), 80–91.

Tinto, V. (1987). *Leaving college: Rethinking the causes and cures of student attrition*. Chicago, IL: University of Chicago Press.

Tinto, V. (1993). *Leaving college: Rethinking the causes and cures of student attrition* (2nd ed). Chicago, IL: University of Chicago Press.

Tinto, V. (1998). Colleges as communities: Taking research on student persistence seriously. *Review of Higher Education, 21*(2), 167–177.

Tinto, V. (2000). Linking learning and leaving: Exploring the role of the college classroom in student departure. In J. M. Braxton (Ed.), *Rethinking the departure puzzle: New theory and research on college student retention* (pp. 81–94). Nashville, TN: Vanderbilt University Press.

Yosso, T. J. (2005). Whose culture has capital? A critical race theory discussion of community cultural wealth. *Race Ethnicity and Education, 8*(1), 69–91.

Acknowledgments

We would like to thank those who made the publication of this text possible. First, we thank all of the chapter authors who helped shape this volume through their writings. Second, we thank Dr. Robert Reason for contributing the Foreword and Dr. D. Jason DeSousa for contributing the Afterword. Third, we thank Dr. Virginia Stead, our series editor, for investing in our vision for the text. Fourth, we thank Chris Myers, Stephen Mazur, Bernadette Shade, and Phyllis Korper—all at Peter Lang—for all that they brought to the production of this volume. Finally, we thank a host of family, friends, and colleagues, whose love and support keep us going each day.

Introduction

KRISTA M. SORIA, JOHN A. GIPSON AND
DONALD MITCHELL JR.

In 2010, there were just over 18 million undergraduate students enrolled in colleges and universities across the United States (U.S. Department of Education, 2012). Of that total, 60.5% were White, 13.8% were African American/Black, 11.5% were Hispanic American/Latino/a, 6.3% were Asian/Pacific Islander, and less than 1% were Native American/Alaskan Native (the remaining percentage of students identifying as international; U.S. Department of Education, 2012). As recently as 2009, the six-year college graduation rates for African American, Hispanic American/Latino/a, and Native American students at four-year institutions were 39%, 49%, and 38%, respectively, which lagged behind the respective graduation rates of 61% and 69% for White and Asian/Pacific Islander students (U.S. Department of Education, 2012). In addition, higher education achievement gaps exist for first-generation college and/or low-income students. For example, in 2005, only 54% of low-income students went directly to college compared to an 81% rate for higher-income students (Engle & Tinto, 2008). First-generation, low-income college students are four times more likely to drop out of college than middle- to high-income, non-first-generation college students and the national six-year graduation rate for low-income students was 11% in 2005 compared to a 55% graduation rate for their more advantaged peers (Engle & Tinto, 2008).

DeAngelo, Franke, Hurtado, Pryor, and Tran (2011) found that first-generation students and members of underrepresented racial populations graduate from college at lower rates across institutional types compared to their White and

Asian/Pacific Islander counterparts. While Asian/Pacific Islanders as a monolithic group appear to be doing well academically, disaggregating this diverse population proves that many students are, in fact, underrepresented and struggling, just as other "recognized" underrepresented populations (Chang, 2011; Museus, 2011). Obtaining a college degree is often viewed as a critical component of upward social mobility; however, first-generation college students, students from underrepresented racial minority backgrounds, and students from lower- or working-class backgrounds are less likely to be eligible to choose a four-year college, enroll, attend, and persist to graduation regardless of their academic ability than their counterparts from higher-income families or those who are not the first in their families to attend or graduate from college (Astin, 1993; Astin & Oseguera, 2004; Cabrera, Burkhum, & La Nasa, 2005; Engle & O'Brien, 2007; McDonough, 1997; Pascarella & Terenzini, 1991, 2005; Tinto, 2006; Walpole, 2007). For students from underrepresented minority, low-income, or first-generation college backgrounds, the effects of these disparities in educational attendance and attainment can yield many negative long-term outcomes.

Disparities in degree attainment rates between students from historically underrepresented backgrounds can perpetuate socioeconomic differences, causing greater "gaps between the 'haves' and 'have nots'" (Dickbert-Conlin & Rubenstein, 2007, p. 1) and denying students from lower-income families the wealth of opportunities provided to students from higher-income families (Mortenson, 2010). Concerns that colleges and universities are "reproducing social advantage instead of serving as an engine of mobility" (Leonhardt, 2004, p. A1) are renewing calls for scholarship to suggest ways to enhance higher education degree attainment rates among students from underrepresented backgrounds, including research related to the programmatic measures in which higher education institutions can invest to promote students' success. In addition, researchers have sought to better understand underrepresented students' experiences that may prohibit students from achieving their educational goals. For example, Engle and O'Brien (2007) note that low-income students are more likely to delay entry into postsecondary education, enter two-year institutions, work full-time, and stop in and out of college. Berkner, He, and Cataldi (2002) describe low-income students as more likely to attend less selective public institutions, which tend to have fewer economic resources, serve students with greater academic and financial needs, and have lower overall graduation rates. Low-income students are also more likely to earn a nontraditional high school credential (such as a GED), often do not enter college immediately following high school, and are less likely to attend college full time (King, 2005; U.S. Government Accountability Office, 2007). These factors place students from underrepresented backgrounds at greater disadvantages for college completion.

A goal of President Barack Obama's agenda is to have the United States become the most highly college-educated nation in the world by the year 2020

(Mitchell & Daniele, in press). Soon after the President announced this goal, educational foundations like the Lumina Foundation and the Bill and Melinda Gates Foundation joined President Obama's education initiative. Niemann and Maruyama (2005) suggest that racial and ethnic diversity in higher education is a matter of national need as demographics shift, and we suggest the same for first-generation college and low-income students. Ultimately, to reach President Obama's goal and improve the economic prosperity of the United States, postsecondary outcomes for diverse college student populations must improve.

In summary, even as access to higher education has widened considerably over the last century, diverse college students (i.e., first-generation, low-income, and racial minorities) face greater challenges regarding their access to college, choice of college, sense of belonging, and success in graduating from college (Choy, 2001; Fischer, 2007; Hossler, Schmit, & Vesper, 1999; Karabel & Astin, 1975; McDonough, 1997; Mauk & Jones, 2006; Mortenson, 2007; Pascarella & Terenzini, 2005; Paulsen & St. John, 2002; Smith, 2009; Walpole, 2007). According to Rendón, Jalomo, and Nora (2011):

> While traditional theories of student retention and involvement have been useful in providing a foundation for the study of persistence, they need to be taken further, as much more work needs to be done to uncover race, class, and gender issues (among others) that impact retention for diverse students in diverse institutions. (p. 244)

Perhaps further documentation of ways to support diverse student populations could improve postsecondary outcomes. We propose that one area of emphasis might include documenting effective ways to involve underrepresented and diverse college students.

INVOLVEMENT IN HIGHER EDUCATION

Several decades' worth of scholarship in higher education has affirmed the positive benefits of college students' involvement in their respective colleges and universities (Astin, 1993; Kuh et al., 2010; Pascarella & Terenzini, 1991, 2005). For example, Tinto's (1993) paradigmatic retention theory identifies the importance of students' participation in formal extracurricular activities and informal peer group interactions in predicting students' social integration—a factor which, in turn, predicts students' institutional commitment. Pascarella and Terenzini's (1991, 2005) comprehensive review of this subject suggests that students' interactions with peers and faculty, fraternity and sorority affiliations, intercollegiate athletics involvement, community service participation, diversity experiences, work responsibilities, and on-campus residence status are positively associated with their learning (e.g., critical thinking and writing skills). Kuh and colleagues

(2010) highlighted institutions that documented effective engagement practices (or DEEP institutions), which includes practices such as study abroad, undergraduate research, and living-learning communities. Astin's (1993) comprehensive study of undergraduate college students found that several types of involvement were positively associated with students' grade point averages (GPAs) after the effects of input and environmental characteristics were controlled. Some forms of involvement included tutoring other students, number of hours per week spent studying, participating in internships or study abroad, and number of hours per week spent talking with faculty outside of class. Several scholars have challenged these foundational studies, as the research does not always fully explain the experiences of students from diverse or underrepresented experiences (Fischer, 2007; Guiffrida, 2006; Mayo, Murguia, & Padilla, 1995; Pascarella & Terenzini, 2005; Thayer, 2000). This suggests further complexities underlying all-encompassing involvement strategies and the various associated academic outcomes for certain activities.

Within the growing literature knowledge base regarding the many benefits of student involvement in higher education, gaps still exist about the potential benefits of involvement for diverse college students' academic success in higher education. Researchers who have previously examined the benefits of diverse students' involvement in higher education have received relatively mixed results. For example, while broader theories suggest students' involvement on campus increases students' institutional commitment and social integration, the nature of the involvement, whether formal or informal, within social networks of peers from similar backgrounds, or among off-campus connections all have varying effects on diverse students' academic achievement (Fischer, 2007). As colleges and universities grow increasingly diverse, and the number of students from diverse backgrounds continues to climb, new scholarship is needed to investigate the relationships between "nontraditional" students' involvement in a variety of activities and subsequent academic outcomes. Studies about students' academic achievements are important, as they can yield new insights into specific involvement opportunities that could leverage diverse college students' persistence and graduation rates.

REFRAMING INVOLVEMENT

Astin's (1993) comprehensive study measured five broad categories of involvement: (1) academic involvement (e.g., attending classes, studying); (2) involvement with faculty (e.g., conducting research with faculty); (3) involvement with student peers (e.g., fraternity or sorority membership, intercollegiate athletics); (4) involvement in work (e.g., working full time or part time); and (5) other forms of involvement (e.g., exercising, participating in religious services). Astin broadly suggests that the effect of college on students depends upon the length of exposure in addition to the intensity of exposure.

Applied to college student involvement, but with a bit of a twist, we propose that the length of time in which students are involved in an experience is an important factor in predicting the outcome, as is the quality of the involvement experience. These two separate factors are likely interrelated and difficult to discern from each other; for example, we hypothesize that the longer students are involved in an experience, the more opportunities there are for interpersonal relationships to develop, for deep reflection to occur, and for leadership and promotion opportunities to arise—all of which may carry great significance for students. More directly, we argue length and quality both matter, and might matter independently of each other for different populations. We also acknowledge the importance of examining a greater range of involvement activities, programs, and opportunities in which students may be involved in higher education, including leadership experiences, employment, connections to families and home communities, and highly enriching educational practices. Further, we believe it is important to examine involvement through an "academic outcomes–based" lens; ultimately, any activity a student is involved in has an effect on academic outcomes and, thus, these activities and involvements should be documented and understood to improve postsecondary outcomes, particularly for diverse student populations.

OUTCOMES AND ORGANIZATION OF THIS VOLUME

This volume furthers the literature base related to the academic achievement benefits of involvement for diverse college students. Specifically, this text aims to offer evidence regarding the academic benefits and drawbacks of involvement for diverse college students. Therefore, the text is organized into the following categories:

- Theoretical and Research Advancements
- High-impact Involvement
- Student Organization Involvement
- Institutional Involvement
- Employment
- Family and Friends

Our aim is to:

- Improve scholarly discourse surrounding involvement and engagement by explicitly linking involvement to academic achievement (i.e., GPA, graduation rates, persistence) through theory, research, and practice.

- Document research-based practices to help institutions and researchers gauge the effect of certain involvement and engagement practices within various institutional contexts.
- Highlight practices that may hinder academic achievement for diverse student groups.
- Offer successful practical strategies that can be easily leveraged within colleges and universities to enhance underrepresented students' academic success.

In bringing together the authors of this volume, we believe this collection will help improve the experiences of diverse students in U.S. higher education contexts, and help advance higher education as it becomes increasingly and complexly diverse.

REFERENCES

Astin, A. W. (1993). *What happens in college? Four critical years revisited.* San Francisco, CA: Jossey-Bass.

Astin, A. W., & Oseguera, L. (2004). The declining "equity" of American higher education. *Review of Higher Education, 27*(3), 321–341.

Berkner, L., He, S., & Cataldi, E. F. (2002). *Descriptive summary of 1995–96 beginning postsecondary students: Six years later.* Washington, DC: National Center for Education Statistics.

Cabrera, A. F., Burkum, K. R., & La Nasa, S. M. (2005). Pathways to a four-year degree: Determinants of transfer and degree completion. In A. Seidman (Ed.), *College student retention: A formula for student success.* Westport, CT: ACE/Praeger.

Chang, M. (2011). Asian American and Pacific Islander millennial students at a tipping point. In F. A. Bonner, A. F. Marbley, & M. F. Howard-Hamilton (Eds.), *Diverse millennial students in college: Implications for faculty and student affairs* (pp. 55–68). Sterling, VA: Stylus.

Choy, S. (2001). *Students whose parents did not go to college: Postsecondary access, persistence, and attainment.* (NCES Rep. No. 2001–126). Washington, DC: National Center for Education Statistics.

DeAngelo, L., Franke, R., Hurtado, S., Pryor, J. H., & Tran, S. (2011). *Completing college: Assessing graduation rates at four-year institutions.* Los Angeles: Higher Education Research Institute, University of California Los Angeles.

Dickbert-Conlin, S., & Rubenstein, R. (Eds.). (2007). *Economic inequality and higher education: Access, persistence, and success.* New York, NY: Russell Sage Foundation.

Engle, J., & O'Brien, C. (2007). *Demography is not destiny: Increasing the graduation rates of low-income college students at large public universities.* Washington, DC: Pell Institute for the Study of Opportunity in Higher Education.

Engle, J., & Tinto, V. (2008). *Moving beyond access: College success for low-income, first-generation students.* Washington, DC: Pell Institute for the Study of Opportunity in Higher Education.

Fischer, M. J. (2007). Settling into campus life: Differences by race/ethnicity in college involvement and outcomes. *Journal of Higher Education, 78*(2), 125–156.

Guiffrida, D. A. (2006). Toward a cultural advancement of Tinto's model. *Review of Higher Education, 29*(4), 451–472.

Hossler, D., Schmit, J., & Vesper, N. (1999). *Going to college: How social, economic, and educational factors influence the decisions students make.* Baltimore, MD: Johns Hopkins University Press.

Karabel, J., & Astin, A. W. (1975). Social class, academic ability, and college "quality." *Social Forces, 53*, 381–398.

King, J. E. (2005). Academic success and financial decisions: Helping students make crucial choices. In R. S. Feldman (Ed.), *Improving the first year of college: Research and practice* (pp. 3–25). Mahweh, NJ: Lawrence Erlbaum.

Kuh, G. D., Kinzie, J., Schuh, J. H., Whitt, E. J., et al. (2010). *Student success in college: Creating conditions that matter* (2nd ed.). San Francisco, CA: Jossey-Bass.

Leonhardt, D. (2004, April 22). As wealthy fill top colleges, concerns grow over fairness. *New York Times*, p. A1.

Mauk, A. J., & Jones, W. A. (2006). African American students. In L. A. Gohn & G. R. Albin (Eds.), *Understanding college student subpopulations: A guide for student affairs professionals* (pp. 69–90). Washington, DC: National Association of Student Personnel Administrators.

Mayo, J. R., Murguia, E., & Padilla, R. V. (1995). Social integration and academic performance among minority university students. *Journal of College Student Development, 36*, 542–552.

McDonough, P. M. (1997). *Choosing colleges: How social class and schools structure opportunity.* Albany: State University of New York Press.

Mitchell, Jr., D., & Daniele, E. (in press). Diversity in United States graduate education admissions: 21st century challenges and opportunities. Forthcoming in V. Stead (Ed.), *International perspectives in higher education admission policy: A reader.* New York, NY: Peter Lang.

Mortenson, T. G. (2007, April). Educational attainment in the United States, 1940 to 2006. *Postsecondary Education Opportunity, 178*, 7–16.

Mortenson, T. G. (2010). Family income and educational attainment 1970 to 2009. *Postsecondary Education Opportunity, 221*, 1–16.

Museus, S. D. (2011). Living at the intersection of diversification, digitization, and globalization. In F. A. Bonner, A. F. Marbley, & M. F. Howard-Hamilton (Eds.), *Diverse millennial students in college: Implications for faculty and student affairs* (pp. 69–88). Sterling, VA: Stylus.

Niemann, Y. F., & Maruyama, G. (2005). Inequities in higher education: Issues and promising practices in a world ambivalent about affirmative action. *Journal of Social Issues, 61*(3), 407–426.

Pascarella, E. T., & Terenzini, P. T. (1991). *How college affects students: Findings and insights from twenty years of research* (Vol. 1). San Francisco, CA: Jossey-Bass.

Pascarella, E. T., & Terenzini, P. T. (2005). *How college affects students: A third decade of research* (Vol. 2). San Francisco, CA: Jossey-Bass.

Paulsen, M. B., & St. John, E. P. (2002). Social class and college costs: Examining the nexus between college choice and persistence. *Journal of Higher Education, 73*(2), 189–236.

Rendón, L. I., Jalomo, R. E., & Nora, A. (2011). Theoretical considerations in the study of minority student retention in higher education. In S. R. Harper & J. F. L. Jackson (Eds.), *Introduction to American education* (pp. 229–248). New York, NY: Routledge.

Smith, M. J. (2009). Right directions, wrong maps: Understanding the involvement of low-SES African American parents to enlist them as partners in college choice. *Education and Urban Society, 41*(2), 171–196.

Thayer, P. B. (2000). Retention of students from first-generation and low-income backgrounds. *Journal of the Council of Opportunity in Education*, 2–8.

Tinto, V. (1993). *Leaving college: Rethinking the causes and cures of student attrition* (2nd ed.). Chicago, IL: University of Chicago Press.

Tinto, V. (2006). Research and practice of student retention. What's next? *Journal of College Student Retention, 8*(1), 1–19.

U.S. Department of Education, National Center for Education Statistics (2012). *The condition of education 2011* (NCES 2012–045). Washington, DC: Author.

U.S. Government Accountability Office. (2007). *Poverty in America: Consequences for individuals and the economy* (No. GAO-07-343T). Washington, DC: Author.

Walpole, M. (2007). Economically and educationally challenged students in higher education: Access to outcomes [Monograph]. *ASHE Higher Education Report, 33*(3). San Francisco, CA: Jossey-Bass.

Theoretical AND Research Advancements

CHAPTER ONE

Rethinking Student Involvement AND Engagement

Cultivating Culturally Relevant and Responsive Contexts for Campus Participation

SAMUEL D. MUSEUS AND VARAXY YI

A Chinese American college student named Maya, at a large rural predominantly White research university, was enrolled in an introductory American literature course during her first semester in college. During the first class session of the semester, she noticed that almost all of the authors of assigned readings were White and most of them were men. After class, she scheduled a meeting with the White female faculty member who was teaching the course. When Maya asked the instructor if they could read some Asian American authors in class, the faculty member responded by saying, "That's what Asian Studies is for." The faculty member was apparently unaware that Asian Studies on this campus was actually East Asian Studies and did not include curricula focused on Asian American experiences. The interaction left Maya invalidated and frustrated, and led to her contemplating dropping the course.

A Chicano undergraduate named Mason, who was majoring in biology at a mid-sized public urban research university, took an ethnic studies course that focused on race and racism in American society during his first year. Over the course of the semester, he scheduled a couple of meetings with the instructor, during which they engaged in conversations about the student's experiences growing up Chicano and navigating racist environments, how those experiences shaped his aspirations, and his potential involvement in an undergraduate research project focused on health disparities in Latino/a communities. These experiences, combined with Mason's growing recognition that his biology courses were not as engaging as he had hoped, led him to develop a growing interest in ethnic studies and begin considering a major change.

These two scenarios are grounded in actual undergraduate experiences. We share these two real-life stories because their juxtaposition can stimulate valuable thought and discourse around student involvement and engagement. Together, they illuminate how a single type of student involvement or engagement in college—interactions with a faculty member—can be experienced within different types of environments, vary significantly in the extent to which it is relevant to students' identities, and generate very different outcomes.

In the first vignette, Maya encounters a situation in which she is excluded from the curriculum of a liberal arts course. This exclusion sent a message to Maya that she is not relevant to the course, while the curriculum is not relevant to Maya's ethnic community, identity, or life. Equally important, because the course was focused on "American" literature and did not include Asian American voices, it sent a message that Maya and her community were irrelevant to the evolution of American thought. In addition, Maya's interactions with the faculty member who was teaching the course confirmed these messages and evoked feelings of invalidation. Furthermore, through her remarks, the faculty member essentialized Asians and Asian Americans into one homogenous group, diminishing the significance of Maya's identity as an American and otherizing Asian Americans as foreigners.

The second scenario paints a very different picture: Mason was enrolled in a course focused on how the voices of people of color are marginalized. Through the course, Mason connected with an instructor who engaged him in conversations that validated his experiences, connected the curriculum of the course to those experiences, and linked those experiences to opportunities to engage in educationally meaningful activities that are aimed at improving lives within his own community. These encounters made Mason realize that he can be involved in environments that are relevant, validate his experiences, and serve his communities.

While an analysis of the stories above underscores the importance of intentionally constructing involvement and engagement opportunities in culturally relevant and responsive ways, research and discourse on involvement and engagement are often constructed in de-racialized and acultural ways. In this chapter, we explore how postsecondary educators can more meaningfully construct culturally relevant and responsive involvement and engagement activities that increase diverse students' interest in the curriculum and enhance students' satisfaction with courses, as well as the benefits that accrue from them. We utilize the Culturally Engaging Campus Environments (CECE) model as a framework to reexamine how the environment may shape involvement activities (Museus, 2014). Then, we take a closer look at how the CECE model can be employed to assist educators in understanding how to cultivate specific involvement and engagement opportunities that are characterized by the culturally relevant and culturally responsive elements of the model. Finally, we conclude with some recommendations for educators who seek to engage in campus-wide transformation to cultivate culturally engaging environments across their respective institutions.

THEORETICAL FOUNDATIONS OF COLLEGE
STUDENT INVOLVEMENT AND ENGAGEMENT

Over the last three decades, higher education research and discourse on student success has generated valuable insights regarding how educators can facilitate behaviors that contribute to student learning, persistence, and degree completion. The concepts of student integration, involvement, and engagement have largely driven this research and discourse (Astin, 1984, 1999; Kuh, 2001, 2003, 2009; Tinto, 1975, 1987, 1993). We focus on the concepts of student involvement and engagement herein, because they are currently two of the most widely utilized concepts in efforts to assess and increase student success.

Astin (1984) first introduced the theory of student involvement, which emphasized both the "quantity and quality of the physical and psychological energy that students invest in the college experience" (p. 528). Involvement theory hypothesizes that students' levels of involvement in college are associated with greater levels of success. Activities in which students invest physical and psychological energy may include, but are not limited to, academic work, extracurricular participation, and interactions with faculty and staff. Thus, involved students are those who spend time studying, participate in student organizations, spend time on campus, and participate in frequent interactions with faculty and students on campus. On the other hand, uninvolved students neglect their studies, do not participate in student organizations, and do not interact with faculty and other students. Finally, involvement theory acknowledges that student time and energy are finite resources, which is a reality that can inform the creation of activities that increase student involvement and, thus, college success.

Kuh (2001, 2003, 2009) spearheaded the development of the concept of student engagement, which focuses on the time and energy students spend engaging in specific educationally purposeful activities and what institutions do to induce such participation. The original five engagement benchmarks outlined by the National Survey of Student Engagement (NSSE, 2014) from 2000 to 2012 include the following:

1. *Level of academic challenge* measures how institutions challenge the intellectual and creative work of students considered central to student learning and collegiate quality. Academic challenge is measured as the time spent preparing for class, the quantity of assigned books and written papers for class, and whether there is an emphasis on the depth of learning.

2. *Active and collaborative learning* considers that students learn more when intensely involved in their education. Active and collaborative learning is measured by questions related to the extent of students' class participation,

asking questions or contributing to class discussions, tutoring, and involvement with community-based projects.

3. *Student-faculty interaction* focuses on the opportunities that encourage students to make connections with faculty. Student-faculty interactions are measured by how often students discuss grades or assignments with instructors, discuss career plans, work with faculty on activities outside of coursework, and receive prompt feedback.

4. *Enriching educational experiences* considers the complementary learning opportunities inside and outside of the classroom. Enriching educational experiences are measured by questions that ask students about the extent of interactions they have had with students from different backgrounds; the extent to which they have had discussions with others who have differing religious, political opinions, and values; and their participation in activities such as study abroad, internships, and community service, among others.

5. *Supportive campus environment* refers to the extent to which the campus encourages students to perform better, experience increased satisfaction with their campus, and to engage in social relations among different groups. The supportive campus environment is measured through perceptions of students that the campus assists in helping them succeed academically and socially as well as the quality of relationships students have with students, faculty members, and administrative personnel.

In 2013, NSSE (2014) revised the aforementioned benchmarks to delineate ten engagement indicators grouped under four themes:

1. *Academic challenge* consists of four indicators: higher-order learning, reflective and integrative learning, learning strategies, and quantitative reasoning.

2. *Learning with peers* consists of two indicators: collaborative learning and discussions with diverse others.

3. *Experiences with faculty* consists of two indicators: student-faculty interactions and effective teaching practices.

4. *Campus environment* consists of two indicators: quality of interactions and supportive environment.

Moreover, the NSSE outlines six types of high-impact practices that increase engagement and success in college. These high-impact practices include the following:

- Learning communities
- Courses with community-based projects (e.g., service learning)
- Research project work with faculty members

- Internships, co-ops, field experiences, student teaching, and clinical placements
- Study abroad
- Culminating senior projects (e.g., capstone courses, senior projects, theses, comprehensive exams, and portfolios)

Like the theory of student involvement, the concept of student engagement acknowledges that the activities in which students participate consist of both quantitative and qualitative elements. Regarding quantity, both frameworks underscore the importance of the *extent* to which students participate in campus activities. With regard to quality, both concepts highlight the value of student participating in specific *types* of activities on campus. In addition, both the original *supportive environments* engagement benchmark and new *campus environments* engagement indicator explicitly focus on measuring the quality of students' interactions with agents on campus and their perceptions of the level of support in the campus environment.

The concepts of student involvement and engagement have made significant contributions to current levels of understanding regarding how to improve students' experiences and outcomes. However, while these frameworks have advanced knowledge of how to serve students, they have also been critiqued for their limitations in understanding and explaining the experiences and outcomes of racially diverse college students. It has been noted, for example, that the concept of student involvement is self-deterministic, in that it underscores the role of students in determining their own college success while insufficiently acknowledging the role of institutions in facilitating that success (Rendón, Jalomo, & Nora, 2000). And scholars have critiqued research utilizing the concept of student engagement for not giving adequate attention to the role that culture plays in shaping racial and ethnic minority students' connections to their institutions (Dowd, Sawatsky, & Korn, 2011). They have underscored the need for new, more culturally relevant and responsive frameworks to assess, understand, and maximize students' connections to their institutions and success. We focus on one such model in the following section.

THE CULTURALLY ENGAGING CAMPUS ENVIRONMENTS (CECE) MODEL OF COLLEGE SUCCESS

Over the last few decades, higher education researchers have shed considerable light on the types of environments that hinder or facilitate success among diverse populations (Guiffrida, 2003, 2005; Harper & Hurtado, 2007; Hurtado & Carter, 1997; Jun & Tierney, 1999; Museus, 2011; Museus & Neville, 2012; Museus & Quaye, 2009; Rendón, 1994; Rendón, Jalomo, & Nora, 2000). One strand of this research suggests that campus environments characterized by hostility, prejudice, and discrimination are negatively associated with student outcomes (Harper & Hurtado, 2007; Hurtado & Carter, 1997; Museus, Nichols, & Lamert, 2008). Another body of scholarship illuminates how campus environments that are characterized by cultural relevance and responsiveness contribute to the conditions for diverse populations to thrive (Guiffrida, 2003, 2005; Jun & Tierney, 1999; Museus, 2011; Museus & Neville, 2012; Museus & Quaye, 2009; Rendón, 1994; Rendón et al., 2000). Museus (2014) used this research in conjunction with more than 100 qualitative interviews to construct the CECE model of college success, which synthesizes the types of campus environments that allow diverse populations to thrive and can be used to consider the ways in which campuses can construct involvement opportunities that are more likely to maximize success among diverse undergraduate student bodies.

The CECE model suggests that external influences (e.g., financial factors, employment, and family influences) and precollege characteristics (e.g., demographics and precollege academic preparation) partially shape individual influences (e.g., sense of belonging, academic predispositions, and academic performance) and college success outcomes (e.g., learning, satisfaction, persistence, and degree completion; Museus, 2014). The focal point of the CECE framework emphasizes that culturally engaging campus environments are associated with more positive individual factors (e.g., greater sense of belonging, more positive academic dispositions, and better academic performance). Finally, the model posits that both the existence of culturally engaging campus environments and individual factors are related to greater likelihood of success (e.g., learning, satisfaction, persistence, and degree completion).

The CECE model hypothesizes that there are nine indicators of culturally engaging campus environments, which can be separated into two subgroups of *cultural relevance* and *cultural responsiveness*. The first five indicators focus on the ways that campus environments are relevant to the cultural backgrounds and communities of diverse college students:

1. *Cultural familiarity* is the extent to which college students have opportunities to physically connect with faculty, staff, and peers who share and understand their backgrounds and experiences.
2. *Culturally relevant knowledge* refers to opportunities for students to learn and exchange knowledge about their own cultures and communities of origin.
3. *Cultural community service* refers to the extent to which students have opportunities to give back to and positively transform their communities.
4. *Meaningful cross-cultural engagement* involves students in positive and purposeful interactions with peers from diverse backgrounds.

5. *Culturally validating environments* refer to environments that validate students' cultural knowledge, backgrounds, and identities.

The remaining four indicators focus on the ways in which campus environments respond to the cultural norms and needs of diverse students:

6. *Collectivist cultural orientations* are cultural values that encourage collaboration and mutual success, rather than individualism and competition, on campus.
7. *Humanized educational environments* are characterized by institutional agents who care about, are committed to, and who develop meaningful relationships with students.
8. *Proactive philosophies* drive the practice of institutional agents who go above and beyond providing information, opportunities, and support to ensure that students have access to that information, opportunities, and support.
9. *Holistic support* is characterized by the extent to which postsecondary institutions provide students with access to at least one faculty and staff member who those students trust to provide the information and offer the assistance that they need, or connect them with a source of support who will provide that information or assistance.

The CECE indicators outlined above can be used to rethink the way academic and student affairs units are structured on college campuses, how curricula and educational programs and practices are delivered across institutions, and the ways in which individual faculty and staff cultivate relationships and interactions with students on their respective campuses. Therefore, the CECE indicators can also be utilized in conjunction with involvement and engagement frameworks to better understand how college educators can structure environments that are conducive to the types of involvement and engagement opportunities that will lead to positive experiences for diverse students, increase those students' interest in becoming more engaged, and generate positive outcomes among those undergraduates.

Evidence suggests that students' access to culturally engaging environments is associated with stronger connections to their respective campuses, greater sense of belonging, more positive academic self-efficacy, and higher levels of academic motivation in higher education (Museus, 2014; Museus & Smith, in press). Consequently, we believe that postsecondary educators who utilize the CECE indicators to (re)think and (re)construct involvement and engagement opportunities on their campuses will witness increased levels of student involvement and engagement, more positive educational experiences among students, and improvements in diverse students' academic outcomes. In the next section, we discuss how educators can begin to engage in such (re)thinking and (re)structuring toward more culturally relevant and responsive involvement and engagement opportunities.

RETHINKING COLLEGE STUDENT INVOLVEMENT AND ENGAGEMENT

The first five CECE indicators outlined above—the indicators of cultural relevance—encourage the consideration and integration of the cultural backgrounds and identities of the student in the development of spaces, programs, practices, and activities that are designed to foster involvement or engagement on college campuses. For example, engaging students in activities that encourage them to give back to their communities via community service or problem-based research opportunities can simultaneously strengthen both students' connections to their respective campuses and cultural communities. Therefore, college educators should intentionally cultivate spaces, programs, practices, and activities that provide students with opportunities to connect with people from similar cultural backgrounds, engage the experiential knowledge of the communities from which participating students come in meaningful ways, provide mechanisms for students to give back to their respective cultural communities, facilitate positive and meaningful cross-cultural interactions, and send positive messages to participating students that the experience and knowledge of their communities are valued. Educators interested in creating an involvement or engagement opportunity and who want to do so in a culturally relevant way should consider the following questions:

- Which cultural groups will be involved in this space or program (and the activities that will transpire within them)? Is an appreciation for the different cultural groups that will be represented in this space or program made explicit?
- Will participants be able to connect with peers from similar cultural backgrounds via this space or program?
- Are the voices and knowledge of members of their respective cultural communities incorporated into this space or program? Will students from each of these groups be able to learn about their own cultural communities or share their own experiences as members of their respective communities?
- Will this involvement or engagement opportunity provide tools for participating students to positively impact their own cultural communities? Is this made explicit to participants?
- Does this opportunity provide participating students with the space to engage in meaningful interactions that are aimed at solving real-world problems with students who are different from them?

The last four CECE indicators can stimulate consideration of how college educators can create involvement and engagement opportunities in ways that are responsive to the cultural norms and needs of diverse populations. For example, many students of color come from collectivist-oriented families and communities and face increased challenges in individualistic and competitive campus environments. Therefore, rather than encouraging competition, educators should emphasize collaboration and mutual success in the cultivation of campus spaces, programs, practices, and activities. Many students of color also come from communities that place heavy emphasis on relationships, proactively engage and welcome outsiders, and do not possess high levels of knowledge about how to navigate the higher education system; thus, educators should seek to structure involvement opportunities around the pursuit of mutual goals and provide proactive and holistic support to ensure that students are aware of the wide array of involvement and engagement opportunities on their campuses and are likely to encounter spaces where they will develop meaningful connections with agents across their campuses. College educators seeking to cultivate more culturally responsive involvement opportunities should consider the following questions:

- Does this space or program encourage collaboration toward a common goal?
- Is the space or program structured so that participants will spend prolonged engagement with specific faculty, staff, or peers?
- Have sufficient efforts been made to ensure that all potential participants have acquired information about the space or program? Have they been given sufficient information for forming their own perspectives about what the experience in this program will be like and how they will benefit from it?
- Have program planners sent more than an email to potential participants?
- Have potential participants been encouraged or pressured to engage by someone they know?

These types of questions can help college educators begin the process of rethinking how they can make their programming and practices more culturally relevant and responsive. Equally important to integration of cultural relevance and responsiveness into specific involvement and engagement activities, however, is engaging in transformation efforts that can lead to more culturally engaging campus environments across institutions.

PURSUING SYSTEMIC TRANSFORMATION AND CREATING MORE INCLUSIVE ENVIRONMENTS FOR STUDENT INVOLVEMENT AND ENGAGEMENT

As previously mentioned, conversations around college student involvement and engagement often focus on facilitating particular types of behaviors, but often do not adequately consider how opportunities to become involved or engaged in those behaviors can be structured in culturally relevant or responsive ways to maximize the positive outcomes experienced by participants. In the section above, we offered some recommendations for postsecondary educators who seek to create more culturally relevant and responsive involvement or engagement opportunities to advance such goals. Yet, college educators should also construct long-term visions to cultivate cultures that drive the type of thinking illuminated above across the academic and student affairs units on their campuses, so that faculty and staff are compelled to more automatically integrate cultural relevance and responsiveness into their work. To begin bending the cultures of their respective colleges, departments, programs, and offices toward greater cultural relevance and responsiveness, postsecondary educators should consider engaging in holistic transformation efforts that include the following elements.

Focus on Cultural and Structural Transformation

First, colleges and universities should focus their energies on transforming the cultures and structures of their campuses to create more culturally relevant and responsive environments across their institutions. Oftentimes, targeted diversity, retention, and support initiatives that are designed to support marginalized populations are created as isolated efforts. The CECE model is intended to prompt institutional leaders and college educators to think more deeply about how they can (re)shape the cultures of their academic departments, student affairs units, and other support programs and practices so that they reflect the cultural communities of their students. The framework stimulates educators to (re)envision how their campus systems might be redesigned to create more collectivist, humanized, proactive, and holistic structures. This (re)envisioning is necessary for educators to pursue deep and pervasive institutional transformation to create more culturally engaging campus environments.

Coalition Building and Creating Networks

Second, those who seek to (re)shape the cultures and structures on their campuses must engage the voices and perspectives of all stakeholders internal and external to their organization—including executive administrators, faculty and staff members, college students, and community organizations and members. Engaging these voices can help facilitate the development of coalitions and networks that can drive the reculturing and restructuring mentioned above. The CECE model is one framework that can provide a centerpiece for conversations among these various constituents because it provides a common vision toward which transformation efforts can be aimed. As such, the model has the potential to not only transform practices and environments for students but also to positively change relationships among institutional members who can coalesce around a common vision.

Moreover, while individual departments or programs might easily integrate some CECE indicators into their work and find it challenging to adopt others, developing networks across the institution can help these units leverage other resources in their broader campus networks to address their own limitations and advance an agenda aimed at cultivating more culturally engaging campus environments. For example, some academic advising units might be more equipped to provide humanized and proactive support while not having sufficient time and resources to provide holistic support. However, they can serve as conduits to other departments and programs on campus by (1) ensuring that they have strong relationships and partnerships with counseling services, academic departments, financial aid offices, and the like; and (2) making concerted efforts to meaningfully connect students who need support that they cannot provide with the agents who work within the appropriate support offices. Such efforts require that units break down silos and construct more collaborative and integrated support systems.

Creating Space for Collective Analysis and Strategic Planning

As mentioned, some of the CECE indicators might be more easily integrated into the work of some units than others. Identifying how some CECE indicators might be more effectively incorporated into the practice of a unit through short-term goals and how others might be integrated through long-term transformation initiatives can inform more effective and efficient transformation planning and efforts. For this strategic planning to occur, however, campuses must provide space for educators to engage in deeper analysis and reflection to understand how to effectively cultivate culturally engaging campus environments in seemingly incompatible spaces via long-term efforts. In such spaces, educators can work collectively to figure out how to ensure that all incoming students on large campuses are able to find spaces of cultural familiarity, make an engineering curriculum more culturally relevant, or restructure entire advising systems to ensure that all students have access to holistic support.

It is important to clarify that, while it might be easy for educators to prematurely conclude that the integration of some CECE indicators into their work is too difficult, such assumptions can be misleading, self-defeating, and hinder positive transformation efforts; for example, while it might be easy to imagine how cultural familiarity, culturally relevant knowledge, and cultural community service can be integrated into social science courses, many would not intuitively conclude that such indicators could be easily incorporated into math or science curricula. Nevertheless, while educators might teach courses in which the curricular content is not centered on issues of culture and diversity, such as math and science, it is certainly possible for them to construct more culturally relevant and culturally responsive environments in the classroom (Armstrong, 2011). Indeed, educators around the nation are already making such courses more culturally relevant through the integration of culturally diverse problems, examples, and test questions that provide support for this notion.

Nurturing and Scaling Up Models of Success

There are salient examples of spaces or programs that perpetuate culturally engaging campus environments on many college and university campuses. At institutions in which such programs do exist, campus leaders should make an effort to nurture, leverage, and make more visible those units so that other departments and programs can learn from them. Kezar (2012) notes that many leaders across campus who have been engaged in work to better serve diverse populations for many years have often gone unrecognized. Kezar also asserts that the work of leaders is often to scale up the advances made in particular units by grassroots efforts across campuses in order to advance institutional transformation and equity efforts. Identifying units that have been particularly effective at cultivating culturally engaging campus environments, nurturing them to maximize their impact, and scaling their efforts up across campuses can be invaluable in efforts to create more systemic change.

Conducting Assessment and Continuous Learning

Finally, using assessment tools to analyze and better understand both larger campuses and specific units across institutions can reveal where environments that allow diverse populations to thrive exist, as well as opportunities for the implementation of the CECE model to generate more culturally engaging environments. Indeed, a clear understanding of the current environment and how it shapes the experiences of all students should inform the strategic planning and pursuit of long-term transformation efforts. The National CECE survey, which will be launched in 2015, provides one instrument that can be effectively used to measure, assess, and understand how well institutions are cultivating culturally relevant and responsive campus environments. Such tools can be used to conduct continuous assessments, which are critical to ensuring that campuses are utilizing evidence-based decision making as they advance their efforts to create more culturally engaging campus environments across their institutions.

CONCLUSION

The intent of this chapter is to begin shifting the discourse around student involvement and engagement in a more culturally conscious direction. While the concepts of involvement and engagement are invaluable and serve as the foundation for critical efforts to create conditions for students to thrive across the nation, we argue herein that educators who wish to foster environments that induce the participation of diverse populations and allow those students to thrive must begin thinking intentionally about how to make those environments more culturally relevant and responsive. If college educators can rethink college student involvement and engagement in these ways, higher education can re-envision the ways in which institutions are structured, rethink how postsecondary education is delivered, and advance the transformation toward more inclusive college campuses in the twenty-first century.

REFERENCES

Armstrong, M. A. (2011, Fall). Small world: Crafting an inclusive classroom (no matter what you teach). *Thought & Action*, 51–61.

Astin. A. W. (1984). Student involvement: A developmental theory for higher education. *Journal of College Student Personnel, 25,* 297–307.

Astin, A. W. (1999). Student involvement: A developmental theory for higher education. *Journal of College Student Development, 40*(5), 518–529.

Dowd, A. C., Sawatzky, M., & Korn, R. (2011). Theoretical foundations and a research agenda to validate measures of intercultural effort. *Review of Higher Education, 35*(1), 17–44.

Guiffrida, D. A. (2003). African American student organizations as agents of social integration. *Journal of College Student Development, 44*(3), 304–319.

Guiffrida, D. A. (2005). Othermothering as a framework for understanding African American students' definitions of student-centered faculty. *Journal of Higher Education, 76*(6), 701–723.

Harper, S. R., & Hurtado, S. (2007). Nine themes in campus racial climates and implications for institutional transformation. In S. R. Harper & L. D. Patton (Eds.), *Responding to the realities of race on campus: New Directions for Student Services* (No. 120, pp. 7–24). San Francisco, CA: Jossey-Bass.

Hurtado, S., & Carter, D. (1997). Effects of college transition and perceptions of the campus racial climate on Latina/o college students' sense of belonging. *Sociology of Education, 70,* 324–345.

Jun, A., & Tierney, W. (1999). At-risk urban students and college success: A framework for effective preparation. *Metropolitan Universities: An International Forum, 9*(4), 49–62.

Kezar, A. J. (2012). Shared leadership for creating campus cultures that support students of color. In S. D. Museus and U. M. Jayakumar (Eds.), *Creating campus cultures: Fostering success among racially diverse student populations* (pp. 150–167). New York, NY: Routledge.

Kuh, G. D. (2001). Assessing what really matters to student learning: Inside the National Survey of Student Engagement. *Change, 33*(3), 10–17, 66.

Kuh, G. D. (2003). What we're learning about student engagement from NSSE. *Change, 35*(2), 24–32.

Kuh, G. D. (2009). The National Survey of Student Engagement: Conceptual and empirical foundations. In R. Gonyea and G. Kuh (Eds.), *Using student engagement data in institutional research. New Directions for Institutional Research* (No. 141, pp. 5–20). San Francisco, CA: Jossey-Bass.

Museus, S. D. (2011). Using cultural perspectives to understand the role of ethnic student organizations in Black students' progress to the end of the pipeline. In D. E. Evensen and C. D. Pratt (Eds.), *The end of the pipeline: A journey of recognition for African Americans entering the legal profession* (pp. 162–172). Durham, NC: Carolina Academic.

Museus, S. D. (2014). The Culturally Engaging Campus Environments (CECE) Model: A new theory of college success among racially diverse student populations. In M. B. Paulsen (Ed.), *Higher education: Handbook of theory and research* (pp. 189–227). New York, NY: Springer.

Museus, S. D., & Neville, K. (2012). Delineating the ways that key institutional agents provide racial minority students with access to social capital in college. *Journal of College Student Development, 53*(3), 436–452.

Museus, S. D., Nichols, A. H., & Lambert, A. (2008). Racial differences in the effects of campus racial climate on degree completion: A structural model. *Review of Higher Education, 32*(1), 107–134.

Museus, S. D., & Quaye, S. J. (2009). Toward an intercultural perspective of racial and ethnic minority college student persistence. *Review of Higher Education, 33*(1), 67–94.

Museus, S. D., & Smith, E. (in press). *The culturally engaging campus environments model and survey: New tools for assessing the impact of campus environments on diverse college student outcomes.* Washington, DC: NASPA.

National Survey of Student Engagement (NSSE). (2014). *From benchmarks to engagement indicators and high-impact practices.* Retrieved from http://nsse.iub.edu/pdf/Benchmarks%20to%20Indicators.pdf

National Survey of Student Engagement (NSSE). (n.d.). *Benchmarks of effective educational practice.* Retrieved from http://nsse.iub.edu/pdf/nsse_benchmarks.pdf

Rendón, L. I. (1994). Validating culturally diverse students: Toward a new model of learning and student development. *Innovative Higher Education, 19*(1), 33–51.

Rendón, L. I., Jalomo, R. E., & Nora, A. (2000). Theoretical considerations in the study of minority student retention in higher education. In J. Braxton (Ed.), *Reworking the student departure puzzle* (pp. 127–156). Nashville, TN: Vanderbilt University Press.

Tinto, V. (1975). Dropout from higher education: A theoretical synthesis of recent research. *Review of Educational Research, 45*(1), 89–125.

Tinto, V. (1987). *Leaving college: Rethinking the causes and cures of student attrition.* Chicago, IL: University of Chicago Press.

Tinto, V. (1993). *Leaving college: Rethinking the causes and cures of student attrition* (2nd ed.). Chicago, IL: University of Chicago Press.

CHAPTER TWO

Multiracial Border Work

Exploring the Relationship Between Validation, Student Involvement, and Epistemological Development

AMANDA SUNITI NISKODE-DOSSETT AND ELIZABETH A. JOHN

The multiracial population is one of the fastest growing demographic groups in the United States. In 2010, the U.S. Census data revealed 9,009,073 individuals (2.9% of the population) self-identified with two or more races, a 32% increase from the 2000 U.S. Census data (N. A. Jones & Bullock, 2012). Furthermore, 92% of those multiracial individuals who marked identification with two or more races, 7.5% marked identification with three or more, and less than 1% marked identification with four or more races (N. A. Jones & Bullock, 2012). Given the substantial growth within the multiracial population, the number of multiracial college students is also likely to increase (Renn, 2004, 2009), which poses a challenge for higher education because many institutional policies and practices do not support multiracial identity development, including the limited ways students are able to racially and ethnically self-identify (Renn, 2004, 2009; Renn & Lunceford, 2004). Additionally, the accentuation of monoracial student services limits multiracial students' opportunities to engage in multicultural spaces (Literate, 2010).

Although the scholarship around multiracial college students has increased in the last 10 years (e.g., see Kellogg & Liddell, 2012; Literate, 2010; Renn, 2004), there is still a need for expansion, particularly in examining the relationship between student involvement and academic outcomes for multiracial students. The purpose of this chapter is to push the conversation about this relationship with a new conceptual model. Throughout the article, we utilize the term "multiracial" to refer to individuals who have two or more racial heritages (Root, 1996). We recognize that some people who are multiracial may also be multiethnic (i.e., two or more ethnicities), although some multiethnic individuals are monoracial.

THE NEED FOR A NEW CONCEPTUAL MODEL
FOR MULTIRACIAL COLLEGE STUDENTS

Much of the research on multiracial college students centers on multiracial identity development (Renn, 2004; Rockquemore, 1999; Wallace, 2001), multiracial categorization and identification (Sanchez, 2010; Townsend, Markus, & Bergsieker, 2009), and multiracial student experiences within the college setting (Johnston & Nadal, 2010; Kellogg & Liddell, 2012; Literate, 2010). Thus, as we searched for the relationship between student involvement and academic outcomes for multiracial students, we identified a significant gap. Yet, how is this research gap distinctive for multiracial students as opposed to monoracial students and other populations who are marginalized, underrepresented, or both? Also, how can understanding the connection between student involvement and academic outcomes for this population change educational practice? As we reflected upon these questions, we concluded that the concepts of contemporary multiracial identity development (Renn, 2004; Wijeyesinghe, 2001), borders and border work (Giroux & McLaren, 1994; Higonett, 1994; Hesse-Biber & Leckenby, 2003), validation theory (Rendón, 1994), student involvement (Astin, 1993), and epistemological development (Baxter Magolda, 2001) play distinct roles for multiracial students. To illustrate the relationships among these concepts and to guide future research and practice, we developed a conceptual model (Figure 2.1). The remainder of this chapter describes each concept within the model, how they work together, and what this means for practice.

Contemporary Theoretical Approaches and Research

The approach to multiracial identity development research and theory has evolved over time. Our model draws upon the ecological approach—where the environment plays a key role in identity formation—because it recognizes race is socially constructed (McEwen, 1996; Rockquemore, Brunsma, & Delgado, 2009) and is unique in its assumption that "(a) racial identity varies, (b) racial identity often changes over the life course, (c) racial identity development is not a predictable linear process with a single outcome, and (d) social, cultural, and spatial context are critical" (Rockquemore et al., 2009, pp. 20–21). Notably distinctive of this approach is the malleable nature of multiracial identity construction, one that does not follow stage-based theories (Renn, 2004; Wijeyesinghe, 2001, 2012). Moreover, "it is precisely the focus on the pathways toward different racial identities, as

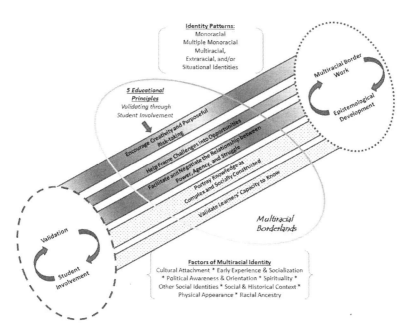

Fig 2.1. Supporting Multiracial Border Work and Epistemological Development through Validation and Student Involvement.

opposed to a circumscribed end point, that make ecological theories useful in the post–Civil Rights racial landscape" (Rockquemore et al., 2009, p. 23).

Multiracial Identity Development and Border Work

Our model draws upon Renn (2004) and Wijeyesinghe's (2001) scholarly work within the ecological approach to multiracial identity. Renn's ecological theory of mixed race identity development has two components: (1) ecological factors and (2) identity patterns. Ecological factors significant to multiracial identity development include peer culture and physical and psychological spaces. The identity patterns of racial identification are monoracial (identify with one race), multiple monoracial (identify with two monoracial identities), multiracial (identify using terms such as "mixed," "multiracial"), extraracial (oppose racial constructs), and situational (identity is dependent on situation). The five identity patterns are fluid, change over time and within context, and the student can reside in multiple patterns at one time (Renn, 2004). Wijeyesinghe's factor model of multiracial identity (FMMI) outlines environmental factors that affect multiracial individuals' identity choice. The FMMI consists of eight factors including racial ancestry, early experiences and socialization, cultural attachment, physical appearance, social and historical context, political awareness and orientation, other social identities, and spirituality. These theories highlight the role that student involvement and validation play in student racial identity development—and we argue—the way they can support students in developing their ability to do border work, as we subsequently describe.

Multiple scholars have used the concepts of borders and borderlands as framework for analysis of various topics, including personal identity (Anzaldúa, 1987), organizational identity (Niskode-Dossett, 2011), pedagogy (Giroux & McLaren, 1994), research methodology (S. R. Jones & Abes, 2014), and feminism (Hesse-Biber & Leckenby, 2003; Higonett, 1994). Higonett (1994) offered a useful definition of borders:

> A border is a complex construction that defines and localizes what it strives to contain or release. It is rarely a smooth seam; an edge may ravel, gape open at interstices, or leak in both directions. Borders mark sites of rupture, connection, transmission, and transformation. (pp. 2–3)

According to Anzaldúa (1987), the areas between borders are called borderlands and are "places that are safe and unsafe … vague and undetermined … [and] in a constant state of transition" (p. 2). Scholars have used the concepts of borders and borderlands to talk about individuals or the relationship individuals have with organizations and society (Chávez, 2009). How people or groups make their way through these borderlands is termed "border work," or how one negotiates "the relationship between agency, power, and struggle" (Giroux & McLaren, 1994, p. ix). According to Hesse-Biber and Leckenby (2003), navigating the contradictions and tensions that are part of border work "requires creativity and risk taking" (p. 4), which allows "new forms of knowledge to arise" and to create opportunities out of challenges (p. 5).

Navigating borders is inherent to the multiracial population, although multiracial students experience and express their racial identity differently (Renn, 2000; Rockquemore, 1999; Root, 1996; Wallace, 2001). Borders can be seen as racial constructs, which Root (1996) describes as "border crossing" (p. xx). We propose that the ways multiracial college students understand and respond to these racial constructs and borders is a distinct type of border work related to their racial identity development, ecological constructions, and epistemological development, as subsequently discussed.

Epistemological Development as an Academic Outcome for Multiracial Students

In our experience, when "multiracial students" and "academic outcomes" are discussed together, the tendency is to examine how multiracial students are faring academically and, if they are doing well (e.g., good GPAs, retention, persistence), do nothing more for these students. Additionally, multiracial students are often grouped within students of color in data and/or individuals' assumptions, which does not always accurately represent how the students see themselves or experience the campus, nor does it point to how this population may benefit from a distinct type of support to succeed academically. Because of these realities, we propose another way to frame academic outcomes—one that may be particularly beneficial to the success of multiracial students. We assume that epistemological development is itself an academic outcome for all students because it is the foundation for cognitive maturity (Baxter Magolda & King, 2001); however, we propose that it should be fostered in distinctive ways for multiracial students.

The epistemological dimension of development addresses how individuals "use assumptions about the nature, limits, and certainty of knowledge to make knowledge claims" (Baxter Magolda & King, 2004, p. 8). Epistemological development is instigated when students have to make meaning of unclear situations and problems without an easy answer or where students must reevaluate their own way of knowing based on new information (Baxter Magolda, 1992). This form of development is not only related to abstract reasoning but also "developing an identity based on a strong internal sense of self and using this internal foundation to guide oneself through one's understanding of contextual knowledge construction processes" (Chaudhari & Pizzolato, 2008, p. 446).

The epistemological growth of college students is one dimension of Baxter Magolda's (1992, 2001) theory of self-authorship. Briefly defined, students' capacity within epistemological, intrapersonal, and interpersonal development intertwine to form self-authorship to support students' cognitive maturity, integrated identity, mature relationships, and effective citizenship. Baxter Magolda and King (2004) described the journey toward self-authorship in each dimension at three points—(1) external formulas, (2) crossroads, and (3) self-authorship. As we reflected upon the epistemological dimension at each of these points, we realized that a multiracial person's approach to border work might follow a similar path. Thus, for the purposes of this chapter, we focus on the epistemological development dimension because it is the foundation for cognitive maturity. We further maintain that the skills and abilities of cognitive maturity—"intellectual power, reflective judgment, mature decision making, and problem solving in the context of multiplicity" (Baxter Magolda & King, 2004, p. 6)—align with the intellectual and practical skills that are essential learning outcomes for college graduates (*The LEAP Vision for Learning*, 2011). Therefore, epistemological development should itself be considered an academic outcome.

Epistemological development has not been studied for multiracial students specifically; however, epistemological development has been examined among multiethnic students. For example, Chaudhari and Pizzolato (2008) found that cognitive development serves as an impetus for "further ethnic identity develop-ment" for multiethnic students because—different from monoethnic students—multiethnic students "are faced with simultaneously understanding, accepting or rejecting, evaluating, and affirming *multiple* ethnicities as opposed to just one" (p. 456). The authors noted that

> Given the number of disequilibrizing situations multiethnic students may encounter in college that call into question their self-understanding, it seems then that mixed students may have the opportunity to make much progress in epistemological development as they grapple with their complex ethnic identities. (p. 446)

Similarly, we maintain that there is a relationship between the racial identity and epistemological development of multiracial students; however, our interest is more specifically about the grappling process Chaudhari and Pizzolato described. How does this grappling—what we refer to as "border work"—develop and change be-cause of their college experience? Specifically, how does the way in which students are involved and validated by educators play a role?

Although theories about multiracial identity represent development as fluid and nonlinear, perhaps there is a progressive way in which multiracial college stu-dents develop the ability to do this border work. How do they learn to be creative, take risks, turn challenges into opportunities (Hesse-Biber & Leckenby, 2003), and negotiate the relationship "between agency, power, and struggle" (Giroux & McLaren, 1994, p. ix) in relation to their racial identity? Perhaps this progression is related to their epistemological growth. To represent this possibility, our model proposes a mutually reinforcing relationship between multiracial students' episte-mological development and their increasingly complex approach to border work. Table 2.1 outlines our comparison of two developmental journeys, epistemological development (Baxter Magolda & King, 2004) and our proposed elements of bor-der work for multiracial students grounded in the work of Giroux and McLaren (1994) as well as Hesse-Biber and Leckenby (2003).

Because of these parallels, we believe there is a mutually reinforcing relation-ship between epistemological development and multiracial border work. Accord-ingly, educators should support the border work of multiracial students, not only because it can help with their overall identity development but also because it can lead toward epistemological development—the foundation for cognitive maturity—an essential learning outcome.

Involvement and Validation for Multiracial Students

The concept of student involvement has been used by colleges to create offices and programs to support student involvement and activities that foster student success (Wolf-Wendel, Ward, & Kinzie, 2009). Thus, when "student involvement" and

Table 2.1. A Comparison of Developmental Journeys: Epistemology and Multiracial Border Work.

	External formulas	Crossroads	Self-authorship
Epistemological Dimension (Baxter Magolda & King, 2004, p. 12)	View knowledge as certain or partially certain, yielding reliance on authority as source of knowledge; lack of internal basis for evaluation knowledge claims results in externally defined beliefs	Evolving awareness and acceptance of uncertainty and multiple perspectives; shifts from accepting authority's knowledge claims to personal processes for adopting knowledge claims; recognize need to take responsibly for choosing beliefs	View knowledge as contextual, develop an internal belief system via constructing, evaluation, and interpreting judgments in light of available evidence and frames of reference
Border Work	• View borders as impermeable and inflexible, yielding reliance on authority to understand the nature of borders • Lack of internal basis for critically examining borders, resulting in acceptance of monoraciality as the norm. • Borders are seen as limitations and a means of containment, not places of possibilities or release. • Is uncomfortable with the vague and undetermined nature of border work • Does not recognize the "relationship between agency, power, and struggle" (Giroux & McLaren, 1994, p. ix) that exist for multiracial persons living in a monoracial paradigm	• Evolving awareness that borders can be permeable and flexible • Explore the many approaches to border work by evaluating multiple perspectives on the monoracial and multiracial paradigms • Borders are seen as places that are safe and unsafe and potential possibilities are recognized • Understand the vague and undetermined nature of border work • Recognize struggle that exists for multiracial persons living in a monoracial paradigm	• View borders as permeable, flexible, and fluid • Use creativity and purposeful risk-taking to navigate safe and unsafe feelings of identity • Develop an internal belief system for critically analyzing borders, resulting in approaching the world through a multiracial paradigm • Borders are seen as possibilities and sites of rupture, connection, transmission, and transformation • Comfort with the vague and undetermined nature of border work • Recognizes the "relationship between agency, power, and struggle" (Giroux & McLaren, 1994, p. ix) that exist for multiracial persons living in a monoracial paradigm

"multiracial students" are discussed together, educators may quickly go to helping develop a multiracial student organization, creating a multiracial student services office, or making sure there are more multiracial students involved in existing campus activities. Such efforts increase the quantity of services and opportunities for multiracial students. Although these are steps in the right direction, we advocate for conceptualizing student involvement for multiracial students also in terms of quality. While the length and intensity of exposure to student involvement experiences influences the effect of college on students (Astin, 1993), the quality of the involvement experience is also critical. Yet, how might educators improve the quality of student involvement for multiracial students specifically? To answer this question, we turn to the concept of validation.

Validation theory was introduced by Rendón (1994) in order to support students to success in college, particularly first-generation, low-income students and those returning to school after some time away:

> As originally conceived, validation refers to the intentional, proactive affirmation of students by in- and out-of-class agents (i.e., faculty, student, and academic affairs staff, family members, peers) in order to: 1) validate students as creators of knowledge and as valuable members of the college learning community and 2) foster personal development and social adjustment. (Rendón-Linares & Munoz, 2011, p. 12)

Validation also is an important condition that challenges and supports students to move toward self-authorship (Baxter Magolda, 2001).

Within multiracial identity development theory and research, a validating and affirming environment fosters multiracial student identity formation and experiences (John, 2012; Kellogg & Liddell, 2012; Renn, 2004; Rockquemore, 1999; Wallace, 2001). For example, Kellogg and Liddell (2012) identified four critical incidents that affect students' understanding of their own racial identity. One of the critical incidents—affirming racial identity—includes experiences that provide "opportunities for multiracial students to learn more about their racial background, and cultivate safe and comfortable spaces for students to connect with others" (p. 539). Moreover, John (2012) found that the college environment affected multiracial identity development in several ways, including providing supportive contexts specific to racial identity. Supportive contexts include institutional size and location and various forms of student involvement—student and faculty/staff relationships, co-curricular experiences, peer culture, and academic experience. These examples demonstrate the important role that affirmation and validation play in the quality of multiracial student involvement.

In summary, it is asserted that the quality of multiracial students' involvement is related to the validation they receive for the unique aspects of their racial identity development. We believe one of those unique aspects is learning how to do border work. In addition—as indicated earlier—we contend that learning how to do border work reinforces epistemological development and leads to cognitive maturity—an essential academic outcome.

PRACTICAL IMPLICATIONS

Our model proposes five principles for supporting multiracial students in their navigation of borders related to their identity and epistemological development. We believe that they serve as a good starting point to describe how educators can provide validation through the multiracial students' curricular and co-curricular involvement and foster the ability for these students to do border work and develop epistemologically. Our objective is to push the conversation about multiracial students' involvement and academic outcomes and identify areas for future research.

The first three principles stem from elements of border work: encourage creativity and risk taking; help frame challenges into opportunities (Hesse-Biber & Leckenby, 2003); and facilitate students "negotiating the relationship between agency, power, and struggle" (Giroux & McLaren, 1994, p. ix). The last two principles are based on two of the conditions that challenge and support students' development in self-authorship (Baxter Magolda, 2001). For the epistemological dimension, Baxter Magolda indicates that by portraying "knowledge as complex and socially constructed" (p. 41) students' "capacity to wisely choose from among multiple alternatives" (p. 42) is fostered; this helps students develop an internal set of beliefs (Baxter Magolda & King 2004). A corresponding principle— "validating learners' capacity to know" welcomes students into the process of knowledge construction, encourages them to share their ideas, and provides respect that builds confidence (Baxter Magolda & King, 2004, p. 42). This is consistent with Rendón's validation theory that calls for educators to engage in "a process that affirms, supports, enables, and reinforces their capacity to fully develop themselves as students and as individuals" (p. 45).

Validation theory is particularly important in our model because it places onus on the institution to intentionally, proactively affirm students inside and outside of the classroom (Rendón, 1994). We use validation as our foundation along with the ideas presented in the border work literature and elements of promoting epistemological development. To illustrate the use of the five principles, we propose the following practical strategies of validation: (1) intentionally build relationships; (2) cultivate reflective conversations; (3) create curricular and co-curricular opportunities; and (4) advocate for inclusive institutional policy and practice. These originate from our review of several key bodies of literature, including border work (Giroux & McLaren, 1994; Hesse-Biber & Leckenby, 2003), dimensions of self-authorship (Baxter Magolda, 2001; Baxter Magolda & King, 2004, 2008), validation theory (Rendón, 1994), and multiraciality (John, 2012; Johnston & Nadal, 2010; Renn, 2000, 2004, 2009; Root, 1993/1994, 1996, 2004). We illustrate the use of the principles and validation strategies through our analysis of the following case study:

> You serve as the Student Government Association advisor for David, a second-year student. David identifies as multiracial and has Southeast Asian and White lineage. David's phenotype is ambiguous and he is often navigating the "What are you?" question, which causes him to habitually feel that he has to prove his racial heritage. David is also enrolled in a course that centers on racial identity development. He was drawn to the course because of the content; however he has recently shared with you that he feels left out of the conversation because concepts are discussed through a monoracial lens (e.g., no readings have been assigned that relate to multiracial identity development). Additionally, he just filled out a campus survey, which did not allow him to racially identify with two or more races. He shares with you how he feels "like the only one" at the institution.

David's experience is, unfortunately, too common for multiracial college students given that many campuses still function within a monoracial paradigm. The recommended validation strategies provide context for how student affairs professionals can use our five proposed principles to support multiracial students in their border work.

- *Intentionally Build Relationships*: The core of student affairs work involves building relationships with students. In David's case, he is more likely to open up to an advisor when he feels there is an investment in him as a student and his multiracial identity feels validated. Strong relationships may lead to mentorships, which could allow for support around creating opportunities out of challenges, such as working with David to determine how his frustration with his identity course could lead to constructive recommendation to the faculty member that will help other multiracial students. Building relationships can create space for critical dialogue, opportunities to serve as a resource, and provide mentorship and a supportive environment.
- *Cultivate Reflective Conversations*: Encouraging students to reflect and interpret their experiences within their ecological context can be very valuable (see Baxter Magolda & King's Reflective Conversation Guide, 2008). Engaging students in reflective conversations is an example of how students' capacity to know can be validated, and they can recognize knowledge as complex and socially constructed. For example, engaging in critical dialogue about how David navigates the complexity and social construction of race could help him view identity-related borders as permeable, flexible, and fluid.
- *Create Curricular and Co-curricular Opportunities*: Risk-taking and creativity are needed to create a campus climate of inclusion for multiracial students, especially when funds may not be available for dedicated staff or physical

space and the monoracial paradigm is ingrained in the campus culture. Perhaps you could work with David to co-facilitate an affinity group (see Ortiz, 2013). You could also develop a student affairs–academic affairs partnership with academic departments that focus on identity and culture to co-sponsor an educational speaker series about multiracial topics and theory.

- *Advocate for Inclusive Institutional Policy and Practice*: As an advisor, you can serve as an advocate for David and encourage self-advocacy. For example, you could help David understand why the survey he completed did not have an option to identify with more than one race by dialoging about the monoracial paradigm. Such a dialogue may help him critically analyze the borders that are part of the institution and identify ways that these challenges could be opportunities for his own identity expression and other multiracial students. You could help him figure out an appropriate, potentially effective way to voice his concerns to the survey administrator. Doing so would support David as he negotiates the "relationship between, agency, power, and struggle" (Giroux & McLaren, 1994, p. ix).

We conclude that our principles and validation strategies support students in their journey in doing border work and developing epistemologically. The mutually reinforcing relationship between border work and epistemology demonstrates how validating multiracial students through their curricular and co-curricular involvement can lead to the intellectual and practical skills that are essential learning outcomes for college graduates (*The LEAP Vision for Learning, 2011*). Thus, we call for educators to be intentional about validating multiracial students' identity and navigation of borders in order to support their development and academic success. In doing so, readers are invited to engage in their own border work to push the conversation about multiracial student success, reframe perceived challenges into opportunities, and foster the development of practices, structure, policies, and research that further address the relationship between multiracial college students and student involvement and academic success.

REFERENCES

Anzaldúa, G. (1987). *Borderlands/La frontera: The new mestiza*. San Francisco, CA: Spinsters Aunt Lute.

Astin, A. W. (1993). *What matters in college: Four critical years revisited*. San Francisco, CA: Jossey-Bass.

Baxter Magolda, M. B. (1992). *Knowing and reasoning in college: Gender-related patterns in students' intellectual development*. San Francisco, CA: Jossey-Bass.

Baxter Magolda, M. B. (2001). *Making their own way: Narratives for transforming higher education to promote self-development*. Sterling, VA: Stylus.

Baxter Magolda, M. B., & King, P. M. (Eds.). (2004). *Learning partnerships: Theory & models of practice to educate for self-authorship*. Sterling, VA: Stylus.

Baxter Magolda, M. B., & King P. M. (2008). Toward reflective conversations: An advising approach that promotes self-authorship. *Peer Review, 10*(1), 8–11.

Chaudhari, P., & Pizzolato, J. E. (2008). Understanding the epistemology of ethnic identity: Development in multiethnic college students. *Journal of College Student Development, 49*(5), 443–458.

Chávez, A. F. (2009). Leading in the borderlands: Negotiating ethnic patriarchy for the benefit of students. *NASPA Journal about Women in Higher Education, 2*(1), 39–65.

Giroux, H., & McLaren, P. (1994). (Eds.). *Between borders: Pedagogy and politics of cultural studies*. New York, NY: Routledge.

Hesse-Biber, S. N., & Leckenby, D. (2003). Introduction. In S. N. Hesse-Biber & D. Leckenby (Eds.), *Women in Catholic higher education: Border work, living experiences, and social justice* (pp. 1–13). Lanham, MD: Lexington.

Higonett, M. R. (1994). *Borderwork*. Ithaca, NY: Cornell University Press.

John, E. (2012). *How college affects the racial identity development of multiracial students at two predominantly White private institutions*. Unpublished doctoral dissertation, Edgewood College, Madison, WI.

Johnston, M. P., & Nadal, K. L. (2010). Multiracial microaggressions: Exposing monoracism in everyday life and clinical practice. In D. W. Sue (Ed.), *Microaggressions and marginality: Manifestation, dynamics, and impact* (pp. 123–144). New York, NY: Wiley.

Jones, S. R., & Abes, E. S. (2013). *Identity development of college students: Advancing frameworks for multiple dimensions of identity*. San Francisco, CA: Jossey-Bass.

Jones, N. A., & Bullock, J. (2012, September). The two or more races population: 2010. *2010 Census Briefs*. Washington, DC: U.S. Census Bureau.

Kellogg, A. H., & Liddell, D. L. (2012). "Not half, but double": Exploring critical incidents in the racial identity of multiracial college students. *Journal of College Student Development, 53*(4), 524–541.

The LEAP vision for learning: Outcomes, practices, impact, and employers' view. (2011). Washington, DC: Association of American Colleges and Universities.

Literate, P. E. (2010). Revising race: How biracial students are changing and challenging student services. *Journal of College Student Development, 51*(2), 115–134.

McEwen, M. K. (1996). New perspectives on identity development. In S. R. Komives & D. B. Woodward Jr. (Eds.), *Student services: A handbook for the profession* (3rd ed., pp. 188–217). San Francisco, CA: Jossey-Bass.

Niskode-Dossett, A. S. (2011). *Examining the culture of a Catholic, liberal arts, women's college: An ethnography*. Unpublished doctoral dissertation, Indiana University, Bloomington.

Ortiz, A. J. (2013). Understanding and supporting multiracial students. In L. M. Landreman (Ed.), *The arts of effective facilitation: Reflections from social justice educators*. Sterling, VA: Stylus.

Rendón, L. I. (1994). Validating culturally diverse students: Toward a model of learning and student development. *Innovative Higher Education, 19*(1), 33–51.

Rendón-Linares, L. I., & Munoz, S. M. (2011). Revisiting validation theory: Theoretical applications, foundations and extensions. *Enrollment Management Journal, 5*(2), 12–33.

Renn, K. A. (2000). Patterns of situational identity among biracial and multiracial college students. *Review of Higher Education, 23*(4), 339–420.

Renn, K. A. (2004). *Mixed race students in college: The ecology of race, identity, and community on campus*. Albany: State University of New York Press.

Renn, K. A. (2009). Educational policy, politics, and mixed heritage students in the United States. *Journal of Social Issues, 65*(1), 165–183.

Renn, K. A., & Lunceford, C. J. (2004). Because the numbers matter: Transforming postsecondary education data on student race and ethnicity to meet the challenges of a changing nation. *Educational Policy, 18*(5), 752–783.

Rockquemore, K. A. (1999). Between Black and White: Exploring the "biracial" experience. *Race & Society, 1*(2), 197–212.

Rockquemore, K. A., Brunsma, D. L., & Delgado, D. J. (2009). Racing to theory or retheorizing race? Understanding the struggle to build a multiracial identity development theory. *Journal of Social Issues, 65*(1), 11–34.

Root, M. P. P. (1993/1994). *Bill of rights for people of mixed heritage.* Retrieved from http://www.drmariaroot.com/doc/BillOfRights.pdf

Root, M. P. P. (1996). The multiracial experience: Racial borders as a significant frontier in race relations. In M. P. P. Root (Ed.), *The multiracial experience: Racial borders and the new frontier* (pp. xiii–xxviii). Thousand Oaks, CA: Sage.

Root, M. P. P. (2004). *Multiracial oath of social responsibility.* Retrieved from http://www.drmariaroot.com/doc/OathOfSocialResponsibility.pdf

Sanchez, D. T. (2010). How do forced-choice dilemmas affect multiracial people? The role of identity autonomy and public regard in depressive symptoms. *Journal of Applied Social Psychology, 40*(7), 1657–1677.

Townsend, S. S. M., Markus, H. R., & Bergsieker, H. B. (2009). My choice, your categories: The denial of multiracial identities. *Journal of Social Issues, 65*(1), 185–204.

Wallace, K. R. (2001). *Relative/outsider: The art and politics of identity among mixed heritage students.* Westport, CT: Ablex.

Wijeyesinghe, C. L. (2001). Racial identity in multiracial people: An alternative paradigm. In C. L. Wijeyesinghe & B. W. Jackson (Eds.), *New perspectives on racial identity development* (pp. 129–152). New York: New York University Press.

Wijeyesinghe, C. L. (2012). The intersectional model of multiracial identity: Integrating multiracial identity theories and intersectional perspectives on social identity. In B. W. Jackson & C. L. Wijeyesinghe (Eds.), *New perspectives on racial identity development: Integrating emerging paradigms into racial identity models* (pp. 81–107). New York: New York University Press.

Wolf-Wendel, L., Ward, K., & Kinzie, J. (2009). A tangled web of terms: The overlap and unique contribution of involvement, engagement, and integration to understanding college student success. *Journal of College Student Development, 50*(4), 407–428.

High-impact Involvement

Elevating THE Academic Success OF Working-class College Students through High-impact Educational Practices

KRISTA M. SORIA

Scholars continue to point toward the importance of social class in understanding undergraduate students' success in higher education. In particular, scholars have long substantiated that students from working-class backgrounds remain historically underrepresented in higher education—especially at four-year institutions—are less prepared for college, have lower grade point averages while in college, and are significantly less likely to persist to graduation as compared to their peers from middle- or upper-class families (Dickbert-Conlin & Rubenstein, 2007; Pascarella & Terenzini, 2005; Soria & Stebleton, 2013; Terenzini, Cabrera, & Bernal, 2001; Tinto, 2006, 2012). Working-class students tend to be the first in their families to earn a college education, come from low-income families, and are often students of color (Soria, 2012; Soria & Barratt, 2012). Additionally, working-class students' parents are often employed in occupations that are low in prestige, power, and income (Barratt, 2011). Parental resources—including finances, social networks, and knowledge of high-status culture—greatly advantage affluent students in nearly every aspect of the college-going experience from admission to graduation (Armstrong & Hamilton, 2013; Goldrick-Rab, 2006; Lucas, 2001); consequently, working-class students tend to be disadvantaged in several aspects of college attendance, including their academic and social integration (Rubin, 2012; Soria, 2012; Soria & Bultmann, in press; Soria, Stebleton, & Huesman, 2013-2014).

After several decades of analysis, it is apparent that students from lower-social-class families are significantly less likely than their peers to achieve their dreams of attaining college degrees. From 1980 to 2010, the rate of disparate baccalaureate degree attainment levels between students in the upper and lower quartiles of family income doubled. In effect, students in the top quartile of family income were ten times more likely than students in the bottom quartile to earn a baccalaureate degree by the age of 24 in 2010 compared to 1980, when the difference in graduation rates was only five times (Mortenson, 2010). Higher education institutions are just as culpable as other social institutions in systematically reproducing social and economic inequalities in our nation, and the time has come for institutions to more actively support working-class students' academic success in higher education. The purpose of this chapter is to understand more about how social class operates in higher education and discover whether high-impact educational practices (Kuh, 2008) can support working-class college students' academic achievement in higher education.

Higher education practitioners have commonly sought to support undergraduate students' academic success through institutional measures designed to facilitate students' engagement, foster a sense of belonging among students, and strengthen students' commitment to their collegiate experiences. While there are many ways for students to become more engaged and invested in their academic pursuits, high-impact educational practices have been highlighted for their unique, enriching, and powerful effects on students' experiences. Examples of high-impact educational practices outlined by Kuh (2008) include learning communities, first-year experience programs, common book-reading experiences, service learning and community service, diversity experiences, student-faculty research collaborations, senior capstone experiences, writing-intensive courses, internships, and study-abroad opportunities. Such opportunities for student involvement are particularly effective in promoting students' development, active learning, deep learning, engagement, and retention (Kuh, 2008).

Kuh (2008) suggests high-impact activities are uniquely beneficial for at least three reasons. First, these practices require students to spend significant time and energy in the completion of intentionally designed tasks. Second, high-impact educational practices require students to have frequent and engaged interactions with faculty and peers as they are embedded in active forms of learning. Third, students who participate in these activities are more likely to experience diversity by working with other classmates, staff, or faculty who differ from them in several ways. Kuh argues students who participate in high-impact practices typically receive regular feedback on their performances, a factor that could enhance students' academic success. Furthermore, within high-impact educational practices, students are more likely to receive opportunities to apply their learning within practical, real-world settings, in turn, seeing how learning functions in a variety of dynamic contexts.

The cumulative effects of participation in high-impact practices should not go overlooked—students who participate in five to six different high-impact practices over the course of their collegiate experiences reported 9.4% to 16.9% higher gains in general education, practical competence, and personal and social development over their peers who participated in one to two high-impact practices (Finley & McNair, 2013). Students who participated in five to six high-impact practices also reported between 18.1% and 24.1% higher gains than their peers who did not participate in any high-impact practices. Additionally, students who participated in five to six high-impact practices reported greater engagement in deep learning practices—integrative, reflective, synthesized, and applied learning—nearly 20 points higher than their peers who did not participate in any high-impact practices (Nelson Laird, Shoup, & Kuh, 2005).

While all students benefit from participation in high-impact practices, Kuh (2008) discovered that historically underserved students, including students of color and first-generation students, tend to benefit *more* from engagement in high-impact educational activities. Although first-generation students, students with lower ACT scores, and students of color are less likely to participate in high-impact practices (Finley & McNair, 2013), the act of participation tends to have a compensatory effect among these groups of students (Kuh, 2008). Although Kuh (2008) and Finley and McNair (2013) explored the benefits of involvement in high-impact practices among these groups of historically underrepresented and underserved students, to date, no studies have explored the potential academic benefits of high-impact practices among students from working-class backgrounds. The purpose of this study is therefore to examine whether working-class students' participation in high-impact educational practices is associated with working-class students' academic achievement in higher education.

STUDENTS' INVOLVEMENT IN HIGHER EDUCATION

Distinct from engagement and integration (Wolf-Wendel, Ward, & Kinzie, 2009), students' involvement in campus life has been conceptualized as the amount of physical or psychological energy students devote to their academic experiences (Astin, 1984). Students' involvement is broadly associated with their success in higher education, although the majority of research exploring the benefits of students' involvement is somewhat limited in its focus on the amount of time students spend participating in extracurricular activities, engaging in residence-life contexts, or socializing with peers or faculty members (Astin, 1993; Hernandez, Hogan, Hathaway, & Lovell, 1999; Pascarella & Terenzini, 2005). Several outcomes that matter most to higher education institutions—students' persistence, satisfaction, and graduation—are linked to students' extracurricular involvement, although researchers suggest that students' academic involvement tends to have more significant effects on those measures than other social involvement (Astin, 1993; Pascarella & Terenzini, 2005).

Involvement theory provides a theoretical link between students' participation in a variety of higher education activities, the influence of environmental contributions, and students' outcomes (Astin, 1984). There are several ways in which involvement benefits students' experiences; for example, when students are involved in campus activities, they have increased interactions with their peers—a factor highly important in fostering students' social integration on campus and contributing to larger developmental outcomes (Pascarella & Terenzini, 2005). The many benefits of student interactions with their peers can positively influence academic development, analytical and problem-solving skills, and self-esteem (Kuh, 1995). According to Astin (1993), peers are "the single most potent source of influence" on college students (p. 398)—and these important socialization agents, in addition to students' involvement experiences, affect students' cognitive, identity, affective, psychological, psychosocial, and behavioral development (Foubert & Grainger, 2006; Guardia & Evans, 2008; Harper & Quaye, 2007; Pascarella & Terenzini, 2005).

While the benefits of social and academically oriented interactions with peers are clearly established, working-class students are significantly less likely than their middle- and upper-class peers to participate in the social life of campus—including being involved in organized student groups or extracurricular activities, participating in informal social activities, and feeling socially integrated within their colleges and universities (Armstrong & Hamilton, 2013; Rubin, 2012; Soria et al., 2013–2014; Stuber, 2011; Walpole, 2003). Barratt (2012) stressed that "social class is a powerful and often unrecognized influence on student participation in the extracurriculum" (p. 1). In addition to the broad base of literature that describes the lower retention and graduation rates of working-class students (Carnevale & Rose, 2004; Engle & Lynch, 2011; Haveman & Wilson, 2007; Mortenson, 2007), scholars have found evidence that social class is strongly related to students' integration and sense of belonging in higher education (Ostrove, 2003; Ostrove & Long, 2007; Soria et al., 2013–2014). As a result, working-class students are more likely to feel alienated and marginalized at college, which in turn negatively affects their academic performance and retention (Ostrove, 2003; Ostrove & Long, 2007).

THEORETICAL PERSPECTIVES

Several theories can be utilized to describe the mechanisms generating working-class students' lower involvement on campus—and the roots of these disparities happen as early as childhood. Middle-class parents engage in the process of concerted cultivation by deliberately encouraging their children's development through involvement in afterschool activities, developing their children's interests in education, and playing a highly active and involved role in their education (Lareau, 2003). Working-class parents facilitate the accomplishment of natural growth in their children and do not consider organized activities as important in their children's development (Lareau, 2003). While middle-class parents elicit the opinions and thoughts of their children and engage them in reasoning activities, working-class parents tend to use directives and tell their children what to do as opposed to persuading them with logic and reasoning (Lareau, 2003). These different socialization techniques lead to the "transmission of differential advantages to children" (Lareau, 2003, p. 5)—differences leading middle-class children to acquire greater verbal agility with larger vocabularies and greater ease with authority figures. The different ways in which children are socialized also impacts their ability to interact within institutions and shapes their ability to "engage in the rules of the game" (Lareau, 2003, p. 6).

These early patterns in socialization carry over to students' experiences in higher education and are associated with the different types of cultural capital and social capital students acquire from growing up in distinct social classes. Developed by Bourdieu (1986) as a "partial explanation for the less tangible or less immediately visible inequalities" in society (Winkle-Wagner, 2010, p. 5), cultural capital functions as a form of social currency and is a function of the class-based acquisition of culturally situated norms, preferences, and skills. In social situations, cultural capital acts as a "power resource" (Swartz, 1997, p. 75) in exchange for social rewards, including social mobility, recognition, or acceptance (Winkle-Wagner, 2012). Within the form of cultural attitudes, preferences, and behaviors, cultural capital "selects and conditions some students for success while identifying others as unworthy of academic or social distinction" (Stuber, 2011, p. 10). In higher education, middle- and upper-class cultural capital is manifested by reading the right books, having the right values and priorities, and participating in the right activities.

Distinct from cultural capital, social capital—the knowledge and resources garnered through social connections and social networks—can work as a form of capital in social settings to enhance the social and economic well-being of individuals who belong to communities, groups, and organizations (Bourdieu, 1979, 1986). Working-class students are often the first in their families to enter into higher education; consequently, they do not inherit the same types of social capital (e.g., knowledge and resources) as their peers whose parents attended higher education (Gofen, 2009; Soria & Stebleton, 2013; York-Anderson & Bowman, 1991). Middle/upper-class students are more likely to possess the types of social capital to be successful in higher education; for example, illustrating the powerful effects of this type of social capital, Stuber (2011) discovered that middle/upper-class first-year students arrived on campus already involved in campus activities before classes even officially commenced. The social capital gained through increased social interactions and social networks on college campuses can increase students' social integration, and thus retention, on campus (Tinto, 2003, 2006, 2012); subsequently, students with less-privileged forms of social capital who are not as involved on campus may not accrue the cumulative effects of social capital.

In additional to cultural and social capital, researchers focusing on the role of social class in higher education are interested in Bourdieu's (1986) notion of "habitus," a "common set of subjective perceptions held by all members of the same group or class that shapes an individual's expectations, attitudes, and aspirations" (p. 9). Within the context of higher education, students from working classes leave behind their habitus to join the new, more elite habitus of the middle-class university environment (Berger, 2000; Hurst, 2010; Stuber, 2011). Working-class students who enter higher education often encounter challenges negotiating the social and cultural norms within the middle-class habitus of higher education; for example, Borrego (2001) noted that "students who come from a working-class or poor background often describe a sense of bewilderment about the educational environment, more often related to the social codes and norms than actual coursework" (p. 31). It is often this presumed lack of fit or lack of belonging that supports most scholarship addressing the higher dropout rates of working-class students (Lehmann, 2007); working-class students withdraw from higher education because they feel alienated and marginalized in higher education, experience challenges connecting with their wealthy peers, perceive that they are imposters who do not really belong in college, and encounter significant challenges becoming integrated into the social fabric of institutional life (Aries & Seider, 2005; Granfield, 1991; Lehmann, 2007, 2013; Rubin, 2012).

Working-class students' social capital prior to entrance in higher education may have included family and friends of similar social-class backgrounds; however, upon entrance into a new middle-class habitus, working-class students struggle to develop social capital as they develop networks of support among staff, faculty, and students who more closely conform to the middle-class culture of higher education. Thus, the educational system—reflective of middle-class values, culture, and customs—contributes to the reproduction of power relationships between classes by systematically excluding working-class students who do not fit into the elite middle-class habitus of higher education. Higher education reinforces privileged forms of cultural capital and maintains power distinctions between the classes by systematically reproducing the distribution of elite forms of cultural capital among social classes (Bourdieu, 1979); in other words, because middle- and upper-class students are more likely to persist and attain their degrees, their elite forms of cultural capital (which are highly prized in higher education) are maintained and reproduced throughout generations.

The effects of those factors on working-class students' involvement in higher education translates into lower involvement in several respects; for example, scholars have suggested middle- and upper-class students are better positioned to interact with their peers than working-class students because middle-class students feel comfortable on display and possess the ability to talk to strangers (Lareau, 2003; Stuber, 2011). Accordingly, students from middle- and upper-class backgrounds possess the cultural capital that helps them know the rules of involvement on campus in addition to the economic capital that makes it easier for them to have the time and money to participate in campus life (Barratt, 2012).

Students engage in coalition building with students from similar backgrounds (Tienda, 2013)—a factor that also translates into their involvement in activities with students from similar social classes; for example, Barratt (2012) suggested that students who perceive that an event, activity, or organization does not include students from their class background will not be as likely to participate. Similarly, students who possess different forms of cultural capital will most likely engage in those types of campus activities that align with their cultural preferences and knowledge. Middle- and upper-class students whose parents attended college are more familiar with opportunities afforded from membership in fraternities and sororities—or have parents who belonged to fraternities and sororities—and are therefore more likely to be involved in such organizations themselves due to their comfort in those particular cultural settings (Soria, 2013; Stuber, 2011; Walpole, 2011).

While several forms of involvement and activities listed above are voluntary, in some cases, high-impact educational practices are opportunities that can more easily be undertaken by all students; for example, writing-intensive courses, senior capstone classes, globally infused courses, and common book-reading experiences are required at some institutions, so students cannot opt-out of participating in those high-impact practices. These activities therefore stand the potential to ease working-class students' transitions into higher education, increase their social integration, and help them to feel more secure in their identities as college students. Although extant literature suggests working-class students struggle most in terms of their social isolation (Soria et al., 2013–2014), working-class college students also have significantly lower grade point averages than their peers (Aries, 2008; Soria & Stebleton, 2013; Terenzini et al., 2001; Walpole, 2003). Given these considerations, it is important for higher education practitioners to discover whether high-impact educational practices can potentially promote the success of working-class college students. In this chapter, I focus on the potential academic benefits of high-impact practices for working-class students.

METHOD

I utilized student survey data derived from the Student Experience in the Research University (SERU) survey, which was distributed to all eligible undergraduate students enrolled at six large public research institutions in spring 2012. In the survey, students were asked to report their social-class background and participation in high-impact practices. I used additional items in the survey in factor analysis to develop independent control variables (academic engagement, sense of belonging, and perception of campus climate for social class). The participating institutions provided additional control variables while students provided other controls by answering items in the survey. After factor analysis, I conducted multiple regression analyses to examine relationships between working-class students' participation in high-impact practices and their cumulative grade point average controlling for additional measures.

Instrument

The SERU survey is based at the Center for Studies of Higher Education at the University of California-Berkeley and administered every year to several institutions that participate in the SERU consortium. The SERU survey sampling plan is a census scan of the undergraduate experience; all undergraduates enrolled at participating institutions in spring 2012 were included in the web-based questionnaire, with the majority of communication occurring by e-mail. In the survey, each student answered a set of core questions and was randomly assigned one of four modules containing items focused specifically on a research theme. Items used in this analysis were derived from a module assessing students' involvement in high-impact practices.

Participants

The SERU survey was administered to more than 147,170 undergraduate students across six large public universities classified by the Carnegie Foundation as having very high research activity. The average institutional level response rate was 27% (n = 39,736). Students were asked to identify their social class through the question, "Which of the following best describes your social class when you were growing up?" Students could select one of the following categories: wealthy, upper middle or professional middle, middle class, working class, and low income or poor. In the entire sample, 5.3% of students identified as low-income or poor (n = 1,607), 18.2% as working class (n = 5,529), 43.4% as middle class (n = 13,158), 30.5% as upper-middle or professional-middle class (n = 9,263), and 2.5% as wealthy (n = 770).

I only used items embedded in an academic and global engagement module of the SERU survey randomly assigned to between 20% and 40% of students, depending upon the institutions' preferences. The items in that module asked students to indicate whether they had ever participated or were currently participating in several types of high-impact practices. After deleting missing data listwise, the final sample of low-income and working-class students (which I combined into one category of working-class students) was reduced to 1,165 students. Among the working-class students used in analysis, 62.4% were female and 37.6% male. Additionally, 0.6% of respondents were American Indian or Alaskan Native, 8.9% African American, 17.7% Chicano or Latino, 23.4% Asian, Filipino, or Pacific Islander, 41.1% White, 4.6% other or unknown racial background, 2.4% multiracial, 1.3% international, and 54.6% first generation (the first in their families to pursue a bachelor's degree). In the sample, students' academic levels, as determined by number of credits accumulated (e.g., freshman = 1–30 credits, sophomore = 31–60 credits, etc.), were 20.2% freshmen, 24.6% sophomores, 21.5% juniors, and 33.7% seniors. Many of the participating institutions accepted students' AP credits or other precollege credits, which skewed the sample to appear as though it was primarily composed of juniors and seniors.

Measures

Dependent variable

The dependent variable used in this analysis was students' cumulative grade point average. Students' cumulative grade point average was derived from their fall semester (as the survey was administered in the middle of the spring semester) and provided by the institutions in the sample. Within the respondent group, the mean grade point average was 3.08 (SD = .64).

Block one

Several precollege variables were used as control measures in analyses. Gender, race/ethnicity, and first-generation status were all dummy-coded. Students' ACT scores were derived from institutional records. When students had SAT but not ACT scores, the SAT scores were converted to ACT scores using concordance tables. Students' academic majors were provided by institutions participating in the study and were dummy-coded into several broader categories (e.g., STEM, arts/humanities, etc.).

Block two

Additional college experiences were also captured from the survey, including whether students lived on or off campus and whether students were employed. These variables were dummy-coded (i.e., 0 = lived off campus, 1 = lived on campus; 0 = not employed, 1 = employed). Within the sample, 63.6% of low-income and working-class students were employed while 46.8% lived on campus.

Additional control variables were used that examined students' sense of belonging, academic engagement, and perceptions of campus climate for social class. Ten survey items measuring these constructs were used in factor analysis.

To obtain these factors, I conducted a principal component analysis (PCA) with oblique rotation (promax) on the 10 survey items. Given the large sample size, Kaiser's criteria for components, and the convergence of a scree plot that showed inflexions that justify retaining three components, the final analysis retained three factors: sense of belonging, academic engagement, and campus climate.

Block three

The primary independent variables examined in analyses included students' participation in several high-impact practices. In the survey module, students were asked whether they had previously or were currently participating in living-learning communities, community service (either service as a stand-alone activity or service-learning in classes), first-year seminars, learning communities, writing-intensive courses, courses that involve themes related to diversity or global learning, internships, study abroad, and undergraduate research or creative scholarship. Additional questions about participation in honors programs and enrollment in senior capstone courses were asked of students; however, I removed those from analyses because enrollment in honors programs often requires a very high grade point average and only a small percentage of students in the sample were advanced enough to pursue senior or capstone courses. Within the sample, students were most likely to have enrolled in a writing-intensive course, enrolled in a course that involved themes related to diversity or global learning, or to have participated in community service or service learning (Table 3.1).

Table 3.1. Working-class Students' Participation in High-impact Practices.

Experiences	No		Yes, Doing Now or Have Done	
	n	%	n	%
Writing-intensive courses	198	17.0	967	83.0
Courses that involve themes related to diversity or global learning	277	23.8	888	76.2
Community service or service learning	414	35.5	751	64.5
First-year seminar	602	51.7	563	48.3
Learning communities	807	69.3	358	30.7
Internship	879	75.5	286	24.5
Reading a book common across the university	802	68.8	363	21.2
Undergraduate research or creative scholarship	983	84.5	180	15.5
Study abroad affiliated with home campus	1,025	88.0	140	12.0
Living-learning programs	1,045	89.7	120	10.3

Analysis

I analyzed the data using hierarchical multiple regression and entered independent and control variables in three blocks: (1) precollege demographic indicators; (2) college experiences; and (3) high-impact practices. I tested the independent variables for violations of regression assumptions and the multicollinearity, tolerance, and VIF collinearity diagnostics indicated that assumptions were not violated.

RESULTS AND DISCUSSION

The results of the hierarchical linear regression analysis suggest participation in high-impact educational practices explains a significant amount of variance in working-class students' cumulative grade point average above and beyond the variance explained by students' background characteristics (e.g., gender, race, first-generation status); students' ACT scores; students' academic majors, academic engagement, sense of belonging, and perceptions of campus climate; and whether students were employed or lived on campus (Table 3.2). While several demographic characteristics were positively and negatively associated with working-class students' grade point averages, the only collegiate experience positively associated with the outcome variable was students' sense of belonging, illustrating the power of belongingness to support the success of working-class students.

Furthermore, the results suggest specific high-impact educational practices are positively associated with working-class students' academic achievement, including participation in common book-reading programs; enrollment in writing-intensive courses and courses involving themes related to diversity or global learning; and participation in internships, study abroad, and undergraduate research (Table 3.2). These particular types of high-impact educational practices may therefore prove to be the most effective in supporting the academic achievement of working-class college students above and beyond students' other collegiate experiences and the characteristics they bring with them to college.

The results of this study provide fresh perspectives into the benefits of high-impact educational practices for students who are traditionally marginalized in higher education; yet, the results also warrant critical examination and discourse. For example, some of the high-impact educational practices, such as common book-reading programs, may be relatively affordable opportunities for student engagement and development (Soria, in press); yet, other opportunities, such as study abroad, are significantly more expensive and may therefore be out of the reach of a lot of working-class students (only 12% of the students in this sample had studied abroad). Some high-impact practices can be built into the curriculum so that all students receive more democratic opportunities to be involved; for example, courses can

Table 3.2. Hierarchical Regression Analysis Predicting Working-class Students' Grade Point Average.

Predictor	B	SE	β	p
(Constant)	1.787	.149		***
Student Background Characteristics				
Female	.161	.037	.122	***
Multiracial	−.428	.127	−.094	**
Hispanic or Latino	−.200	.052	−.119	***
American Indian or Alaskan Native	.128	.223	.016	
Asian American	−.049	.045	−.032	
Black	−.089	.066	−.040	
Pacific Islander	.118	.264	.012	
International	.071	.157	.013	
First-generation	−.049	.036	−.038	
ACT	.042	.005	.278	***
R^2			.138	***
College Experiences				
Academic engagement	.028	.019	.045	
Sense of belonging	.059	.019	.092	**
Campus climate for social class	−.017	.019	−.027	
STEM majors	−.017	.046	−.012	
Arts and humanities majors	.034	.056	.018	
Social sciences majors	.008	.066	.004	
Business majors	−.010	.062	−.005	
Education majors	.032	.136	.006	
Employed	−.059	.038	−.044	
Lived on campus	−.046	.038	−.036	
R^2 *change*			.029	***
High-impact Practices				
First-year seminar	.050	.036	.039	
Learning communities	−.053	.042	−.038	
Living-learning programs	−.006	.061	−.003	
Reading a book common across the university	.079	.041	.057	*
Writing-intensive courses	.113	.050	.067	*
Courses that involve themes related to diversity or global learning	.094	.044	.063	*
Internship	.108	.045	.073	*
Study abroad affiliated with home campus	.112	.056	.057	*
Undergraduate research or creative scholarship	.131	.052	.074	*
Community service or service learning	.064	.038	.048	
R^2 *change*			.032	***
R^2			.199	***
F			9.278	***

Note: $^*p < .05$; $^{**}p < .01$; $^{***}p < .001$.

involve internship experiences, better leveling the playing field for students who might otherwise not have the time, social connections, or resources to engage in internships. Likewise, internationalization at home experiences—such as on-campus globally themed courses—can also promote learning and development among students so that students do not have to study abroad to gain global, international, and intercultural competencies (Soria & Troisi, 2014).

An additional critical question lies in the directionality of these results—students who study abroad and participate in undergraduate research might have needed high grade point averages to be competitive candidates for more elite opportunities. There are additional factors surrounding students' involvement in high-impact practices that could also explain these results; for example, students who participate in formal undergraduate research opportunities may be more likely to make use of their academic libraries, which has been positively associated with students' academic achievement and retention (Soria, Fransen, & Nackerud, 2013, 2014). While many of these factors are unknown in the present study, scholars are encouraged to unpeel all the very complex layers associated with students' involvement in high-impact educational practices, including the various ways in which these important opportunities can support working-class students' academic achievement and retention. Furthermore, as some high-impact practices were not significantly associated with working-class students' grade point average in this model (i.e., first-year seminars, learning communities, living-learning programs, and community service), scholars are encouraged to investigate why some high-impact practices may be more beneficial than others in supporting students' success.

CONCLUSION

Scholars and practitioners alike should not ignore the powerful effects of social class on students' experiences in higher education. As alternatives to voluntary forms of involvement on campus, some high-impact educational practices can be built into students' educational experience and leveraged to support working-class students' academic achievement in higher education. Many high-impact practices can be incorporated into existing systems within higher education, allowing working-class students even more opportunities to participate in these valuable opportunities for social integration, development, and achievement.

REFERENCES

Aries, E. (2008). *Race and class matters at an elite college.* Philadelphia, PA: Temple University Press.
Aries, E., & Seider, M. (2005). The interactive relationship between class identity and the college experience: The case of lower income students. *Qualitative Sociology, 28*(4), 419–443.

Armstrong, E. A., & Hamilton, L. T. (2013). *Paying for the party: How college maintains inequality.* Cambridge, MA: Harvard University Press.

Astin, A. W. (1984). Student involvement: A developmental theory for higher education. *Journal of College Student Personnel, 25*(4), 297–307.

Astin, A. W. (1993). *What matters in college: Four critical years revisited.* San Francisco, CA: Jossey-Bass.

Astin, A. W., & Oseguera, L. (2005). Pre-college and institutional influences on degree attainment. In A. Seidman (Ed.), *College student retention: Formula for student success* (pp. 245–276). Westport, CT: American Council on Education & Praeger.

Barratt, W. (2011). *Social class on campus: Theories and manifestations.* Sterling, VA: Stylus.

Barratt, W. (2012). Social class and the extracurriculum. *Journal of College and Character, 13*(3), 1–7.

Berger, J. B. (2000). Optimizing capital, social reproduction, and undergraduate persistence: A sociological perspective. In J. M. Braxton (Ed.), *Reworking the student departure puzzle* (pp. 95–124). Nashville, TN: Vanderbilt University Press.

Borrego, S. (2001). Social class in the academy. *About Campus, 6*(5), 31–32.

Bourdieu, P. (1979). *Distinction—a social critique of the judgment of taste.* London: Routledge.

Bourdieu, P. (1986). The forms of capital. In J. Richardson (Ed.), *Handbook of theory and research for the sociology of education* (pp. 241–258). Westport, CT: Greenwood.

Bourdieu, P. (1990). *In other words: Essays toward reflexive sociology.* Stanford, CA: Stanford University Press.

Carnevale, A. P., & Rose, S. J. (2004). Socioeconomic status, race/ethnicity, and selective college admissions. In R. D. Kahlenberg (Ed.), *America's untapped resource: Low-income students in higher education* (pp. 101–156). New York, NY: Century Foundation.

Dickbert-Conlin, S., & Rubenstein, R. (Eds.). (2007). *Economic inequality and higher education: Access, persistence, and success.* New York, NY: Russell Sage Foundation.

Engle, J., & Lynch, M. G. (2011). Demography is not destiny: What colleges and universities can do to improve persistence among low-income students. In A. Kezar (Ed.), *Recognizing and serving low-income students in higher education: An examination of institutional policies, practices, and culture* (pp. 161–175). New York, NY: Routledge.

Finley, A., & McNair, T. (2013). *Assessing underserved students' engagement in high-impact practices.* Washington, DC: Association of American Colleges & Universities.

Foubert, J. D., & Grainger, L. U. (2006). Effects of involvement in clubs and organizations on the psychological development of first-year and senior college students. *NASPA Journal, 43*(1), 166–182.

Gofen, A. (2009). Family capital: How first-generation higher education students break the intergenerational cycle. *Family Relations, 58*(1), 104–120.

Goldrick-Rab, S. (2006). Following their every move: An investigation of social-class differences in college pathways. *Sociology of Education, 79*(1), 61–79.

Granfield, R. (1991). Making it by faking it. *Journal of Contemporary Ethnography, 20*(3), 331–351.

Guardia, J. R., & Evans, N. J. (2008). Factors influencing the ethnic identity development of Latino fraternity members at a Hispanic Serving Institution. *Journal of College Student Development, 49*(3), 304–319.

Harper, S. R., & Quaye, S. J. (2007). Student organizations as venues for Black identity expression and development among African American male student leaders. *Journal of College Student Development, 48*(2), 127–144.

Haveman, R., & Wilson, K. (2007). Access, matriculation, and graduation. In S. Dickbert-Conlin & R. Rubenstein (Eds.), *Economic inequality and higher education: Access, persistence, and success* (pp. 17–43). New York, NY: Russell Sage Foundation.

Hernandez, K., Hogan, S., Hathaway, C., & Lovell, C. (1999). Analysis of the literature on the impact of student involvement on development and learning: More questions than answers? *NASPA Journal, 36*(3), 1–15.

Hurst, A. L. (2010). *The burden of academic success: Loyalists, renegades, and double agents.* New York, NY: Rowman & Littlefield.

Kuh, G. D. (1995). The other curriculum: Out-of-class experiences associated with student learning and personal development. *Journal of Higher Education, 66*(2), 123–155.

Kuh, G. D. (2008). *High-impact educational practices: What they are, who has access to them, and why they matter.* Washington, DC: Association of American Colleges & Universities.

Lareau, A. (2003). Concerted cultivation and the accomplishment of natural growth. In A. Lareau (Ed.), *Unequal childhoods: Class, race, and family life* (pp. 1–13). Berkeley: University of California Press.

Lehmann, W. (2007). "I just didn't feel like I fit in": The role of habitus in university drop-out decisions. *Canadian Journal of Higher Education, 37*(2), 89–110.

Lehmann, W. (2014). Habitus transformation and hidden injuries: Successful working-class university students. *Sociology of Education, 87*(1), 1–15.

Lucas, S. R. (2001). Effectively maintained inequality: Education transitions, track mobility, and social background effects. *American Journal of Sociology, 106*(6), 1642–1690.

Mortenson, T. (2007). *Bachelor's degree attainment by age 24 by family income quartiles, 1970 to 2005.* Oskaloosa, IA: Postsecondary Education.

Mortenson, T. G. (2010). Family income and educational attainment 1970 to 2009. *Postsecondary Education Opportunity, 221,* 1–16.

Nelson Laird, T. F., Shoup, R., & Kuh, G. D. (2005, May). *Measuring deep approaches to learning using the National Survey of Student Engagement.* Paper presented at the Association for Institutional Research Forum, Chicago, IL.

Ostrove, J. M. (2003). Belonging and wanting: Meanings of social class background for women's constructions of their college experiences. *Journal of Social Issues, 59*(4), 771–784.

Ostrove, J. M., & Long, S. M. (2007). Social class and belonging: Implications for college adjustment. *Review of Higher Education, 30*(4), 363–389.

Pascarella, E. T., & Terenzini, P. T. (2005). *How college affects students: A third decade of research.* San Francisco, CA: Jossey-Bass.

Rubin, M. (2012). Social class differences in social integration among students in higher education: A meta-analysis and recommendations for future research. *Journal of Diversity in Higher Education, 5*(1), 22–38.

Soria, K. M. (2012). Creating a successful transition for working-class first-year students. *Journal of College Orientation and Transition, 20*(1), 44–55.

Soria, K. M. (2013, May). Social class reconsidered: Examining the role of class and privilege in fraternities and sororities. *Association of Fraternity and Sorority Advisors Essentials,* 1–4.

Soria, K. M. (in press). Common reading, learning, and growing: An examination of the benefits of common book reading programs for college students' development. *Journal of the First-Year Experience and Students in Transition.*

Soria, K. M., & Barratt, W. (2012, June). *Examining class in the classroom: Utilizing social class data in institutional and academic research.* Association for Institutional Research Forum, New Orleans, LA.

Soria, K. M., & Bultmann, M. (in press). Advising scholars from blue collar backgrounds: Supporting working-class students' success in higher education. *NACADA Journal.*

Soria, K. M., Fransen, J., & Nackerud, S. (2013). Library use and undergraduate student outcomes: New evidence for students' retention and academic success. *portal: Libraries and the Academy, 13*(2), 147–164.

Soria, K. M., Fransen, J., & Nackerud, S. (2014). Stacks, serials, search engines, and students' success: First-year undergraduate students' library use, academic achievement, and retention. *Journal of Academic Librarianship, 40*(1), 84–91.

Soria, K. M., & Stebleton, M. J. (2013). Social capital, academic engagement, and sense of belonging among working-class college students. *College Student Affairs Journal, 31*(2), 139–153.

Soria, K. M., Stebleton, M. J., & Huesman, R. L. (2013–2014). Class counts: Exploring differences in academic and social integration between working-class and middle/upper-class students at large, public research universities. *Journal of College Student Retention: Research, Theory, and Practice, 15*(2), 215–242.

Soria, K. M., & Troisi, J. N. (2014, July). Internationalization at home alternatives to study abroad: Implications for students' development of global, international, and intercultural competencies. *Journal of Studies in International Education, 18*(23), 261–280.

Stuber, J. M. (2011). *Inside the college gates: How class and culture matter in higher education.* Lanham, MD: Lexington.

Swartz, D. (1997). *Culture & power: The sociology of Pierre Bourdieu.* Chicago, IL: University of Chicago Press.

Terenzini, P. T., Cabrera, A. F., & Bernal, E. M. (2001). *Swimming against the tide: The poor in American higher education.* Princeton, NJ: College Board.

Tienda, M. (2013). Diversity ≠ inclusion: Promoting integration in higher education. *Educational Researcher, 42*(9), 467–475.

Tinto, V. (2003). *Learning better together: The impact of learning communities on student success.* (Higher Education Monograph Series, 2003–1). School of Education, Syracuse University, NY, Higher Education Program.

Tinto, V. (2006). Research and practice of student retention. What's next? *Journal of College Student Retention, 8*(1), 1–19.

Tinto, V. (2012). *Completing college: Rethinking institutional action.* Chicago, IL: University of Chicago Press.

Walpole, M. (2003). Socioeconomic status and college: How SES affects college experiences and outcomes. *Review of Higher Education, 27*(1), 45–73.

Walpole, M. (2011). Academics, campus administration, and social interaction: Examining campus structures using post-structural theory. In A. Kezar (Ed.), *Recognizing and serving low-income students in higher education: An examination of institutional policies, practices, and cultures* (pp. 99–120). New York, NY: Routledge.

Winkle-Wagner, R. (2010). *Cultural capital: The promises and pitfalls in educational research.* (ASHE Higher Education Report, Vol. 36, No. 1). San Francisco, CA: Jossey-Bass.

Wolf-Wendel, L., Ward, K., & Kinzie, J. (2009). A tangled web of terms: The overlap and unique contribution of involvement, engagement, and integration to understanding college student success. *Journal of College Student Development, 50*(4), 407–428.

York-Anderson, D., & Bowman, S. (1991). Assessing the college knowledge of first-generation and second-generation students. *Journal of College Student Development, 32*(2), 116–122.

CHAPTER FOUR

National Survey OF Student Engagement Findings AT A Historically Black Institution

Does Student Engagement Impact Persistence?

MONDRAIL MYRICK, D. JASON DESOUSA AND DONALD MITCHELL JR.

How can historically Black colleges and universities (HBCUs) improve student degree completion rates? To the credit of HBCUs, many students who otherwise would not have had an opportunity for college access and success have enrolled and graduated with degrees. In practical numbers, HBCU enrollment increased from 223,000 to 324,000, or by 45%, between 1976 and 2011 (National Center for Education Statistics, 2011). Today, HBCUs enroll 9% of all African American men and women in American higher education, although they continue to enroll diverse populations. In spite of the increase in college-going rates, fall-to-fall retention, and six-year graduation rates, students at HBCUs lag noticeably behind students attending predominantly White institutions (PWIs). This may not be surprising given HBCUs commitment to access and success of underserved populations and students with diverse learning styles, backgrounds, talents, and learning differences.

The changing landscape of American higher education presents formidable challenges for many HBCUs, including increased competition in the market, especially from proprietary schools; decreased and rigid federal financial assistance, particularly firmer Parent Plus Loan requirements; and heightened measures of institutional accountability, primarily manifested through accreditation standards.

In fact, state and federal governments are increasingly mandating that colleges and universities improve the effectiveness of institutional stewardship of resources while providing quality education at a practical cost to students and families (Commission on the Future of Higher Education, 2006).

Yet, if HBCUs are to thrive, more must be done to improve the rates at which students persist to graduation, as retention and graduation metrics have become critical measures of institutional performance and accountability. The National Survey of Student Engagement (NSSE) helps measure the extent to which students are engaged in important personal learning and development domains, making it a widely used instrument to inform institutional quality (Gonyea & Kuh, 2009). Student engagement, which is connected to higher retention and graduation rates (Harper & Quaye, 2009), as measured by NSSE, should be an HBCU imperative given current persist-to-graduation rates at such schools. In this chapter, we explore the extent to which students are actively engaged in activities and experiences associated with NSSE. We are also interested in comparing students who returned and those who did not based on their level of engagement.

A GLIMPSE OF CURRENT RETENTION AND GRADATION RATES AT HBCUs

For the purposes of this chapter, we examined African Americans' degree completion rates at HBCUs. The data are organized into three categories: (1) retention rates, (2) six-year graduation rates by sex, and (3) overall graduation rates. These categories are also examined by institutional type (i.e., private and public HBCUs).

Overall, retention rates for first-year students who entered an HBCU in the fall 2011 cohort and returned the following fall challenge HBCUs to better create "staying environments" for students. As Table 4.1 shows, about three of five (62%) students who enrolled at an HBCU in the fall 2011 cohort returned fall 2012 for their second year.

However, when retention data are disaggregated by institutional type (i.e., public versus private institutions), a more holistic picture emerges. For first-year students enrolled in public HBCUs, the retention rates were modestly higher than for students attending private HBCUs (i.e., 62% versus 60%, respectively). At best, public HBCUs retained a minimum of 7 of 10 first-time students from fall 2011 to fall 2012. Specifically, nine public HBCUs can make such a claim: Elizabeth City State University (79%), Winston-Salem State University (78%), Fayetteville State University (76%), North Carolina A&T (74%), Norfolk State University (74%), Jackson State University (73%), Morgan State University (72%), Savannah State University (72%), and Bowie State University (71%). While private HBCUs

Table 4.1. A Comparison of HBCU Retention and Six-year Graduation Rates.

HBCU	Location	Type	Retention Rate % All	Six-year Graduation Rates % Men	Women	Total
Alabama A&M	Normal, AL	Public	68	26	38	32
Alabama State University	Montgomery, AL	Public	62	19	32	26
Albany State University	Albany, GA	Public	67	31	42	39
Alcorn State University	Alcorn, MI	Public	69	27	35	31
Allen University	Columbia, SC	Private	61	20	23	21
Arkansas Baptist College	Little Rock, AR	Private	41	0	8	5
Benedict College for Women	Columbia, SC	Private	57	25	33	29
Bethune–Cookman University	Daytona, FL	Private	64	23	25	24
Bluefield State College	Bluefield, WV	Public	53	32	19	25
Bowie State University	Bowie, MD	Public	71	27	40	35
Central State University	Wilberforce, OH	Public	43	23	31	27
Cheyney University of PA	Cheyney, PA	Public	65	19	26	23
Claflin University	Orangeburg, SC	Private	74	34	48	44
Clark Atlanta University	Atlanta, GA	Private	62	37	40	39
Concordia College–Selma	Selma, AL	Private	50	5	6	6
Coppin State University	Baltimore, MD	Public	66	12	18	17
Delaware State University	Dover, DE	Public	60	29	36	33

(To be continued)

HBCU	Location	Type	Retention Rate %	Six-year Graduation Rates %		
			All	Men	Women	Total
Dillard University	New Orleans, LA	Private	68	22	35	31
Edward Waters College	Jacksonville, FL	Private	54	19	29	23
Elizabeth City State University	Elizabeth City, NC	Public	79	35	38	43
Fayetteville State University	Fayetteville, NC	Public	76	28	33	31
Fisk University	Nashville, TN	Private	85	56	53	54
Florida A&M University	Tallahassee, FL	Public	80	31	46	40
Florida Memorial University	Miami Gardens, FL	Private	70	39	42	41
Fort Valley State University	Fort Valley, GA	Public	58	22	36	29
Grambling State University	Grambling, LA	Public	69	22	38	31
Hampton University	Hampton, VA	Private	65	53	63	59
Harris–Stowe State University	St. Louis, MO	Public	44	7	9	8
Howard University	District of Columbia	Private	81	57	66	63
Huston–Tillotson University	Austin, TX	Private	57	20	29	25
Jackson State University	Jackson, MI	Public	73	37	51	45
Jarvis Christian College	Hawkins, TX	Private	55	10	17	13
Johnson C. Smith University	Charlotte, NC	Private	72	36	46	42
Kentucky State University	Frankfort, KY	Public	45	10	19	14
Lane College	Jackson, TN	Private	50	-	48	36

(To be continued)

HBCU	Location	Type	Retention Rate % All	Six-year Graduation Rates % Men	Women	Total
Langston University	Langston, OK	Public	57	13	20	16
Le Moyne-Owen College	Memphis, TN	Private	50	2	13	8
Lincoln University	Jefferson City, MO	Public	36	20	29	24
The Lincoln University	Lincoln University, PA	Public	67	25	44	37
Livingstone College	Salisbury, NC	Private	48	18	30	23
Miles College	Fairfield, AL	Private	52	11	20	15
Mississippi Valley State University	Itta Bena, MS	Public	61	18	27	22
Morehouse College	Atlanta, GA	Private	82	55	–	55
Morgan State University	Baltimore, MD	Public	72	22	34	29
Morris College	Sumter, SC	Private	40	26	35	31
Norfolk State University	Norfolk, VA	Public	74	30	39	36
North Carolina A&T State University	Greensboro, NC	Public	74	35	50	42
North Carolina Central University	Durham, NC	Public	71	36	46	43
Oakwood College	Huntsville, AL	Private	76	30	43	38
Paine College	Augusta, GA	Private	52	26	21	22
Paul Quinn College	Dallas, TX	Private	44	1	0	1
Philander Smith	Little Rock, AR	Private	63	29	32	31
Prairie View A&M University	Prairie View, TX	Public	67	28	42	36

(To be continued)

HBCU	Location	Type	Retention Rate % All	Six-year Graduation Rates % Men	Women	Total
Rust College	Holly Springs, MI	Private	66	24	36	32
Savannah State University	Savannah, GA	Public	72	20	44	32
Selma University	Selma, AL	Private	38	46	44	45
Shaw University	Raleigh, NC	Private	39	19	30	26
South Carolina State University	Orangeburg, SC	Public	61	30	38	34
Southern University and A&M College	Baton Rouge, LA	Public	69	21	32	28
Southern University at New Orleans	New Orleans, LA	Public	61	14	19	17
Southwestern Christian College	Terrell, TX	Private	50	25	32	28
Spelman College	Atlanta, GA	Private	90	–	73	73
St. Augustine College	Raleigh, NC	Private	46	30	42	35
Talladega College	Talladega, AL	Private	39	28	24	25
Tennessee State University	Nashville, TN	Public	56	28	39	35
Texas College	Tyler, TX	Private	44	16	18	17
Texas Southern University	Houston, TX	Public	61	9	15	12
Tougaloo College	Tougaloo, MI	Private	79	46	53	51
Tuskegee University	Tuskegee, AL	Private	73	40	50	46
University of Arkansas at Pine Bluff	Pine Bluff, AR	Public	55	23	33	28

(To be continued)

HBCU	Location	Type	Retention Rate % All	Six-year Graduation Rates % Men	Women	Total
University of Maryland Eastern Shore	Princess Anne, MD	Public	69	30	32	31
University of the District of Columbia	District of Columbia	Public	51	17	15	16
University of the Virgin Islands	St. Croix, VI	Public	–	–	–	–
Virginia State University	Petersburg, VA	Public	65	39	47	44
Virginia Union	Richmond, VA	Private	49	21	41	30
Virginia University of Lynchburg	Lynchburg, VA	Private	100	–	–	–
Voorhees College	Denmark, SC	Private	46	25	34	29
West Virginia State University	Institute, WV	Public	50	20	22	21
Wilberforce University	Wilberforce, OH	Private	78	45	27	33
Wiley College	Marshall, TX	Private	51	21	10	15
Winston-Salem State University	Winston-Salem, NC	Public	78	36	42	40
Xavier University of Louisiana	New Orleans, LA	Private	65	41	49	47

Note: Retention rates reflect the percentage of first-year students who began their enrollment in the fall 2011 and returned fall 2012. The six-year graduation rate represents students who entered an HBCU in the 2006 cohort as first-time students. Overall graduation rates are the percentage of full-time students who graduated or transferred out within 150% of normal time of degree completion. The HBCUs presented on this table were derived from the White House Initiative on Historically Black Colleges and Universities (n.d.) List of Accredited HBCUs.

had slightly lower retention rates (60%), some of these institutions can be credited for retaining a minimum of four of five students: Spelman College (90%), Fisk University (85%), Morehouse College (82%), and Howard University (81%).

Six-year Graduation Rates

Based on the most recent data from the National Center for Education Statistics (NCES), for students entering an HBCU in the 2006 cohort, 32%, on average, graduated in six years. The six-year graduation rates at HBCUs fluctuate from as low as 1% to as high as 73%. By institutional control, private HBCUs graduated, on average, 34% of the students who entered school in the 2006 cohort. In contrast, an average of 30% of students who entered a public HBCU in 2006 graduated in six years. The six-year graduation rates between private and public HBCUs differed sharply. For instance, among private HBCUs, Spelman College (73%), followed by Howard University (63%), graduated a considerably larger proportion of students. This compared to Jackson State University (45%), Elizabeth City State University (43%), North Carolina A&T University (43%), North Carolina Central University (43%), and Virginia State University (42%).

ASSESSING STUDENT ENGAGEMENT

As a backdrop, student engagement reflects more than the amount of time students spend in activities. Kuh (2009), for example, defines engagement as "the time and effort students devote to activities that are empirically linked to desired outcomes of college and what institutions do to induce students to participate in these activities" (p. 683). In practice, student involvement entails the extent to which a student is actively immersed in educationally purposeful activities, practices, and experiences, such as co-curricular organizations; quality interactions with faculty; opportunities that develop student leadership; and experiences that enhance student learning and other desirable outcomes outside the classroom, laboratory, and studio settings (Astin, 1993; Kuh, Kinzie, Schuh, Whitt, & Associates, 2005; Kuh et al., 1991).

A widely used tool to assess student engagement is the NSSE. NSSE 1.0, which is composed of five scales (i.e., Level of Academic Challenge, Active and Collaborative Learning, Student-Faculty Interaction, Enriching Educational Experiences, and Supportive Campus Environment), measures the extent of student engagement as well as the degree to which colleges and universities facilitate effective learning environments among other institutional dimensions (Kuh, 2001).

NSSE RESULTS

The purpose of this research was to investigate NSSE benchmarks at a public HBCU in southeast North Carolina—a state with the predominant number of HBCUs nationally. It currently enrolls approximately 6,000 undergraduate students through a college of arts and sciences, school of education, and school of business and economics. All together, the institution offers 43 undergraduate majors. Two questions formed the basis of this research at an HBCU:

1. Was there a significant difference in the NSSE benchmarks between seniors who graduated and those who did not?
2. Was there a significant difference in the NSSE benchmarks between first-year students who were retained and those who withdrew prematurely at the HBCU?

METHOD

Participants

The total sample size was 2,831 students from the years of 2007, 2008, 2009, and 2010. Over this period, the first-year, first-time combined SAT score, on average, was 852, with students in the 2008 cohort earning the highest combined SAT score (i.e., 865). The high school grade point average (HSGPA) ranged from 2.77 to 2.88, with an average HSGPA of 2.82.

Of the total sample, 72% were African American, 17% White, 5% Hispanic, 2% Asian American/Pacific Islander, 1% Native American/American Indian, and 3% other/unknown. In terms of sex, 77% were female with 23% male. There were 1,171 first-year students and 1,660 seniors included in the sample.

Measures

The NSSE benchmarks are measured on a 1–100 score to facilitate comparisons over time (NSSE, 2009). There are 42 items that make up the five NSSE benchmarks. The benchmarks are as follows: Level of Academic Challenge (11 items), Active and Collaborative Learning (7 items), Student-Faculty Interaction (6 items), Enriching Educational Experiences (12 items), and Supportive Campus Environment (6 items). The Level of Academic Challenge benchmark determines the rigor of coursework in terms of academic effort and higher order thinking (Pike, Kuh, McCormick, Ethington, & Smart, 2011). The Active and Collaborative Learning benchmark measures the degree in which students can reflect on and apply their learning with other students (Campbell & Cabrera, 2011). The Student-Faculty Interaction benchmark measures students' interaction with faculty in and outside the classroom. The Enriching Educational Experience benchmark measures a variety of learning experiences and interactions students have in and out the classroom. Last, the Supportive Campus Environment benchmark measures the students' perceptions of the quality of their interactions on campus and the supportiveness of the university. Reliability coefficients indicate consistency among the NSSE benchmarks. Cronbach alphas range from 0.70 to 0.79. George and Mallery (2003) indicate 0.7 to be acceptable.

Two variables were employed: retained and graduated. The retention variable was used for the first-year students and the graduated variable for the senior students. A first-year student was coded as 1 (reenroll) or 0 (dropped out) and determined if the student was still enrolled at the university one year after taking the survey. Senior students were coded as 1 (graduated) or 0 (did not graduate), depending on whether the student graduated within one year of taking the survey.

Data Analyses

Separate analyses were conducted for first-year and senior students using Statistical Product and Service Solutions (SPSS). Reliability analysis was used to test the consistency of the NSSE benchmarks. Independent sample t tests were used to compare the NSSE benchmarks for first-year students and seniors.

RESULTS

Overall, first-year and senior students who were more engaged in all five NSSE benchmarks persisted in school at statistically higher levels than their peers who prematurely withdrew. These are described below separately.

First-year Students

Independent sample t tests were used to compare NSSE benchmark scores for 1,171 first-year students who participated in the study. Of the 1,171 first-year students, 949 who were retained had significantly higher levels of engagement on Academic Challenge ($t[1095] = -3.57, p < .001$), Active and Collaborative Learning ($t[1162] = -3.47, p < .01$), Student Faculty Interaction ($t[1108] = -4.15, p < .001$), Enriching Educational Experiences ($t[1062] = -2.70, p < .01$), and Supportive Campus Environment benchmarks ($t[1039] = -3.90, p < .001$) than the 222 first-year students who prematurely withdrew from school after their first year, equating to an 81% retention rate.

Seniors

For seniors, independent sample t tests were also employed to compare six-year graduation rates among 1,660 senior-level students from 2007 to 2010 who graduated as compared to the 581 seniors who did not persist to graduation within one year of participating in the survey during the same time period. In examining the benchmark scores, seniors who graduated had significantly higher levels of Academic Challenge ($t[1597] = -6.91, p < .001$), Active and Collaborative Learning ($t[1647] = -7.85, p < .001$), Student-Faculty Interaction ($t[1605] = -7.81, p < .001$), and Enriching Educational Experiences ($t[1570] = -8.43, p < .001$). This equated to a 65% persistence to graduation rate.

DISCUSSION

The results of this study suggest that HBCU first-year and senior students who persisted generally demonstrated high levels of educational effort (i.e., Academic Challenge); exhibited intense involvement in their academic tasks and collaborated with their peers frequently (i.e., Active and Collaborative Learning); interacted with a high degree of substance with their faculty members (i.e., Student-Faculty Interaction); engaged in robust educationally purposeful experiences that complemented academic endeavors (i.e., Enriching Educational Experiences); and interacted formally and informally with diverse students, building important interpersonal skills. This may not be surprising given HBCUs have a history of providing African Americans with supportive environments (Mitchell, 2013a) and experiences that inspire students' confidence (Chen, Ingram, & Davis, 2006).

HBCUs must redouble efforts to improve both retention and graduation rates. These metrics may be at the heart of new legislation related to the reauthorization of the Higher Education Act as "Congress is looking to accreditation to help assure that attending college … is encouraged and that information is available to students and parents about outcomes such as graduation rates and employment and earnings for graduates" (Eaton, 2014, p. 1). At this point, the former may not bode well for most of the nation's HBCUs.

Given demands to improve retention and degree completion rates, Kuh (2011) opines that enrolling only well-prepared and academically talented students is the most likely enrollment model to assure student success; however, Kuh et al. (2005) and Keller (2001) make the case that because American higher education now enrolls a more wide-ranging spectrum of student backgrounds and talents such a proposition is problematic. In terms of HBCUs, limiting enrollment to only academically top-notch students deeply chafes against the historical and cultural fiber of such institutions and would be detrimental to their institutional livelihood.

Based on decades of research, however, student engagement appears to be a promising concept to improve student persistence (Kuh et al., 2005). This study reinforces such a claim.

PRACTICAL STUDENT ENGAGEMENT APPLICATIONS AT HBCUs

Based on the findings of this study, the implications are organized around five practical applications for student engagement for HBCUs: Academic Challenge: Promoting High Impact Practices; Active and Collaborative Learning: Focusing on Men of Color; Student-Faculty Interactions: Connect Faculty with Students Early; Educationally Enriching Activities: Invest in Experiences that Matter; and Supportive Campus Environments: Document and Share Aspects of Successful HBCU Environments.

Academic Challenge: Promote High-impact Practices

As Kuh and associates (2005) suggest, "Challenging intellectual and creative work is central to student learning and collegiate quality" (p. 177). It is not necessarily the depth and scope of reading and writing assignments as it is the extent to which the nature of the work expands students' intellectual curiosity "and stretches students to previously unrealized levels of effort" (Kuh et al., 2005, p. 178). As HBCUs consider academically challenging more students, especially underperforming students, engaging them in high-impact practices could be the linchpin to their success, as many of these practices lead to deeper approaches to learning (Brownell & Swaner, 2009). Challenging students to synthesize ideas, apply theories, integrate ideas and diverse perspectives, and judge the value of information are beneficial to most students. These strategies can be particularly beneficial to underrepresented minorities, low-income, and first-generation students (Brownell & Swaner, 2009), students typically enrolled at HBCUs.

Active and Collaborative Learning: Focus on Men of Color

Students in this study who were actively engaged in active and collaborative learning practices, including asking questions in class, making class presentations, and participating in community-based projects, were more likely to persist in college than their peers who were not as engaged in this benchmark. We argue that the findings should be disaggregated by gender, although we can make such a claim for other benchmarks, as it appears that many men of color learn differently and up to now current models have not had the desirable educational outcomes for such students, especially in terms of improving their retention and persistence.

Thus, better engaging men of color in active and collaborative learning could yield more ideal outcomes. For example, getting more men of color to utilize institutional safety nets and services—opportunities in which men of color appear not to engage—may be the sine qua non to their success and persistence.

At one institution, where men of color were academically underperforming, $400,000 was invested in a male initiative to help reverse their declining retention and graduation rates. In its initial year, the initiative helped increase the retention rate of males from 67% in 2010 to 74% in 2011. Also, 82% of first-year men of color who participated in the initiative during the 2012–2013 academic year returned the following fall, which compares to 62% among all first-year males who entered the university during the same cohort (DeSousa, 2014).

Student-Faculty Interactions: Connect Faculty with Students Early

According to Kuh and associates (2005), talking about career plans, discussing ideas with faculty, receiving prompt feedback, working with faculty on research projects, and discussing class assignments and grades typify the Student-Faculty Interaction benchmark. Academic affairs practitioners and others can play a vital role in demonstrating the interconnectedness between student success and student-faculty interactions. The findings of this study support this claim.

In particular, faculty should be attentive to the "talent development" concept (Astin, 1993; Kinzie, Gonyea, Shoup, & Kuh, 2008; Kuh et al., 2005), which encourages faculty and others to "work with the students they have, not those they wish they had … [a] belief that any student can learn anything … provided the right conditions are established for their learning, and [faculty] enact this belief by meeting students where they are—academically, socially, and psychologically" (DeSousa, 2005, p. 2). Strengthening the talent development concept at HBCUs will likely result in more positive results with regard to students' retention.

Educationally Enriching Activities: Invest in Experiences that Matter

First-year and senior students in this study persisted at significantly higher rates when engaged in Educationally Enriching Activities. This benchmark reflects student engagement in experiences that complement learning opportunities inside and outside the classroom, studio, and laboratory, such as participating in internships, civic engagement, field experiences, and an array of co-curricular experiences (Kuh et al., 2005).

Student affairs practitioners should consider organizing student activity fees and other resources more effectively. HBCUs have longstanding traditions and customs that plausibly fall under this benchmark; however, given the current climate of scarce institutional resources, HBCUs must be intrepid enough to put resources in opportunities that are more closely aligned with facilitating learning and persistence than merely bringing students together for modestly enriching activities. Admittedly, this may not be a popular recommendation; however, student activity fees and other resources must reach a wider number of students, with these fees organized around practices that create staying power and not necessarily perpetuate institutional customs that attract few students and are not connected to desired institutional outcomes.

Supportive Campus Environments: Document and Share Aspects of Successful HBCU Environments

In this study, first-year and senior students who persisted had high scores on the Supportive Campus Environment benchmark. While it is well documented that HBCUs provide supportive campus environments for African Americans and other students, HBCUs must be more intentional in documenting the specific aspects of the institutional environment that contribute to a more human scale milieu. Alternatively, are there other practices that better contribute to the unique supportive environments found at HBCUs? By documenting precisely which engagement practices are contributing to students' academic and personal success, HBCUs might improve persistence rates for students.

CONCLUSION

Since the emergence of HBCUs, these institutions have exhibited laudable staying power despite decades of criticism (Willie, Reddick, & Brown, 2006). Yet, higher education's current climate now demands more of them. Preparing today's generation of HBCU students (and future ones) will require these institutions to better engage students in educationally purposeful, compelling, and relevant curricular and co-curricular experiences—many of these experiences are reflected on NSSE. Its institutional utility was recognized in Spellings' (2006) "A Test of Leadership: Chartering the Future of U.S. Higher Education," which recommends its use widely in American higher education. We, therefore, recommend greater use of it at HBCUs in order to improve diverse populations' performance as well as to enhance institutional quality.

REFERENCES

Astin, A. W. (1993). *What matters in college: Four critical years revisited.* San Francisco, CA: Jossey-Bass.
Brownell, J. E., & Swaner, L. E. (2009). High impact practices: Applying the learning outcomes literature to the development of successful campus programs. *AAC&U Peer Review,* 26–30.

Campbell, C. M., & Cabrera, A. F. (2011). How sound is NSSE? Investigating the psychometric properties of NSSE at a public, research-extensive institution. *Review of Higher Education, 35*(1), 77–103.

Chen, P. D., Ingram, T., & Davis, L. K. (2006). *Engaging African American students: Compare student engagement and student satisfaction at HBCUs and their self-identified PWIs using National Survey of Student Engagement (NSSE) data.* Program presented at the Southern Association for Institutional Research Annual Conference, Washington, DC. Retrieved from http://nsse.iub.edu/pdf/conference_presentations/2006/HBCU_Engagement.pdf

Commission on the Future of Higher Education. (2006). *A test of leadership: Chartering the future of U.S. higher education.* Washington, DC: U.S. Department of Education.

DeSousa, D. J. (2014, May 13). *Testimony on strengthening minority serving institutions: Best practices and innovations for student success.* Hearing before the United States Senate Health, Education, Labor, and Pensions Committee, Washington, DC.

DeSousa, D. J. (2005). *Promoting student success: What advisors can do* (Occasional Paper No. 11). Bloomington: Indiana University, Center for Postsecondary Research.

Eaton, J. (2014, March). Maintaining quality and reauthorizing the higher education act. Roll Call. Retrieved from http://www.rollcall.com/news/maintaining_quality_and_reauthorization_the_higher_education_act_commentary-231347-1.html

George, D., & Mallery, P. (2003). *SPSS for Windows step by step: A simple guide and reference. 11.0 update* (4th ed.). Boston, MA: Allyn & Bacon.

Gonyea, R. M., & Kuh, G. D. (2009). Using NSSE in institutional research: Editors' notes. *New Directions for Institutional Research, 2009*(141), 1–4.

Harper, S. R., & Quaye, S. J. (2009). Beyond sameness, with engagement and outcomes for all: An introduction. In S. Harper and S. Quaye (Eds.), *Student engagement in higher education: Theoretical perspectives and practical approaches for diverse populations.* (pp. 1–12). New York, NY: Routledge.

Indiana University, Center for Postsecondary Research. (n.d.). *About NSSE.* Retrieved from http://nsse.iub.edu/html/about.cfm

Keller, G. (2001). The new demographics of higher education. *Review of Higher Education, 24*(3), 219–235.

Kinzie, J., Gonyea, R., Shoup, R., & Kuh, G. D. (2008). Promoting persistence and success of underrepresented students: Lessons for teaching and learning. In J. Braxton (Ed.), *New directions for teaching and learning: The role of the classroom in college student persistence* (pp. 21–38). New York, NY: Wiley.

Kuh, G. D. (2001). *The national survey of student engagement: Conceptual framework and overview of psychometric properties.* Bloomington: Indiana University, Center for Postsecondary Research.

Kuh, G. D. (2009). What student affairs professionals need to know about student engagement. *Journal of College Student Development, 50*(6), 683–706.

Kuh, G. D., Kinzie, J., Schuh, J., Whitt, E. J., & Associates. (2005). *Student success in college: Creating conditions that matter.* San Francisco, CA: Jossey-Bass.

Kuh, G. D., Schuh, J. H., Whitt, E. J., Andreas, R. E., Lyons, J. W., Strange, C. C., Krehbiel, L. E., & MacKay, K. A. (1991). *Involving colleges: Successful approaches to fostering student learning and development outside the classroom.* San Francisco, CA: Jossey-Bass.

Lee, J. M., & Keys, S. W. (2013). *Repositioning HBCUs for the future: Access, success, research & innovation* (APLU Office of Access and Success Discussion Paper 2013–01). Washington, DC: Association of Public & Land-grant Universities.

Mitchell, D., Jr. (2013, Fall). Funding U.S. historically Black colleges and universities: A policy recommendation. *eJournal of Education Policy*. Retrieved from http://nau.edu/COE/eJournal/_Forms/Fall2013/Mitchell/

National Center for Education Statistics. (2011). *The condition of education 2011*. Retrieved from http://nces.ed.gov/pubsearch/pubsinfo.asp?pubid=2011033

National Survey of Student Engagement (NSSE). (2009). *Assessment for improvement: Tracking student engagement over time—annual results 2009*. Bloomington: Indiana University, Center for Postsecondary Research.

Pike, G. R., Kuh, G. D., McCormick, A. C., Ethington, C. A., & Smart, J. C. (2011). If and when money matters: The relationships among educational expenditures, student engagement and students' learning outcomes. *Research in Higher Education, 52*(1), 81–106.

Spellings, M. (2006). *A test of leadership: Chartering the future of U.S. higher education*. Washington, DC: U.S. Department of Education.

White House Initiatives on Historically Black Colleges and Universities. (n.d.). Accredited HBCU listing. Retrieved from http://www.ed.gov/edblogs/whhbcu/one-hundred-and-five-historically-black-colleges-and-universities/

Willie, C., Reddick, R., & Brown, R. (2006). *The Black college mystique*. Lanham, MD: Rowman & Littlefield.

Student Organization Involvement

A Grounded Theory OF THE Influence OF Black Greek-lettered Organizations ON THE Persistence OF African Americans AT A Predominantly White Institution

DONALD MITCHELL JR.

For decades, scholars have documented that predominantly White institutions (PWIs) are not fully meeting the needs of African American students, as these students have reported social isolation, discrimination, and low social integration (Feagin, Vera, & Imani, 1996; Fleming, 1984; Harper, 2013). While the experiences of African American students at PWIs have been well documented, further research on best practices to retain and graduate African American students at PWIs is needed. One particular area where further research is merited concerns African Americans' involvement in Black Greek-lettered organizations (BGLOs). Studies have documented the effects of BGLOs on African American students' experiences at PWIs, particularly in the areas of social support, engagement, and leadership development (Harper, 2008a; Kimbrough, 1995; Kimbrough & Hutcheson, 1998; McClure, 2006; Patton, Bridges, & Flowers, 2011). Still, scholarship on BGLOs and academic outcomes warrants further attention given the many challenges African American students continue to encounter in pursuit of higher education.

There are nine college BGLOs (Alpha Phi Alpha Fraternity, Inc.; Alpha Kappa Alpha Sorority, Inc.; Kappa Alpha Psi Fraternity, Inc.; Omega Psi Phi Fraternity, Inc.; Delta Sigma Theta Sorority, Inc.; Phi Beta Sigma Fraternity, Inc.; Zeta Phi Beta Sorority, Inc.; Sigma Gamma Rho Sorority, Inc.; and Iota Phi Theta Fraternity, Inc.). Founded from 1906 to 1963, college BGLOs became advocates for African Americans as early BGLO members realized that the collective efforts within their organizations were important for racial, educational, and social progress (Bonner, 2006). In this study, I examine students' social experiences in BGLOs to better understand whether, and in what ways, those experiences influence persistence. I define persistence similar to Reason (2009)—a student's progress toward goal attainment—and, in the present study, graduation is defined as a student's goal. To investigate the relationship, I place emphasis on social capital that may be gained through social networks established in BGLOs. The following research questions shaped this study: In what ways, if any, is social capital gained through African American students' participation in BGLOs? In what ways, if any, does social capital influence the persistence of African American students at PWIs?

LITERATURE REVIEW

African American students' academic and social needs are often left unmet at PWIs (Feagin et al., 1996; Harper, 2013; Pascarella & Terenzini, 2005). African American students have reported feeling left out of curricula, having less satisfactory relationships with faculty, feeling more excluded from campus activities, and having inadequate social lives on campus (Harper, 2013; McClure, 2006; Rovai, Gallien, & Wighting, 2005). Subsequently, it is important for PWIs to continue to adopt and improve institutional practices that support and engage African American students.

Tinto's (1975) and Astin's (1993) college student impact models have been foundational, influential, and important in student attrition, involvement, and persistence discourse, as many of their claims are consistent with the experiences of several college students. Yet, some researchers have argued there are limitations to the aforementioned models and recommendations (Fischer, 2007). Alternatively, researchers have focused specifically on African American students' engagement at PWIs (Fischer, 2007; Guiffrida, 2003, 2004; Harper & Quaye, 2007; Harper, 2013). Furthermore, researchers have documented African American students' engagement within minority and African American student organizations as spaces in which African American students actively search to become engaged at PWIs (Guiffrida, 2004; Harper & Quaye, 2007).

Reason (2009) suggests that subcultures are important for underrepresented groups as they help students negotiate the differences between their cultures and dominant cultures and potentially hostile environments. African American student organizations at PWIs are often safe spaces for African American students to learn about and connect with their cultures (Guiffrida, 2003). Researchers have also noted that minority student organizations have positive effects on leadership development (Dugan, Kodama, & Gebhardt, 2012) and racial-identity development (Harper & Quaye, 2007; Renn & Ozaki, 2010), which improve students' college experiences.

Nevertheless, research related to African American student participation in minority and African American student organizations at PWIs in relation to academic outcomes is mixed. Fischer (2007) found that minority students involved in formal social activities are more likely to persist and Guiffrida (2003) found African American student organizations connect students with faculty, which is positively linked to persistence. Nevertheless, Guiffrida (2004) found that overinvolvement in African American student organizations is sometimes harmful to academic achievement. Guiffrida explained, "Overinvolved students with low grades described spending countless hours working on the business of the [Black student] organization, which they believed to have significantly contributed to their low GPAs" (p. 92). This contradiction highlights the need for further research exploring the impact of African American student organizations on academic outcomes of African American students at PWIs. In the present study, I bring focus to the existing gap in the literature concentrating on BGLOs.

Scholars have documented that BGLOs have positive effects on student-faculty relationships (Patton, Bridges, & Flowers, 2011), student involvement and engagement (Kimbrough, 1995; Kimbrough & Hutcheson, 1998), leadership development (Kimbrough, 1995; Kimbrough & Hutcheson, 1998), and social support and integration (Harper, 2008a; McClure, 2006). Still, research related to the impact of fraternities and sororities on academic outcomes—and BGLOs in particular—is inconclusive. Pascarella, Edison, Whitt, Nora, Hagedorn, and Terenzini (1996) found that fraternities and sororities have a negative effect on some areas of cognitive development; however, the authors mention there is a slightly positive effect of fraternity involvement on the cognitive development of men of color. Furthermore, Pascarella, Flowers, and Whitt (2001) found that fraternities and sororities have negative effects on cognitive development during a student's first year; however, in a review of Pascarella, Edison, and colleagues' study, Harper, Byars, and Jelke (2005) noted that most BGLO chapters do not allow students to join during their first year. Accordingly, the academic outcomes associated with students involved in BGLOs may be different than those students involved in historically White Greek-lettered organizations.

Research that has explicitly examined the relationship between BGLOs and academic outcomes has primarily been conducted by Harper (2000, 2008a). According to Harper (2000), after examining the academic standings reports for all fraternities and sororities at 24 colleges and universities, nearly 92% of the BGLO chapters had lower GPA averages than the overall GPA average of all students involved in fraternities and sororities at each institution. Later, Harper (2008a) investigated the effects of BGLO membership on classroom engagement in predominantly White classrooms, interviewing 131 participants at a large, public research university in the Midwest. Harper concluded that the factors that influence classroom engagement positively are underrepresentation, voluntary race representation, collective responsibility, and engaging teaching styles. Harper also found that the factors that negatively affect participation are forced representation and nonengaging teaching styles.

Given the documented benefits of BGLOs on student engagement and social support, researchers should examine how the social aspects of being involved in BGLOs influence persistence. Using a social capital framework, McClure (2006) suggests, "As it relates specifically to connecting members to the university, the fraternity can clearly be considered a mechanism of social integration" (p. 1039). As cultural organizations help socially integrate African Americans on predominantly White campuses, they can be viewed as enclaves of social capital for African American students. Ultimately, in this study, I explore the ways in which BGLOs at a PWI offer participants social capital and the ways in which that capital influences students' persistence.

Social capital is defined through two overarching themes—benefits gained by a community and benefits gained by an individual (Borgatti, Jones, & Everett, 1998; Lin, 1999). Bourdieu's (1986) analysis of social capital places emphasis on the benefits accrued by an individual. I used Bourdieu's definition to shape the present study and also built upon Lin's (1999) network theory of social capital to frame the analysis. Lin's framework highlights the idea that social capital is embedded in resources in social networks and Lin defined social capital as an "investment in social relations with expected returns" (p. 30). Lin's network theory of social capital is explained using three key elements: inequalities, capitalization, and effects.

First, individuals do not possess the same amount of social capital; therefore, there are inequalities in the social capital possessed. Second, individuals capitalize by accessing and mobilizing social capital. Third, the effects are the returns or the benefits associated with the social capital gained. The returns can be explained in two ways: returns to instrumental action and returns to expressive action. Returns to instrumental action are gained resources not originally possessed by the individual, and returns to expressive action are maintaining resources that are already possessed by the individual. I use Lin's network theory of social capital to frame how involvement in BGLOs at a PWI influences persistence.

METHOD

I used a grounded theory methodology to conduct this study. When grounded theory was formed by Glasser and Strauss in 1967, the methodology was unique in that it did not start with a hypothesis (Merriam, 2009). Using a grounded theory methodology allows theories to emerge from the research as participants describe their engagement with, and interpretation of, a given lived experience and researchers seek "not just to understand, but also to build a substantive theory about the phenomenon of interest" (Merriam, 2009, p. 23).

Researchers bring knowledge, assumptions, and biases into qualitative studies (Charmaz, 2006). I am a member of a BGLO, I approached this study as an advocate for BGLOs, and I acknowledge the experiences of African American students studying at PWIs are sometimes negative. Because of my lived experiences and the knowledge I brought to the study, I did not take an objective stance during the study. Rather, I thought that my positionality would be useful in co-constructing the grounded theory that emerged because "constructivist grounded theorists do not attempt to be objective in their data collection or analysis, but instead seek to clarify and problematize their assumptions and make those assumptions clear to others" (Edwards & Jones, 2009, p. 212). Thus, I consider this study a constructivist grounded theory (Charmaz, 2006).

Sample

The participants in the present study were students at a large, public, predominantly White research-intensive university located in the Northeast region of the United States. At the time, the university enrolled approximately 35,000 students with approximately 11% of the students identifying as African American. I recruited participants by introducing my study during a BGLO executive council meeting and, after following up with each BGLO chapter, a total of seven women and five men participated in the study. The participants were all members of one of four BGLO chapters that participated in the study, which included two fraternities and two sororities. Each participant completed a demographic questionnaire. The length of BGLO membership ranged from one academic semester to two academic years. Eleven participants were seniors and one was a junior. All of the participants self-identified as African American or Black. Two of the 12 participants identified as first-generation college students. Their college GPAs were self-reported and ranged from 2.4 to 3.7 on a 4.0 scale.

Data Collection and Analysis

I collected data through focus groups and a series of semi-structured one-on-one interviews. First, all 12 students participated in one of four BGLO focus groups and each focus group was composed of members from one BGLO chapter. Next, I further explored the experiences of eight students through a series of one-on-one interview sessions, totaling 24 one-on-one interviews. I used both focus groups and interviews as a triangulation method, which allowed me to explore how the participants' collective experiences confirmed, enhanced, or rejected the experiences of the one-on-one interview participants, and vice versa. I also conducted culminating focus groups with the one-on-one participants to confirm or reject themes, relationships, and the grounded theory that emerged.

In grounded theory, data collection and analysis are conducted simultaneously, a process referred to as theoretical sampling (Corbin & Strauss, 2008). During the theoretical sampling process, I used codes and themes that emerged from the data to develop questions for the next round of interview questions. This back-and-forth process was employed until I reached data saturation and the grounded theory was formed (Corbin & Strauss, 2008). Examples of focus group and initial interview questions used included the following: In what ways, if any, have the social networks within your organization influenced your college experience? In what ways, if any, have the social networks within your fraternity/sorority influenced your college experience as related to your persistence toward graduation? Examples of round 2 and 3 interview questions used were: In what ways, if any, do your relationships with your line brothers/line sisters (joining a BGLO chapter the same semester) influence your persistence? In what ways, if any, have you ever made academic sacrifices because of the demands of your fraternity/sorority?

I reviewed the transcripts, audiotapes, and my research journal to analyze the data and I used the constant comparative method to analyze the data until a grounded theory emerged (Corbin & Strauss, 2008). The emergence of concepts, themes, and the grounded theory was a result of using processes of open, axial, and selective coding. Open coding is an analysis that identifies emerging concepts from the data; axial coding is the process of identifying subconcepts, properties, and dimensions to fully explain the continua and relationships between concepts; and selective coding is the process of developing a story or creating a grounded theory (Corbin & Strauss, 2008).

I used the criteria credibility, transferability, dependability, and confirmability to ensure the trustworthiness of the study (Merriam, 2009). The techniques I used to ensure trustworthiness were including an audit trail, which is raw data from the study; performing member checks through a culminating focus group with the eight interview participants; triangulating the data by comparing the findings to existing literature and conducting both focus groups and one-on-one interviews; and, by monitoring my biases by documenting my thoughts throughout the study and through member checks. I have also provided detailed information on the participants, the setting, and the procedures used in the study to ensure transferability. In addition, I spent seven months interacting with participants and building relationships with them.

FINDINGS

Within this section, I present the results of the study. First, I introduce the ways in which the participants highlighted inequalities that were present at the institution. Next, I highlight the ways in which the participants decided to join BGLOs and how they used their networks to navigate the campus. Finally, I introduce the returns that were associated with being involved in a BGLO at a PWI. I assigned each interview participant a pseudonym using the first names of African American (s)heroes based on the students' learned identities (e.g., Robin was named after newscaster Robin Roberts because she was a sports management major). Focus group participants were not assigned pseudonyms.

Inequalities

The participants were from different backgrounds, although they were connected by their racial identity. Participants believed their experiences at the institution were different from other students, particularly White students, because they identified as African American. They also articulated differences in being members of BGLOs versus being members of historically White Greek-lettered organizations. These findings are illustrated by the themes: (1) "I want to be normal," which introduces the ways in which the participants highlighted their experiences as African Americans at a PWI; and (2) "getting rid of us," which introduces how the participants articulated their relationships with the department of fraternity and sorority life.

"I want to be normal": Experiences at a PWI

The participants generally believed being an African American influenced and shaped their college experiences. Malcolm simply stated, "Alright, so I'll be straight up. We're always subjected to racism here at this school or any school in general." Amiri referred to his campus's newspaper reports as an example of what he found to be racist:

> So they would have a suspect description and like, this is consistently. They send out a couple of these a week and it [says] Black male and that's it. That's the only description. But if it's a White male, they would just put it's a male, and they would put maybe the height or whatever. But if it's a Black male, they'll put Black male between the ages of 20–25, how they know that, I don't know. But, it's just so broad and applies to like every single Black male.

The students also discussed wanting to feel normal although they did not believe it was possible as African American students studying at a PWI. A member of one fraternity explained his feelings of wanting to be normal:

> I guess a lot of the time, being a Black [person] at a PWI there's this—it's this tendency to want to be "normal." Normal like in America almost always means White. So, you kind of want to fit in, you know, you don't want to be seen as like a sub-group or sub-anything.

While many of the participants talked about these experiences as Black students, two participants told me that they had never experienced these same incidents and feelings on campus. A member of one sorority stated, "Because I am multiracial, I've never experienced any situation where I was discriminated against." Debbie, a member of the same sorority, acknowledged that she does not find the experiences of her peers uncommon, but she explained how she had not experienced what her sorority sisters experienced. She framed it as her being in a "dream world":

> I just don't really see color like that, but cause I really live in a "dream world" … so, as far as being on this campus I can't really pinpoint a moment where I said to myself, "He did that to me because I [am] Black."

While these two students provided a different narrative than the other participants, the theme of racial awareness and wanting to be "normal" was confirmed in seven of the one-on-one interviews and in all four focus groups. Other participants talked about their experiences overcompensating during group work, trying to "sound intelligent" during class discussions, and having to be assigned to groups in academic courses because none of the other students selected them as group members. The participants attributed these feelings and experiences to being Black at a PWI and these feeling transferred to the department of fraternity and sorority life.

"Getting rid of us": Experiences in BGLOs at a PWI

The participants explained that the institution and student affairs professionals in the department of fraternity and sorority life (DFSL) did not appear to value the culture of BGLOs, especially in comparison to historically White Greek-lettered organizations. Malcolm shared that DSFL often threatened BGLOs because of low membership:

> I just know that it's hard being a Black Greek on this campus because everybody is always looking at you and then they always tell you, you must meet these visions, complete these expectations, like thirty something expectations [that doesn't fit BGLOs]. Most of [the BGLO] chapters here … have a [maximum of] seven members. [DSFL tells] us, "You got to have eight. If you don't have eight, you're about to lose your charter."

Robin was disheartened that DSFL and the institution were not supportive of BGLOs, although they are community service–oriented. She could not understand why the university would be so willing to remove the charters for BGLOs on her campus:

> It kind of disheartens me that the campus will still provide that White [Greek-lettered] organization with money and funds to do things that are all socially bound, but [BGLOs] have to struggle for funding, and we have to struggle for that support, and at times [the institution and DSFL] don't even want their name to be behind our particular organization and I feel like that's a huge problem.

These quotes show participants felt they had to constantly fight for their existence even though the groups were important in their college experience and their lives; this was confirmed by all one-on-one interview participants and in all four focus groups. I then asked the participants to reflect on why they joined BGLOs.

Capitalization

The participants capitalized on BGLO membership by first accessing or joining the organizations, then by mobilizing their connections, which helped them navigate the campus. These findings are confirmed by the themes "why I joined," which introduces the ways in which the participants decided to join a BGLO, and "linking with other people," which introduces how the participants mobilized the social capital gained through the social networks within BGLOs.

"Why I joined": Joining a BGLO

Some of the participants were exposed to BGLO membership because they had family members who were also members of the same organization, referred to as "legacy membership." Robin's grandmother suggested that she may want to consider transferring schools after she told her grandmother that she was not interested in her sorority:

> Every member in my family is a member of the organization that I'm in and I completely wanted to be the rebel and go against that. I didn't want to be a part of the organization in the beginning to be honest with you. It was so bad, my grandmother wanted me to transfer schools to see if I would seek to be [states sorority] somewhere else. And she told me before I made any "harsh and rash decisions" that I should do some research on the organization and just find out why so many people in my family chose it.

While Robin did not initially find value in BGLOs, her grandmother pushed her to reconsider. Robin was the only interviewee who identified as a legacy member; however, this theme was supported in three of the four focus groups that included legacy members.

The history and legacy of BGLOs also influenced why the participants decided to become BGLO members; all eight of the interview participants and all four focus groups confirmed this theme. Huey's mom, who is from an African country, loved U.S. African American history and because of her love for African American history, he was attracted to his fraternity:

> A lot of [BGLOs] were born during or before the Civil Rights Movement, which I [have been] real interested in since I was born. Even though it wasn't my country, my mom used to study this kind of stuff. She used to tell about the Civil Rights Movement, [and] the Black Panthers, so that was something I grew up admiring.

Huey linked BGLOs with African American history and because he considered his organization as part of that history, he decided to join. Other participants spoke about African American civil rights leaders, entertainers, athletes, and business executives who shaped African American history and were also members of BGLOs. The participants exuded a sense of pride that these African American pioneers were connected to their BGLO.

BGLO members who joined prior to the participants joining were also influential in the participants' decisions to become members; this was confirmed by all eight interview participants and in all four focus groups. Amiri felt like he was missing brotherhood:

> I got a sense of the support and the brotherhood from the [members] on the campus. That was one of the things I was looking for that I didn't necessarily find it in some of the groups I was in. I like some of the other activities and groups I did outside of school, but I always felt like it was missing something, which was brotherhood … I liked the [members] who are on the campus. I liked what they were doing.

The participants voices describe the impact others had on the participants becoming BGLO members and once they joined they were afforded a new social network of peers.

"Linking with other people": BGLOs as social networks

Once the participants joined their organizations, they used the social networks to gain access to peers, faculty, and staff, and to navigate the campus, which was confirmed by all eight interview participants and in all four focus groups. A member of one fraternity recognized the social networks he gained with some of his peers when he joined his organization. He identified it as "power":

> I can roll up to a party and just walk in as compared to someone who wasn't Greek, who [may have] to sit there and wait in line or need to know somebody. You do get that sense of power over someone who isn't a Greek. To me, honestly you just get popular, you get hip, [and] everyone wants to know you … It's a powerful feeling.

He identified the benefits of his organization and recognized that his organization provided him with what he called "power" and "special privileges" on campus. These experiences were common for participants. Participants described that BGLO networks connected them to unique opportunities and they did not believe their African American peers who were not members of BGLOs shared these networks; these experiences provided the participants "returns."

Returns

Once the participants became members of BGLOs, they were offered returns and these returns influenced the participants' persistence. The returns are documented by the themes: (1) "after 5:00 p.m. connections," which were the relationships and connections established because of being involved in a BGLO; (2) "overnight celebrity," which explains the increased social lives of the participants once they became members of BGLOs; (3) "the pledging starts once you're a member," which explains the administrative and community service experiences BGLO membership provided the participants; (4) "implementing academic plans," which explains the ways in which the participants' academic progress was monitored and supported; and, (5) "I'm a role model," which explains how the participants developed leaderships skills on campus.

"After 5 connections": Relationships and connections within BGLOs

The relationships and connections established through BGLO membership were the most salient returns for the participants; all eight interview participants and all four focus groups confirmed this finding. The relationships established were different than any other relationships established in other student groups on campus. The participants attributed these deeper bonds to intake processes—which is when a BGLO member goes through the requirements to join a chapter—and the amount of time they spent together to sustain the chapter. Oprah and Amiri explained these relationships and connections with their organizational members as "after 5:00 p.m." interactions. Oprah noted while most classes and institutional activities are finished by 5:00 p.m., BGLO activities are never done. Amiri added:

> With non-BGLO [groups] it's like everything turns off after 5 o'clock, after business [hours]. You go home or whatever. But in a BGLO you see your brothers even after 5 [p.m.]. You see them on the weekends. You're more involved in any personal issues they may be going through, or they're involved in your personal issues. It just doesn't turn off, it's a continuous thing.

Oprah and Amiri highlighted the impact of BGLO membership in their lives as they explained BGLO membership goes beyond the traditional nature of student organizations. BGLOs became a part of their whole selves.

The relationships and connections fostered influenced the participants' persistence in many ways; namely, because they were often supported, motivated, impelled by chapter members, and encouraged by role models within their organizations because they had achieved academically. One participant shared how her connections with her sorority sisters had a direct influence on her persistence:

> I went through a hardship sophomore year in college … [There] was a death in my family, someone really close [died]. And at that point it was so bad that I could have dropped out of college. It didn't happen because of the people that I was surrounded with including current chapter [members] and older sisters. But so you know, when you build on such a strong foundation when you stumble, you still have people that will catch you.

This participant directly attributed her persistence to the deeper bonds established through BGLO involvement and the quote further illustrates the deeper bonds that the participants continued to articulate throughout the study. Becoming members of BGLOs also increased the participants' social lives.

"Overnight celebrity": Increased social life

Once the participants became members of their organizations, their social lives increased dramatically, which was confirmed by all eight interview participants and within all four focus groups. Participants spent time with new sorority sisters or fraternity brothers, practiced for step shows, were responsible for membership intake, partied more, and were recognized by more of their college peers. Participants became "instant celebrities" within the Black student community. Amiri explained how his college experience changed once he became a member of his fraternity: "It's almost like an instant celebrity type thing. It's like [people are] looking at you at all times."

Joining a BGLO at this institution pushed the participants into the limelight of the Black student community and that sometimes came with a "party like a rock star" mentality; consequently, with increased social lives also came academic costs. Participating in social events was an integral part of what students did as members of BGLOs, a finding confirmed by seven of the interview participants and all four focus groups. When asked about the social demands of fraternities, Huey said,

> Oh, [the social demands] are major distractions. Because sometimes if you have a step show, I know you're going to have to prepare for it and sometimes practices are going to be after class. So you're going to have to take some time off from your studies. So [social demands] could be, in my opinion, the [biggest] distraction.

The participants shared how the social demands sometimes conflicted with academic assignments and affected grades as participants would temporarily put academics on the back burner. While the social aspects of BGLOs generally appeared to have negative influences on academics, one interview participant and one focus group did highlight the ways in which the social demands positively influenced their persistence. Malcolm said the social demands of his fraternity required him to use any spare time he had wisely:

> [There was] one thing my father always told me when I was growing up. He said, "Whenever you play baseball in the fall or in the spring that's when [you] did the best in school. Because you're so busy with baseball and by the time you get home you don't have any other time but to do homework, so you're so tired you just realize [you] got to study, [you] got to knock this out. You don't have enough free time to just mess around."

While most of the participants articulated the social demands were detrimental to academic outcomes, Malcolm believed BGLO membership and the many social demands made him more time conscious and provided him a structured schedule during his college experience. He noted that the demanding schedule that came along with BGLO membership had positive outcomes on his academics because he did not have time to "mess around" and so he had to use his spare time wisely. Similarly, focus group participants from one sorority maintained set study hours as an organization because of the social demands that came along with BGLO involvement. In addition, because they had to maintain a certain GPA in order to participate in chapter-sponsored social activities, the organization provided them with an extra incentive to excel academically. Not only did increased social lives influence the participants' academics, organizational responsibilities did as well.

"The pledging starts once you're a member": Organizational work

Once the participants became members of their organization, managing chapters and community service immediately became responsibilities. Given the small sizes of their chapters, nearly every member had to hold some type of office and, when they hosted an event, every member had a primary role. Oprah shared as soon as she became a member she was immediately put to work and it was culture shock trying to balance her new life of school, sorority work, and full-time employment. Because of the added responsibilities, her grades suffered that semester:

> You never had that chance to really adjust. It was like all of a sudden you go from not doing it to doing it all in a few weeks. And you just had no way to adjust it. And then on top of that, you had all of this stuff that you have to do ... So on top of trying to save face and try to go everywhere and try to do everything we were [new members] in a chapter. And most of us [were] starting [our] junior and senior years. [Our] classes [were] getting harder, it was just a mess.

The work was demanding for the participants, particularly because of the small number of members in their chapters. Still, the participants took on organizational work as their responsibility and were comfortable with making academic sacrifices for the benefit of their organization, a theme that was confirmed by all eight interview participants and in all four focus groups. Membership in BGLO chapters also provided them academic benefits through a social network that emphasized academics.

"Implementing academic plans": Academic monitoring

The participants' academics were monitored once they joined BGLOs. The monitoring came through GPA requirements for BGLO members, structured academic plans developed by the chapter, and less-formal academic monitoring by advisors, prophytes (older members), and current chapter members. A member of one sorority explained, "Our grades are definitely very important in this organization and to the campus as a whole [and] we have rules and regulations as far as our grades are concerned and they are non-negotiable."

Malcolm, who served as president of his fraternity, referred to an academic plan that he created to help fraternity brothers keep up with academics:

> You had to give this piece of paper, which is signed by the chapter president, to your professor saying, "This is your organization, this is the organization's goal for the [chapter's]

GPA and if you fall under that, please let [the fraternity] know." Every two weeks, you had progress reports where the professor would say what grades you're on target for based on attendance, or participation, or your homework.

Because of BGLO membership, fraternity brothers and sorority sisters, institutional Greek life advisers, and BGLO advisers all monitored their academics. Rather than persisting on their own, the participants were privy to people within their social networks who were concerned about their academics; this was confirmed by all eight interview participants and in all four focus groups. In addition to this academic support, they were inspired by peers who looked to them as role models.

"I'm a role model": Leadership development

After becoming members of BGLOs, the participants became campus leaders, particularly in the Black student community. As members of BGLOs, campus administrators, student affairs professionals, and their peers looked to the participants to lead by example, and the participants accepted their responsibility as leaders. Correspondingly, many participants were often executive board members of other Black student organizations, and BGLOs were primary sources of programming for Black students on campus. Sean shared:

Peers look up to us as leaders in the community cause we are the ones doing all the programs and events and holding leadership positions such as the president of [Black Student Union]. [He] is a member of [Black fraternity] and that's [Black Student Union], one of the largest organizations on campus. So I can say that we have a very strong and positive connection with our peers in the community.

As the participants accepted these leadership roles and developed as leaders, they reflected on what it meant for them and how that influenced their persistence. The participants articulated that the "leadership" title required them to make sure they were setting good examples, particularly in reference to academic achievement. Malcolm was adamant about being a leader and setting examples for other students. He explained:

As a leader I learned in my class you have to model the way. So being a leader you have to show that you have to do good in school. I'm still like everybody else. I want to do well in school [generally] but, I say you have the spotlight on you … So it makes me want to work that much harder knowing that not only are my fellow peers looking at me more, but the University is looking at the [Greek life GPA] statistics over the semester.

By accepting the leadership role, participants realized going to class, striving to make good grades, and leading by example were important characteristics of being student leaders; this was confirmed by all eight interview participants and in all four focus groups.

DISCUSSION

The first research question explored how African Americans may gain social capital through BGLO involvement. In Harper's (2008b) study on high-achieving African American males at predominantly White institutions (PWIs), he noted that African American men access social capital through leadership in student organizations and engagement in campus activities. Harper also noted that minority-focused organizations provide African American men with social networks that generate social capital that they use to navigate a PWI. McClure (2006) added that Black fraternities are important social networks for African American men and provide men social capital. The findings from both studies were replicated in this study; however, this study expands the student affairs literature, as I found that both African American men and African American women who join BGLOs at a PWI gain social capital through the social networks established by becoming BGLO members. In addition, this study highlights and confirms that social capital can be possessed and shared by African American student groups at a large PWI. The social capital the participants gain provides them community and increases the participants' social integration and engagement at the institution.

Furthermore, African American student engagement literature suggests that African American students seek on-campus ties and out-of-classroom experiences to socially integrate on predominantly White campuses and those ties reduce campus departure (Fischer, 2007; Harper & Quaye, 2007; Mayo, Murguia, & Padilla, 1995). These findings are all consistent with the findings in this study, and it adds to the literature by highlighting BGLOs as a specific African American student organization that positively influences the social integration and engagement of participants.

The second research question explored how social capital gained in BGLOs might influence the persistence of African American students at a PWI. It has been noted that being engaged on-campus through formal social integration activities have positive effects on GPA, persistence, and college satisfaction for African American students at PWIs (Fischer, 2007; Harper, 2013; Rovai, Gallien, & Wighting, 2005). This study found engagement in BGLOs is supportive of persistence and college satisfaction for all of the participants; yet, as Guiffrida (2004) found, overinvolvement can be harmful to academic achievement. Within BGLOs in particular, Harper (2000) suggests negative academic influences might include excessive programming and chapter commitments, hazing, and step-show preparation.

While I did not intend to measure GPA in this study, Guiffrida's (2004) and Harper's (2000) findings are supported as "returns," such as increased social lives and chapter administration, and sometimes hindered academic outcomes, such as GPA and completed academic assignments. While persistence was my focus beginning the study, GPA and completed academic assignments emerged as important themes when discussing persistence. Consequently, I included GPA and assignments in the findings because I learned that the participants' definition of persistence included those measures.

RECOMMENDATIONS FOR PRACTICE

Because of the social integration, increased engagement, and positive effects on persistence the participants experienced, this study may present evidence that student affairs professionals at large PWIs might encourage BGLO involvement. In these instances, student affairs administrators should caution interested students about the possibility of becoming overinvolved. Consequently, student affairs administrators should recognize and promote BGLOs as organizations that offer African Americans support, but caution students that overinvolvement sometimes negatively influences academic outcomes.

BGLOs foster leadership development, classroom engagement, and social integration at PWIs. In addition, this study documents the positive influence BGLOs had on the persistence of the participants at a large, predominantly White research-intensive institution. Perhaps this is initial evidence that BGLO governing bodies should fully support petitions for new charters at large PWIs. BGLO governing bodies should closely monitor members' academics once they join because the students in this study expressed possible issues of becoming overinvolved. BGLO governing bodies may also consider limiting the number of programming activities undergraduate chapters host per semester, without moving too far from the missions of the organizations; this practice might be particularly helpful for small chapters similar to the ones included in this study.

This study revealed that the institutional climate was uncomfortable for the students in the study, which is consistent with previous studies. It is documented that out-of-classroom experiences, social integration through extracurricular activities, and minority social networks have positive outcomes for African American students attending PWIs. In support of the literature, the participants stated that BGLOs supported them academically, socially, and assisted them in navigating a predominantly White campus. Given the findings, large PWIs may consider investing in BGLOs and other identity-based support systems on their campuses. BGLOs and other identity-based student organizations might be some of the most cost-effective, immediate ways to invest in student support for African American students.

CONCLUSION

The BGLOs helped the participants in this study persist at a PWI. Yet, other academic outcomes such as GPA and academic assignments were sometimes hindered. Does persistence toward graduation outweigh a higher GPA, or vice versa? Or, why should a student have to choose between the two at any higher education institution? It is important for administrators and student affairs practitioners to reflect on these types of questions because it is the responsibility of institutions to graduate the students they admit.

ACKNOWLEDGMENTS

The author would like to thank the Center for the Study of the College Fraternity at Indiana University, Bloomington, for awarding him the 2012 Richard McKaig Doctoral Research Award for this study.

REFERENCES

Allen, W. R., Epps, E. G., & Haniff, N. Z. (Eds.). (1991). *College in Black and White*. Albany: State University of New York Press.

Astin, A. (1993). *What matters in college? Four critical years revisited*. San Francisco, CA: Jossey-Bass.

Bonner, F. A. (2006). The historically Black Greek letter organization: Finding a place and making a way. *Black History Bulletin, 69*(1), 17–21.

Borgatti, S. P., Jones, C., & Everett, M. G. (1998). Network measures of social capital. *Connections, 21*(2), 27–36.

Bourdieu, P. (1986). The forms of capital. In J. Richardson (Eds.), *Handbook of theory and research for the sociology of education* (pp. 241–258). Westport, CT: Greenwood.

Charmaz, K. (2006). *Constructing grounded theory: A practical guide through qualitative analysis*. Thousand Oaks, CA: Sage.

Corbin, J., & Strauss, A. (2008). *Basics of qualitative research* (3rd ed.). Thousand Oaks, CA: Sage.

Dika, S. L., & Singh, K. (2002). Applications of social capital in educational literature: A critical synthesis. *Review of Educational Research, 72*(1), 31–60.

Dugan, J. P., Kodama, C. M., & Gebhardt, M. C. (2012). Race and leadership development among college students: The additive value of collective racial esteem. *Journal of Diversity in Higher Education, 5*(3), 174–189.

Edwards, K. E., & Jones, S. R. (2009). "Putting my man face on": A grounded theory of men's gender identity development. *Journal of College Student Development, 50*(2), 210–228.

Feagin, J. R., Vera, H., & Imani, N. (1996). *The agony of education: Black students at White colleges and universities*. New York, NY: Routledge.

Fischer, M. (2007). Settling into campus life: Differences by race/ethnicity in college involvement and outcomes. *Journal of Higher Education, 78*(2), 125–161.

Fleming, J. (1984). *Blacks in college*. San Francisco, CA: Jossey-Bass.

Guiffrida, D. A. (2003). African American student organizations as agents of social integration. *Journal of Student College Development, 44*(3), 1–16.

Guiffrida, D. A. (2004). How involvement in African American student organizations supports and hinders academic achievement. *NACADA Journal, 24*(1&2), 88–98.

Harper, S. R. (2000, Fall). The academic standings report: Helping NPHC chapters make the grade. *Association of Fraternity Advisors Perspectives*, 14–17.

Harper, S. R. (2008a). The effects of sorority and fraternity membership on class participation and African American student engagement in predominantly White classroom environments. *College Student Affairs Journal, 27*(1), 94–115.

Harper, S. R. (2008b). Realizing the intended outcomes of Brown: High-achieving African American male undergraduates and social capital. *American Behavioral Scientist, 51*(7), 1030–1053.

Harper, S. R. (2013). Am I my brother's teacher? Black undergraduates, peer pedagogies, and racial socialization in predominantly White postsecondary contexts. *Review of Research in Education, 37*, 183–211.

Harper, S. R., Byars, L. F., & Jelke, T. B. (2005). How membership affects college adjustment and African American undergraduate student outcomes. In T. L. Brown, G. S. Parks, & C. M. Phillips (Eds.), *African American fraternities and sororities: The legacy and the vision* (pp. 393–416). Lexington: University Press of Kentucky.

Harper, S. R., & Quaye, S. J. (2007). Student organizations as venues for Black identity expression and development among African American male student leaders. *Journal of College Student Development, 48*(2), 127–144.

Kimbrough, W. M. (1995). Self-assessment, participation, and value of leadership skills, activities, and experiences for Black students relative to their membership in historically Black fraternities and sororities. *Journal of Negro Education, 64*(1), 63–74.

Kimbrough, W. M., & Hutcheson, P. A. (1998). The impact of membership in Black Greek lettered organization on Black students' involvement in collegiate activities and their development of leadership skills. *Journal of Negro Education, 67*(2), 96–105.

Lin, N. (1999). Building a network theory of social capital. *Connections, 22*(1), 28–51.

Mayo, J. R., Murguia, E., & Padilla, R. V. (1995). Social integration and academic performance among minority university students. *Journal of College Student Development, 36*(6), 542–552.

McClure, S. M. (2006). Voluntary association membership: Black Greek men on a predominantly White campus. *Journal of Higher Education, 77*(6), 1037–1057.

Merriam, S. B. (2009). *Qualitative research: A guide to design and implementation*. San Francisco, CA: Jossey-Bass.

Parks, G. S., & Brown, T. L. (2005). "In the fell clutch of circumstance": Pledging and the Black Greek experience. In T. L. Brown, G. S. Parks, & C. M. Phillips (Eds.), *African American fraternities and sororities: The legacy and the vision* (pp. 437–464). Lexington: University Press of Kentucky.

Pascarella, E. T., Edison, M., Whitt, E. J., Nora, A., Hagedorn, L. S., & Terenzini, P. (1996). Cognitive effects of Greek affiliation during the first year of college. *NASPA Journal, 33*, 242–259.

Pascarella, E. T., Flowers, L., & Whitt, E. J. (2001). Cognitive effects of Greek affiliation in college: Additional evidence. *NASPA Journal, 38*(3), 280–301.

Pascarella, E. T., & Terenzini, P. (2005). *How college affects students: A third decade of research* (Vol. 2). San Francisco, CA: Jossey-Bass.

Patton, L. D., Bridges, B. K., & Flowers, L. A. (2011). Effects of Greek affiliation on African American students' engagement: Differences by college racial composition. *College Student Affairs Journal, 29*(2), 113–123.

Reason, R. D. (2009). An examination of persistence research through the lens of a comprehensive conceptual framework. *Journal of College Student Development, 50*(6), 659–682.

Renn, K. A., & Ozaki, C. C. (2010). Psychosocial and leadership identities among leaders of identity-based campus organizations. *Journal of Diversity in Higher Education, 3*(1), 14–26.

Rovai, A. P., Gallien, L. B., Jr., & Wighting, M. J. (2005). Cultural and interpersonal factors affecting African American academic performance in higher education: A review and synthesis of the research literature. *Journal of Negro Education, 74*(4), 359–370.

Tinto, V. (1975). Dropout from higher education: A theoretical synthesis of recent research. *Review of Educational Research, 45*(1), 89–125.

CHAPTER SIX

Latina/o Students AND Involvement

Outcomes Associated with Latina/o Student Organizations

RICARDO MONTELONGO, HELEN ALATORRE, ANGEL HERNANDEZ,
JOE PALENCIA, RAY PLAZA, DAMARIS SANCHEZ AND
STEPHEN SANTA-RAMIREZ

Extracurricular involvement found in college student organization participation can become a significant factor in a student's college experience. Affective and cognitive changes resulting from extracurricular activities can contribute to intellectual, social, and emotional development in students over time (Astin, 1993; Pascarella & Terenzini, 2005). Outcomes associated with participation in college student organizations include cognitive development or higher intellectual processes such as critical thinking, knowledge acquisition, synthesis, and decision making, as well as personal or affective development of attitudes, values, aspirations, and personality disposition (Astin, 1993). While participation in extracurricular activities has been described as providing these impacts on the college experience of students, problems in generalizing these student outcomes to minority student populations can occur.

Extracurricular involvement outcomes need to be examined further when applying results to diverse student populations. For some studies, researchers failed to provide racial and gender breakdowns of their samples and expressed caution when generalizing to other groups, mainly because White student leaders and predominantly White college student organizations were investigated (Cooper, Healy, & Simpson, 1994; Kuh, 1995). In addition, focus is often placed on identifying statistically significant findings for White students despite researchers' acknowledgment of racial differences in their discussions (Smith & Griffin, 1993). Stage and Anaya (1996) note the difficulty in generalizing studies to all college students because study samples comprised mostly of middle-class Whites provided the "norms" for these experiences where "diverse persons and diverse experiences often appear other than 'normal'" (p. 49). Trevino (1992) adds that it was "particularly problematic [when researchers] use predominantly and traditionally White student organizations such as fraternities, sororities, student government, religious groups, choir groups, and intramural groups" (p. 24) as the focus for their studies. When this occurred, researchers failed to consider the contributions of minority college student organizations present on many campuses (Stage & Anaya, 1996).

When studying student extracurricular opportunities on college campuses, minority student organizations are fairly recent opportunities for extracurricular involvement. These organizations largely came into presence on many predominantly White colleges and universities within the past 45 years (Baker, 2008; Johnson, 1997; Parra, Rios, & Gutierrez, 1976; Rooney, 1985). The more established minority college student organizations can trace their origins to the student movements of the 1960s and 1970s in which "minorities were struggling for identity within society," as well as for "identity, recognition, and integration into the majority community" (Chavez, 1982, p. 15) within higher education. Research investigating minority college student involvement in these organizations indicates that there are many benefits; for example, students' adjustment to college and peer support levels are facilitated by these groups (Bennett, 1999; Hernandez, 2002). Involvement in these organizations also promotes community, cultural, and ethnic awareness (Delgado-Romero, Hernandez, & Montero, 2004; White, 1999) and membership in other campus organizations (Montelongo, 2003; Rooney, 1985). Minority college student organizations have provided generations of minority students opportunities to become involved with campus student life, as well as in community service and leadership development.

LATINA/O STUDENT ORGANIZATIONS

Latina/o student organizations in this chapter are defined as any student or administratively sponsored campus groups that are established for the expressed purpose of representing Latina/o interests and culture in a particular area. According to Davis (1997), Latina/o college student organizations generally include a combination of the following objectives: (1) to support students and increase academic achievement, recruitment, and retention; (2) to provide cultural awareness and education activities for members, the campus, and the larger community, increasing pride and understanding; (3) to provide service activities, for example, tutoring, literacy, mentoring, and other volunteer efforts, for students, youth, and other community members; and (4) to conduct political education and advocacy about issues of concern to Latina/os to improve conditions for them on campus, in the community, and in the nation. Since their initial inception into colleges and universities in the United States during the 1960s, Latina/o campus organizations have provided "a rich legacy of activism, community service, advocacy, and naturally, leadership development" (Davis, 1997, p. 231).

Latina/o college student organizations, like most minority student organizations, gained prominence at predominantly White institutions (PWIs) during the late 1960s and early 1970s as a result of the high levels of youthful energy and activist commitment directed at social and educational issues (Parra, Rios, & Gutierrez, 1976). Latina/o college student organizations addressed a wide array of issues ranging from civil rights and farm laborer rights to concerns regarding the disproportionate number of minorities fighting in the Vietnam War. In response to the rising number of Latina/o students enrolling into colleges and universities at the time, these groups also advocated for more campus counseling and support services for Latina/o students, as well as for increased campus awareness on issues and concerns pertinent to the Latina/o community.

Latina/o students' involvement in college organizations at predominantly White institutions will be investigated in this chapter, with emphasis on the impact of Latina/o student organizations on educational outcomes that enhance academic success. By providing this specific focus, higher education administrators will become aware of the potential effect these groups have on Latina/o identity, leadership, and cognitive development. Practitioners and researchers will also be able to examine these activities with regard to their influence on academic performance, retention, and graduation. Latina/o student organizations at predominantly White institutions have increased and grown, are diverse in their goals and activities, are committed to social change, and provide culturally relevant support systems for Latina/o college students.

LATINA/O STUDENT ORGANIZATION INVOLVEMENT

Latina/o student organizations explicitly educate the campus on issues pertinent to their members, and they advocate for the maintenance of cultural identity in a predominantly White college environment (Davis, 1997). By providing interactions both within and outside the campus, involvement in these groups gives Latina/o college students a feeling of belonging and being at home within their campus community. Participation in Latina/o college student organizations was also reported to provide students a mediating element to handle the effects of hostile adverse educational environments that can sometimes be found at predominantly White institutions (Hurtado & Carter, 1997; Trevino, 1992). The intersection of culture and learning seen through the lens of involvement is important to enhance college environments that are conducive for student success.

Three outcomes that ensue from Latina/o student organization involvement are addressed in this chapter. Outcomes in cultural identity, leadership, and academic engagement connected to Latina/o students' involvement in Latina/o and minority organizations at different institutional types are considered. The selected outcomes are investigated for their potential impact on student learning. First, the social change model of leadership will be analyzed with regard to how Latina/o student organization involvement impacts outcomes of the model. This is a model designed for college students and advocates for leadership practice that is grounded in social responsibility and change on behalf of others for the common good (Higher Education Research Institute [HERI], 1996). Second, Latina/o student organization involvement will be examined for its influence on identity development within students. First-generation Latina/o college students' identity development will be highlighted, with special interest on the role Latina/o Greek organizations play with identity development. Jehangir (2009) found that student support networks, much like those found in student organizations, allow ethnic first-generation students to reflect on and address cultural conflict and cognitive dissonance, which is a clear example on how alternate support networks help students navigate the system at PWIs. When investigating the possible influence involvement has on academic engagement, very few student involvement studies have focused directly on Latina/o organizations. Trevino (1992) found that Latina/o students who were active in co-curricular activities perceive themselves as having strong academic skills. Latina/o student organizations have a deeper purpose and mission than providing social outlets for students. They should be examined for their role in promoting campus involvement and student learning.

Cultural Identity

A majority of Latina/o students attend institutions where they are the minority and as a result often associate with other Latina/os (Stearns, Watanabe, & Snyder, 2002). Oseguera, Locks, and Vega (2009) found that ethnic identity and culture have a strong interpretive influence on students' meaning-making process. Furthermore, the quality and quantity of connections that students of color make with both individuals and organizations determine their likelihood of success (Museus, 2010). Torres (2003) found that students from geographical areas where Latina/os are a critical mass did not see themselves as in the minority until they arrived on a predominantly White college campus. This change in their environment prompts a stronger tie to their ethnicity rather than assimilation.

Providing Latina/o college students with multiple involvement opportunities that reflect their identities and backgrounds will allow Latina/o students to excel at their college or university (Hernandez & Lopez, 2004). As stated by Chavez and Guido-DiBrito (1999), "Deep conscious immersion into cultural traditions and values through religious, familial, neighborhood, and educational communities instills a positive sense of ethnic identity and confidence" (p. 39). For example, a student in Torres' (2003) study who self-identified as bicultural talked about her experiences joining the Latina/o student group on her campus and meeting a friend she related to. She stated:

> As I was growing up, I never really thought of myself as a Latina. Like it wasn't very important in life, and I am just realizing how important it is, and how I want to learn more about the culture, and just to learn more about my family, and my ancestors, and what not. (p. 543)

Extracurricular involvement has been described as assisting identity development for Latina/o college students. Environments that encourage positive identity development for minority college students tend to enhance academic success. Latina/o student organizations have continuously allowed Latina/o students to find their social outlet, learn more about their individual cultures and educate others on them.

According to Guardia and Evans (2008), "One way in which Latina/o college students become involved [and learn more about their identity] is by participation in fraternity and sorority life, specifically Latina/o Greek letter organizations" (p. 168). Guardia and Evans explored various factors that influence the ethnic identity of Latina/o fraternity members at a Hispanic serving institution (HSI), finding that membership in a Latina/o fraternity at an HSI may enhance the ethnic identity development of students. When Latina/o students establish strong connections with fellow ethnic minority members, these connections have a positive impact on academic achievement (Conchas, 2001).

Latina/o students' college success also influences how they navigate hostile campus environments where racism and discrimination still unfortunately exist (Torres & Hernandez, 2007). Longerbeam, Sedlacek, and Alatorre (2007) found that many Latina/o college students cope with these challenges by connecting with the Latina/o community on campus as a means of support in order to maintain their Latina/o cultural identity. Baker (2008) noted that many underrepresented students rely on the support of minority-based student organizations while attending college. Latina/o college students who become involved in activities that promote their Latina/o identity are more likely to graduate in comparison to those who are not involved in similar activities (Hernandez, 2002; Longerbeam et al., 2004). The strong familial influences within the Latina/o community should be taken into consideration when speaking about Latina/o students in higher education.

Family connections and similar strength relationships are key characteristics for Latina/o academic success, especially since Latina/os tend to be first-generation college students. According to Ortiz and Hernandez (2011), "Many Latina/os are the first in their families to participate in higher education, with only 13.2% of all Latina/o holding a bachelor's degree or higher, compared to 29.5% of the total population" (p. 94). With limited guidance, first-generation Latina/o college students often have no one to turn to for support, and many do not have role models to help them understand the expectations and complexities of the higher education system (Abrego, 2008). According to Roberts and Rosenwald (2001), family support and relationships between first-generation students and their parents commonly suffer when the students go to college. This relationship strain is a result of the lack of commonality that develops between first-generation students and their parents who are unable to relate to the contexts that have become such a key aspect of their children's lives (Roberts & Rosenwald, 2001).

In a qualitative study at a large Midwestern public research institution on first-generation Latina/o students' identity development, Schlossberg (1989) found that similar to the theory of marginality and mattering, participants experience the shift from marginalization to belonging. Students who felt marginalized early in their college experience began to feel as if they mattered after meeting other Latina/o students, joined Latina/o-oriented student organizations, and developed relationships with Latina/o-identified mentors (Carrasquillo, Martin, & Santa-Ramirez, 2011). The students maintained regular communication with their families when they began their collegiate career. Many of the students sought out student organizations that allowed them to express their cultures and share similar college experiences with others whose families did not fully understand the collegiate experience. Although the students sought out other avenues to find where they mattered on campus, the students maintained supportive family relationships, which is among the most important aspects of transition for the student and their persistence toward graduation (Hurtado & Carter, 1997).

The establishment of family-like bonds and sense of belonging among Latina/o student organization members was mentioned in studies studying identity development among Latina/o college students. Guardia and Evans (2008) conducted a study on Latin-oriented fraternities and their members, and one of the findings includes the students having feelings that the organization provides the members with "a family atmosphere and Latina/o unity" (p. 177). Torres (2004) highlighted one student's thoughts about being associated with a Latina/o student organization, saying, "I don't know if more comfortable is the word, but I just feel like it's a warmer setting" (p. 465). Latina/o student organizations tend to serve this purpose of establishing and offering a potential home away from home for Latina/os who seek connection and place on campus.

Leadership

As college leadership programs and activities are directed at a larger cross section of the student body, it is particularly important for educators to pay attention to different social identity groups and their distinct leadership needs (Bordas, 2007; Hoppe, 1998). Diverse groups of students present unique developmental needs and influences (Harper & Quaye, 2009) and understanding the nuances is crucial to develop a future generation of leaders that is inclusive of an increasingly diverse student body.

Some research indicates that Latina/o students involved in ethnic associations have a broader purpose of contributing to a Latina/o community than solely individual academic or social gains (Reyes, 2012). When considering Latina/o students' involvement, much of the literature shows that Latina/o college students join Latina/o student organizations to link up with others, creating a greater sense of belonging (Hernandez & Lopez, 2004); however, Reyes (2012) found that many Latina/os see their membership in such organizations as a way of giving back to other Latina/os through political, personal, or professional means.

Considering Reyes' (2012) findings, a leadership model pertinent to this area is the social change model of leadership (HERI, 1996). The social change model is designed for college students and advocates for leadership practice that is grounded in social responsibility and creating change on behalf of others for the common good (HERI, 1996). This model could be used to further understand the leadership experiences of students in Latina/o student organizations or to create programs and activities that support their way of leading. For instance, Latina/os who perceive themselves as activists more likely participate in college extracurricular activities (Davis, 1997; Montelongo, 2003; Johnson, 1997); however, being an activist is often met with stereotypical characteristics that use unpleasant depictions of angry protests and hostile boycotts to describe their involvement (for examples, see Moscoso, 1995; Navarrette, 1993). While these prejudiced descriptions fail to capture the true intent of activists, Latina/o student organizations do provide a leadership opportunity for those whose aim is to make others aware of Latina/o issues and concerns both on and off campus. Latina/o activists likely use college extracurricular involvement to achieve this goal (Davis, 1997; Montelongo, 2003).

Other studies have examined Latina/o students' leadership activities and involvement. Baker (2008) examined the effect of involvement in six different types of student organizations, as well as involvement in a co-ethnic student organization for underrepresented college students. Baker found that political organizations were the most beneficial type of organizational involvement for the academic performance of minority college students. This finding should be noted in that many Latina/o student organizations have a political focus or emphasis. Baker states that political involvement had a positive influence on the academic performance of Black males, Latinos, and Latinas and political involvement was the only type of organizational support that had a positive effect on the grades of both Latinas and Latinos. It was thought that the benefit might be related to increased levels of self-esteem and self-efficacy (Baker, 2008).

For students, involvement in a Latina/o student organization is like rejoining *la familia*—the Latina/o student organizations becomes a place where the student can feel welcomed and supported within an otherwise challenging environment. Being a part of la familia becomes a critical piece for Latina/o student leadership. It is through la familia that students can begin to cope with the stressful environment of college (Cavazos, Johnson, & Sparrow, 2010). Latina/o students that perceive a hostile climate on campus express more difficulty in adjusting academically, socially, and emotionally. Through involvement opportunities in Latina/o student organizations, Latina/o students find a place where they can be themselves and begin to use each other for support. The Latina/o student organization becomes a place where the students can rebuild that sense of connection to the campus, which can then lead to a more positive learning environment. Academic confidence and skills are increased for Latina/o students when positive interactions with other peers occur (Hurtado & Ponjuan, 2005). La familia provides Latina/o students a way to become connected and a way for them to get involved and give back. This engagement is critical in helping students adjust to a new environment but also in helping them to become more academically successful, which further highlights the importance Latina/o student organizations play in creating that la familia atmosphere for students.

While being a part of la familia is important, taking on a leadership role within la familia takes on greater meaning. Becoming a leader within a student organization has been shown to be linked to greater educational involvement, better life-management skills, and increased cultural participation (Foubert & Grainger, 2006). While there is a positive impact in becoming a leader within a student organization, this positive impact is further heightened when this leadership takes place within la familia. The Latina/o student leadership in la familia takes on a deeper meaning as these students become role models for their peers as well as spokespersons for their community. Due to these additional roles, this increased level of responsibility challenges positive impacts. It is critical that those working with these students leaders are aware of these heightened expectations.

Fischer (2007) explained that "for minority students, greater involvement in formal social activities such as school clubs and organizations, was positively related to college grades" (p. 144). After all groups of students were compared, Fischer found that "having more formal (i.e., extracurricular) and informal (i.e., friends) social ties was positively and significantly related to higher levels of satisfaction" (p. 145). Thus, Fischer found higher levels of satisfaction can begin to impact a student's ability to perform better in the classroom as well as reducing the likelihood of leaving college.

When considering leadership and leadership development activities, students involved in leadership activities have higher levels of educational attainment than students who do not participate in these activities (Astin, 1993). Scholars have linked increases in leadership development to varied college outcomes, including academic persistence, career aspirations, academic and work-related performance, the ability to combat stereotype threat, adaptability, and self-efficacy (Day, Harrison, & Halpin, 2009; Hannah, Avolio, Luthans, & Harms, 2008; Van Linden & Fertman, 1998; Wolniak, Mayhew, & Engberg, 2012). These outcomes may be especially relevant for students of color attempting to navigate predominately White institutions.

Academic Development

Astin (1993) postulates that the quality and quantity of a student's involvement in their college experience has a proportional effect on a student's learning and development. Such involvement contributes to intellectual development by promoting awareness of both the educational environment and the resources and learning opportunities available for students to meet academic standards. There are many factors, such as cultural, economic, and social expectations and/or pressures that Latina/o students experience in their educational experience. These external barriers can play a role in decisions on the type of institution Latina/os attend for their higher education. As previous sections note, Latina/os encounter a variety of struggles while attending college; however, Latina/o student organizations provide programs that reaffirm students as capable learners (Gandara & Contreras, 2010). The more confident Latina/o students are in their strategies to succeed academically, the greater their levels of academic achievement.

Montelongo (2003) and Montelongo and Duran-Guzman (2011) surveyed Chicana/o and Puerto Rican students at two large Midwestern PWIs about the nature of their involvement with college student organizations. When comparing Chicana/o students with Puerto Ricans, Chicana/os reported that college student organizations provide members opportunities to become more independent within their educational environment more so than Puerto Ricans. This finding highlights the importance of addressing within-group differences in studying Latina/o college student populations. The difference is explained in part due to the larger number of Chicana/o students within the total Latina/o undergraduate student population.

Culturally relevant factors associated with Latina/o students' involvement also were found that had potential effects on educational outcomes. Students that used cultural activities (i.e., Latina/o student organizations) to establish campus connections and perceptions of the beneficial aspects of Latina/o student organization participation were found to be significant predictors of both satisfaction with college and participation in college extracurricular activities (Montelongo & Duran-Guzman, 2011). Involvement in campus life has a positive effect on Latina/o students' learning, and their perceptions that Latina/o student organizations are supportive of their academic development likely carries over to actual improved academic performance (Montelongo, 2003).

Montelongo found that participation in Latina/o student organizations appear to lower Latina/o students' grade point averages (GPA). If students are members or officers of these organizations, then there may be an increased likelihood that their GPA will be negatively influenced; however, students remarked that academic support is one of the most important functions of minority student organizations. It seems that these organizations would have a positive effect on this outcome. Previous researchers have already shown that holding a leadership position is a negative predictor of undergraduates' GPAs (Astin, 1993). The effect may be the consequence of a high or low GPA, rather than a cause (Astin, 1993). Latina/o students looking to improve their GPA may initially seek help and resources with Latina/o student organizations.

LATINA/O STUDENT INVOLVEMENT AND ACADEMIC OUTCOMES

To effectively increase the positive impacts of cultural identity, leadership, and academic engagement, student affairs professionals must understand the cultural factors that shape Latina/o college student involvement. Understanding these factors can help campuses in developing learning environments that are conducive to academic success. The three outcomes that were examined—cultural identity, leadership, and academic development—have direct effects on academic performance, retention, and graduation. In addition, campus satisfaction, sense of belonging, and community engagement are enhanced, which indirectly can influence academic performance by providing a campus environment where validation and support are recognized.

Latina/o student organizations can help students navigate their own identity by providing supportive elements that allow cultural expression and interactions with others from similar backgrounds. Involvement with these groups produces much needed social capital that can be used to promote student success, despite typically being the minority, especially at predominantly White institutions. The continued rapid growth of Latino-affiliated fraternities and sororities on college campuses highlights the importance belonging has with Latina/o student involvement. Within these groups, members find family-type bonding, which allows for the exploration of their place on campus and in society in general.

Latina/o student organizations are important tools for leadership development. Campus leaders can promote academic success for Latina/os. While some negative perceptions still exist with regard to the political activism of such groups (Montelongo, 2003), political activism is sometimes a response to incite social change. Leadership is also further promoted by instilling a sense of la familia, a cultural characteristic of Latina/o student involvement where opportunities for family-like connections with peers are considered when determining organizational involvement. La familia is crucial especially for first-generation college Latina/o students in that this helps in successfully navigating the complex college academic environments.

Latina/o student organizations promote academic engagement in that members use such groups to find academic resources and peer support. Since students rely on these groups to help them make sense of the academic environment, involvement may be directly related to the academic support that these organizations tend to offer to their members. Latina/o student organizations can also be a helpful tool to direct students toward when encountering academic difficulty.

Today, Latina/o college student organizations on predominantly white campuses have increased in number and have become extremely diverse in regard to their activities and purposes (Delgado-Romero, Hernandez, & Montero, 2004). Presently, numerous Latina/o college student organizations exist on campuses to provide more than social outlets for students (Davis, 1997; Delgado-Romero, Hernandez, & Montero, 2004). These groups have become campus entities whose functions have expanded to advance goals for academic support, career development, and fraternity and sorority life, just to name a few. Despite the diversity apparent among the types of Latina/o college student organizations and their activities, their roots are firmly planted in social change, commitment to the Latina/o community, and the common goal to be student resources for social and emotional comfort and adjustment at PWIs (Davis, 1997; Trevino, 1992). The origins and functions of Latina/o student groups reflect both cultural and sociohistorical factors unique to the Latina/o experience in the United States. It is important for campuses to create supportive niches for Latina/o students to transform college environments into one that welcomes these students. Latina/o student organizations are campus resources where such supportive niches can be found.

REFERENCES

Abrego, S. H. (2008). Recent strategies to increase access and retention. In L. A. Valverde (Ed.), *Latino change agents in higher education: Shaping a system that works for all* (pp. 77–92). San Francisco, CA: Jossey-Bass.

Astin, A. (1993). *What matters in college? Four critical years revisited.* San Francisco, CA: Jossey-Bass.

Baker, C. N. (2008). Under-represented college students and extracurricular involvement: The effects of various student organizations on academic performance. *Social Psychology of Education, 11*(3), 273–298.

Bennett, S. M. (1999). Self-segregation: An oxymoron in Black and White. In K. Freeman (Ed.), *African American culture and heritage in higher education research and practice* (pp. 121–131). Westport, CT: Praeger.

Bordas, J. (2007). *Salsa, soul, and spirit: Leadership for a multi-cultural age.* San Francisco, CA: Berrett-Koehler.

Carrasquillo, M., Martin, B., Santa-Ramirez, S. (2011). *Latino identity student stories.* Poster presented for the Higher, Adult, and Lifelong Learning Program, Department of Educational Administration, College of Education, Michigan State University, East Lansing.

Cavazos, J., Johnson, M. B., & Sparrow, G. S. (2010). Overcoming personal and academic challenges: Perspectives from Latina/o college students. *Journal of Hispanic Higher Education, 9*(4), 304–316.

Chavez, A., & Guido-DiBrito, F. (1999). Racial and ethnic identity and development. *New Directions for Adult and Continuing Education, 1999*(84), 39–48.

Chavez, E. A. (1982). Involvement of minority students in student activities. *Bulletin of the Association of College Unions-International, 50*(4), 15–16.

Coleman, J. (1988). Social capital in the creation of human capital. *American Journal of Sociology, 94*(1), S95–S120.

Conchas, G. (2001). Structuring failure and success: Understanding the variability in Latino school engagement. *Harvard Educational Review, 71*(3), 475–504.

Cooper, D. L., Healy, M. A., & Simpson, J. (1994). Student development through involvement: Specific changes over time. *Journal of College Student Development, 35*(3), 98–102.

Davis, M. (1997). Latino leadership development: Beginning on campus. *National Civic Review, 86*(3), 227–233.

Day, D. V., Harrison, M. M., & Halpin, S. M. (2009). *An integrative approach to leader development.* New York, NY: Taylor & Francis.

Delgado-Romero, E., Hernandez, C., & Montero, H. (2004). Mapping the development of Hispanic/Latina/o student organizations: A model at the University of Florida. *Journal of Hispanic Higher Education, 3*(3), 237–253.

Dugan, J. P., & Komives, S. R. (2007). *Developing leadership capacity in college students.* College Park, MD: National Clearinghouse for Leadership Programs.

Feagin, J. R., & Sikes, M. P. (1995). How Black students cope with racism on White campuses. *Journal of Blacks in Higher Education, 8,* 91–97.

Fischer, M. J. (2007). Settling into campus life: Differences by race/ethnicity in college involvement outcomes. *Journal of Higher Education, 78*(2), 125–161.

Foubert, J. D., & Grainger, L. U. (2006). Effects of involvement in clubs and organizations on the psychosocial development of first-year and senior college students. *NASPA Journal, 43*(1), 166–182.

Gandera, P. & Contreras, F. (2012). *The Latino education crisis: The consequences of failed social policies.* Cambridge, MA: Harvard University Press.

Guardia, J. R., & Evans, N. J. (2008). Factors influencing the ethnic identity development of Latino fraternity members at a Hispanic serving institution. *Journal of College Student Development, 49*(3), 163–181.

Hannah, S. T., Avolio, B. J., Luthans, F., & Harms, P. D. (2008). Leadership efficacy: Review and future directions. *Leadership Quarterly, 19*(6), 669–692.

Harper, S. R., & Quaye, S. J. (2009). *Student engagement in higher education: Theoretical perspectives and practical approaches for diverse populations*. New York, NY: Routledge.

Hernandez, J. C. (2002). A qualitative exploration of the first-year experience of Latino college students. *NASPA Journal, 40*(1), 69–84.

Hernandez, J. C., & Lopez, M. A. (2004). Leaking pipeline: Issues impacting Latino/a college student retention. *Journal of College Student Retention, 6*(1), 37–60.

Higher Education Research Institute (HERI). (1996). *A social change model of leadership development: Guidebook version III*. College Park, MD: National Clearinghouse for Leadership Programs.

Hoppe, M. H. (1998). Cross-cultural issues in leadership development. In C. D. McCauley, R. S. Moxley, & E. Van Velson (Eds.), *Handbook of leadership development: Center for creative leadership* (pp. 336–378). San Francisco, CA: Jossey-Bass.

Hurtado, S., & Carter, D. F. (1997). Effects of college transition and perceptions of the campus racial climate on Latino students' sense of belonging. *Sociology of Education, 70*(4), 324–345.

Hurtado, S., & Ponjuan, L. (2005). Latino educational outcomes and the campus climate. *Journal of Hispanic Higher Education, 4*(3), 235–251.

Jehangir, R. R. (2009). Cultivating voice: First-generation students seek full academic citizenship in multicultural learning communities. *Innovative Higher Education, 34*(1), 33–49.

Johnson, S. (1997). Ethnic/cultural centers on predominantly White campuses: Are they necessary? In K. Lomotey (Ed.), *Sailing against the wind: African Americans and women in education*. Albany: State University of New York Press.

Kezar, A. J., Carducci, R., & Contreras-McGavin, M. (2006). *Rethinking the "L" word in higher education: The revolution in research on leadership*. (ASHE Higher Education Report Vol. 31, No. 6). San Francisco, CA: Jossey-Bass.

Kuh, G. D. (1995). The other curriculum: Out-of-class experiences associated with student learning and personal development. *Journal of Higher Education, 66*(2), 123–155.

Longerbeam, S. D., Sedlacek, W. E., & Alatorre, H. M. (2004). In their own voices: Latino student retention. *NASPA Journal, 41*(3), 538–550.

Montelongo, R. (2003). *Chicana/o and Puerto Rican experiences with Latina/o and minority college student organizations at predominantly White institutions and the potential effects of these organizations on educational outcomes*. Unpublished doctoral dissertation, Indiana University, Bloomington.

Montelongo, R., & Duran-Guzman, N. (2011). *The impact of Latino student organizations on college success: An exploratory study of Latino student involvement*. Program presented at Noel-Levitz Symposium on the Recruitment & Retention of Students of Color, Denver, CO.

Moscoso, E. (1995). Culture comforts: Hispanic organizations help students build a home away from home. *Hispanic, 8*(2), 50–52.

Museus, S. D. (2010). Delineating the ways that targeted support programs facilitate minority students' access to social networks and development of social capital in college. *Enrollment Management Journal, 4*(3), 10–41.

Navarrette, R. (1993). *A darker shade of crimson: Odyssey of a Harvard Chicano*. New York, NY: Bantam.

Ortiz, A. M., & Hernandez, S. (2011). Latino/Latina college students. In M. J. Cuyjet, M. F. Howard-Hamilton, & D. L. Cooper (Eds.), *Multiculturalism on campus: Theory, models, and practices for understanding diversity and creating inclusion* (pp. 87–116). Sterling, VA: Stylus.

Oseguera, L., Locks, A.M., & Vega, I. I. (2009). Increasing Latina/o students' baccalaureate attainment: A focus on retention. *Journal of Hispanic Higher Education, 8*(1), 23–53.

Parra, R., Rios, V., & Gutierrez, A. (1976). Chicano organizations in the Midwest: Past, present and possibilities. *Aztlan, 7*(2), 235–253.

Pascarella, E. T., & Terezini, P. T. (2005). *How college affects students: A third decade of research*. San Francisco, CA: Jossey-Bass.

Reyes, D. I. V. (2012). *Latino student politics: Constructing ethnic identities through organizations.* University of California, Irvine. ProQuest Dissertations and Theses. Retrieved from http://search.proquest.com.ezproxy.shsu.edu/pqdtft/docview/963696930/fulltextPDF/3BF-9780F6A4649E0PQ/1?accountid=7065

Roberts, J. S., & Rosenwald, G. C. (2001). Ever upward and no turning back: Social mobility and identity formation among first-generation college students. In D. P. McAdams, R. Josselson, & A. Lieblich (Eds.), *Turns in the road: Narrative studies of lives in transition* (pp. 91–119). Washington, DC: American Psychological Association.

Rooney, G. D. (1985). Minority students' involvement in minority student organizations: An exploratory study. *Journal of College Student Personnel, 26*(5), 450–456.

Schlossberg, N. K. (1989). Marginality and mattering: Key issues in building community. *New Directions for Student Services, 1986*(48), 5–15.

Schuh, J. H., & Laverty, M. (1983). The perceived long-term influence of holding a significant student leadership position. *Journal of College Student Personnel, 24*(1), 28–32.

Smith, J. S., & Griffin, B. L. (1993). The relationship between involvement in extracurricular activities and the psychosocial development of university students. *College Student Affairs Journal, 13*(1), 79–84.

Stage, F. K., & Anaya, G. A. (1996). A transformational view of college student research. In F. Stage, G. Anaya, J. Bean, D. Hossler, & G. Kuh (Eds.), *College students: The evolving nature of research* (pp. 12–22). Needham Heights, MA: Simon & Schuster/ASHE.

Stearns, C., Watanabe, S., & Snyder, T. D. (2002). *Hispanic serving institutions: Statistical trends from 1990 to 1999*. Darby, PA: Diane.

Torres, V. (2003). Influences on ethnic identity development of Latino college students in the first two years of college. *Journal of College Student Development, 44*(4), 532–547.

Torres, V., & Hernandez, E. (2007). The influence of ethnic identity on self-authorship: A longitudinal study of Latino/a college students. *Journal of College Student Development, 48*(5), 558–573.

Torres, V., Jones, S. R., & Renn, K. A. (2009). Identity development theories in student affairs: Origins, current status, and new approaches. *Journal of College Student Development, 50*(6), 577–596.

Torres, V., & Phelps, R. E. (1997). Hispanic American acculturation and ethnic identity: A bi-cultural model. *College Student Affairs Journal, 17*(1), 53–68.

Treviñó, J. (1992). *Participation in ethnic/racial student organizations*. Unpublished doctoral dissertation, University of California, Los Angeles.

Turner, C. S. (1994). Guests in someone else's house: Students of color. *Review of Higher Education, 17*(4), 355–370.

Van Linden, J. A., & Fertman, C. I. (1998). *Youth leadership: A guide to understanding leadership development in adolescents*. San Francisco, CA: Jossey-Bass.

Williams, M., & Winston, R. B., Jr. (1985). Participation in organized student activities and work: Differences in developmental task achievement of traditional aged college students. *NASPA Journal, 22*(3), 52–59.

Wolniak, G. C., Mayhew, M. J., & Engberg, M. E. (2012). Learning's weak link to persistence. *Journal of Higher Education, 83*(6), 795–823.

CHAPTER SEVEN

First-generation College Students' Leadership Experiences AND Academic Outcomes

KRISTA M. SORIA

Scholarly inquiries about first-generation college students—those who are the first in their families to attend higher education in pursuit of a four-year degree—and their experiences in higher education continue to be underrepresented in the literature (Pike & Kuh, 2005). It is encouraging that more and more first-generation college students are enrolling at college campuses across the nation each year (Choy, 2001); yet, persistent concerns about first-generation students' adjustment, academic engagement, retention, and inclusion in the fabric of campus life (Housel & Harvey, 2009; Jehangir, 2009, 2010; Pascarella, Pierson, Wolniak, & Terenzini, 2004; Pike & Kuh, 2005; Soria & Stebleton, 2012) have led many scholars to critique the system of higher education as one that reproduces existing social-class disparities (Soria, Stebleton, & Huesman, 2013–2014; Stephens, Fryberg, Markus, Johnson, & Covarrubias, 2012). Researchers have demonstrated that first-generation college students have lower grade point averages and greater academic challenges (Soria & Gorny, 2012; Stebleton & Soria, 2012; Terenzini, Cabrera, & Bernal, 2001), are more likely to withdraw from college than students with college-educated parents (Ishitani, 2006), tend to come from backgrounds with fewer financial resources (Horn & Nunez, 2000; Hossler, Schmit, & Vesper, 1990; Soria & Gorny, 2012), and often struggle with the cultural and social norms of higher education (Johnson, Richeson, & Finkel, 2011; Ostrove & Long, 2007; Stephens et al., 2012; Stephens, Townsend, Markus, & Phillips, 2012). Consequently, it is important for colleges and universities to explore measures they can take to better support first-generation college students' success in higher education.

The purpose of this chapter is to examine whether first-generation students' leadership experiences are associated with their academic outcomes in higher education. Scholars have previously found positive relationships between college students' involvement in extracurricular experiences and their academic achievement (Baker, 2008; Broh, 2002; Huang & Chang, 2004; Strapp & Farr, 2009; Webber, Bauer Krylow, & Zhang, 2013); however, the academic outcomes associated with students' leadership participation as a form of involvement in higher education remains underresearched. While not traditionally conceived as a means of advancing students' retention or academic success, college students' leadership experiences can provide tremendous growth and developmental opportunities within their educational journeys (A. Astin, 1993; Cooper, Healy, & Simpson, 1994; Cress, Astin, Zimmerman-Oster, & Burkhardt, 2001; Dugan & Komives, 2010; Kezar & Moriarty, 2000; Logue, Hutchens, & Hector, 2005). Indeed, colleges and universities are increasingly prioritizing college students' development of leadership abilities in recognition of the need to cultivate future leaders who can tackle the most persistent social problems of today—and future leaders who can respond to the emergent social needs of tomorrow (Dugan, 2006; Dugan & Komives, 2007; Hurtado, 2007; Kezar, Carducci, & Contreras-McGavin, 2006; Roberts, 1997).

Contemporary paradigms of leadership counter the notion that leadership is purely positional or hierarchical (Outcalt, Faris, & McMahon, 2001; Roberts, 1997); instead, newer perspectives view leadership as a *process* (H. Astin, 1996; H. Astin & A. Astin, 1996; A. Astin & H. Astin, 2000). Grounded in the social change model of leadership development, leadership is defined as "a purposeful, collaborative, values-based process that results in positive social change" (Komives, Wagner, & Associates, 2009, p. xii). The social change model of leadership development has become nearly paradigmatic in its use as a framework within college leadership programs (Campbell, Smith, Dugan, & Komives, 2012). Within this framework, leadership is collaborative, as opposed to an individual effort, and leadership is based on values as opposed to being a value-neutral, hierarchical process of leaders and followers (H. Astin & A. Astin, 1996). The social change model espouses seven core values corresponding to three broad areas of development: personal, group, and community (H. Astin, 1996). The personal values include consciousness of self (being aware of one's beliefs, values, and emotions), congruence (thinking, feeling, and behaving with consistency), and commitment (possessing the passion and energy that motivates one to action) (H. Astin & A. Astin, 1996). The three group values include collaboration (working with others in common pursuits), common purpose (sharing the aims and values of the group), and controversy with civility (recognizing that differences should be met with civility; H. Astin & A. Astin, 1996). Finally, the value embedded in the community category is known as citizenship—the process whereby individuals and their collective groups become connected to their communities and larger society (H. Astin & A. Astin, 1996). Students who develop those seven values are better positioned to engage in an eighth value—change—which represents students' engagement in socially responsible leadership. The intended goal of leadership development programs grounded in the social change model is to "prepare a new generation of leaders who understand that they can act as leaders to effect change without necessarily being in traditional leadership positions of power and influence" (H. Astin & A. Astin, 1996, p. 12).

While the social change model of leadership development provides a comprehensive and holistic framework around which to understand college students' leadership development, Haber and Komives (2009) discovered co-curricular involvement, formal leadership roles, and leadership training and education programs are important in predicting aspects of students' socially responsible leadership outcomes. Therefore, while conceptualizations of students' leadership as viewed only by their positional leadership involvement are limited because they refer to hierarchical leadership models, students' involvement in leadership positions are nonetheless important in predicting developmental outcomes. For example, college students who held leadership positions reported that their leadership roles had greatest impact on their development of the types of skills valuable in leadership and in the workforce: teamwork, decision making, and organizing-planning skills (Schuh & Laverty, 1983). Cooper, Healy, and Simpson (1994) also discovered that students who held leadership positions in student organizations scored higher than nonleaders on scales including developing purpose, educational involvement, career planning, lifestyle planning, cultural participation, and life management.

College students who participate in leadership opportunities indicate growth in several areas, including civic responsibility; multicultural awareness and community integration; and leadership skills, understanding, and commitment (Cress et al., 2001). Similarly, Soria, Fink, Lepkowski, and Snyder (2013) discovered that students who are positional leaders in college student organizations are more likely to engage in actions to effect social change. Students' positional leadership in specific types of organizations—including advocacy organizations, Greek fraternities or sororities, religious organizations, and service organizations appear to be most important in predicting students' engagement in social change. Beyond holding leadership positions in organizations, researchers have also discovered students' involvement in student organizations or participation in community service to be positively associated with students' development and engagement in socially responsible leadership, growth in cultural awareness, and development of interpersonal skills (A. Astin, 1993; A. Astin & Sax, 1998; Dugan, 2006; Dugan & Komives, 2012; Soria, Nobbe, & Fink, 2013). Extant scholarship suggests that students' involvement in higher education is a stronger predictor of educational and development gains than demographic characteristics or type of institution students attend (Kuh, Kinzie, Schuh, & Whitt, 2005; Pascarella & Terenzini, 2005).

While scholars have investigated the various developmental benefits of positional leadership opportunities, involvement in student organizations, and participation in community service, significantly less is known about the benefits of students' involvement in leadership development programs. Scholars utilizing the social change model as pedagogy have found that students can learn the social change values when they are embedded within academic environments or used as a thematic backdrop in co-curricular settings (Buschlen & Dvorak, 2011; Buschlen & Johnson, 2014). Kezar and Moriarty (2000) discovered students who took leadership courses report higher leadership ability compared to their peers—and that these leadership course experiences are significant for all students across gender and race. Yet others found that participation in formal leadership programming is not associated with the three individual values of the social change model (consciousness of self, congruence, and commitment; Dugan, 2006).

Yet, among the scholarship examining the benefits of students' involvement in higher education—and, in particular, their involvement in leadership positions, student organizations, or in leadership training—little is known about the potential effects of involvement in leadership activities on students' academic outcomes. Students' leadership experiences have the potential to be highly engaging aspects of their collegiate experiences that could translate into enhanced motivation to be academically successful and increased opportunities to collaborate with peers. Scholars have suggested peers play a powerful role in college students' success; for example, the social capital gained through first-generation students' co-curricular involvement can help students acquire the types of academic and cultural capital to help them succeed academically and intellectually (Pascarella et al., 2004). Yet, very few studies have focused specifically on the impact of leadership on first-generation college students. It is important to address this gap in research for several reasons; namely, first-generation college students are significantly less likely than their peers to participate in positional leadership opportunities on campus (Soria, Hussein, & Vue, 2013), although they stand to gain the most from their involvement in these types of student activities (Pascarella et al., 2004). Therefore, in this chapter, I investigate whether first-generation students' participation in formal leadership positions, involvement in student organizations, and participation in leadership trainings, courses, or programs is associated with their academic achievement.

METHOD

I examined the relationships between first-generation college students' participation in leadership opportunities and their self-reported grade point averages utilizing a hierarchical linear regression analysis. I utilized Alexander Astin's (1993) input-environment-outcome (I-E-O) model, which helps to assess the extent to which environmental variables are associated with outcomes above and beyond input characteristics such as demographic or precollege experiences. The data were entered into three blocks according to Astin's model. In block 1, which reflected input variables, I entered demographic variables (race and gender) in addition to students' involvement in leadership or student organizations, leadership efficacy, and cognitive abilities. In the second block, I entered environmental variables including students' college of enrollment, cognitive development, sense of belonging, class standing, residence, and employment off campus. Finally, in block 3, I entered leadership experiences of interest to this student, including students' participation in leadership positions within on-campus or off-campus organizations; participation in community service; general involvement in on-campus or off-campus organizations; involvement in leadership trainings, leadership programs, or leadership courses; engagement in social change; leadership efficacy; and, finally, their scores on all eight socially responsible leadership scales (consciousness of self, congruence, etc.). This analysis provides insights into the significant variance in first-generation students' self-reported grade point averages explained by their leadership experiences above and beyond the variance explained by input and environmental variables.

Instrument

I utilized the Multi-Institutional Study of Leadership (MSL) survey, which features the socially responsible leadership scale (Tyree, 1998) and is based on the social change model of leadership development (H. Astin & A. Astin, 1996). The MSL survey has been previously used in multiple research studies that have examined students' development of socially responsible leadership (Dugan, 2006; Dugan & Komives, 2010; Haber & Komives, 2009).

Participants

In 2009, the MSL survey was distributed to 4,000 randomly selected undergraduate students at a large public research university. The undergraduate student population at this university was more than 29,000 in 2009. The MSL survey was administered online and the response rate (students who responded to at least one item) was 39.0% (n = 1,560). Of these students, 29.1% (n = 453) were first-generation students, which I defined as students whose parents did not earn any college degree. Within the sample, 60.0% were female (n = 272) and 40.0% male (n = 181). The racial-ethnic background of the first-generation students was 72.3% White (n = 327), 3.5% African American (n = 16), 0.2% American Indian or Alaska Native (n = 1), 16.8% Asian American (n = 76), 1.3% Latino or Hispanic (n = 6), 4.4% multiracial or multiethnic (n = 20), and 1.3% other or unknown (n = 6). Given the low numbers of students of color in this sample, I dummy-coded the race variables for analysis (1 = students of color; 0 = White students).

Measures

Block 1: Students' precollege demographics, leadership experiences, and characteristics

Students' precollege experiences are important in predicting their college experiences (A. Astin, 1993). Accordingly, I utilized MSL survey items that asked students about their precollege involvement in leadership positions, confidence conducting leadership tasks (leadership efficacy), and confidence in their cognitive abilities. On a scale from 1 (never) to 4 (very often), students were asked to respond to three items assessing how often they engaged in the following activities during high school: (1) leadership positions in student clubs, groups, or sports; (2) participated in training or education that developed their leadership skills; (3) took leadership positions in community organizations. Four precollege leadership self-efficacy items and five cognitive abilities items began, "Looking back to before you started college, how confident were you that you would be successful at the following?" All nine items were scaled 1 (not at all confident) to 4 (very confident). Examples of leadership efficacy items included "leading others" and "working with a team on a group project," while examples of the cognitive abilities items included "handling the challenge of college-level work" and "analyzing new ideas and concepts."

Block 2: College environmental variables

In considering factors that would influence first-generation students' academic outcomes, I wanted to control for the influence of students' college of enrollment, class standing, sense of belonging, cognitive development, residence, and employment. Students' colleges of enrollment were dummy-coded with the largest college—the liberal arts college—serving as the common referent. Students' class standing was scaled 1–4 (freshman through senior). Residence was dummy-coded (1 = lived on campus, 0 = lived off campus) as was students' employment status (1 = employed off campus, 0 = not employed or employed on campus). Students who live on campus are more likely to be involved on campus while students who are employed may not have the time available to participate in student activities (Blimling, 1993; Pascarella & Terenzini, 2005); consequently, it is important to control for these measures.

Students' sense of belonging was assessed through three items scaled 1 = strongly disagree to 5 = strongly agree (e.g., I feel I belong on this campus). Students' cognitive development was assessed through items asking students to indicate the extent they feel they have grown in four areas. The cognitive development items were scaled 1 = not grown at all to 4 = grown very much (e.g., ability to put ideas together and to see relationships between ideas).

Block 3: Students' leadership experiences

Students were asked to indicate their leadership or general involvement within on-campus or off-campus organizations by responding to an item that began, "Since starting college, how often have you ..." These four items were scaled 1 = never to 5 = much of the time. Students were also asked to indicate how often they had performed community service on a scale of 1 = never to 4 = very often.

Students' involvement in leadership trainings and leadership programs was assessed through the question, "Since starting college, how many times have you participated in the following types of training or education that have developed your leadership skills?" which was scaled 1 (never) to 4 (many). I combined 12 survey items into two primary areas: specific leadership trainings (e.g., emerging or new leaders programs, outdoor leadership programs, multicultural leadership programs) and leadership conferences, workshops, or retreats. I left these variables cumulative as opposed to dummy-coding them to retain variability. Students' enrollment in academic leadership programs was assessed through two items asking students whether they had taken a leadership course or had enrolled in the leadership minor program offered at the institution (dummy-coded, 1 = yes, 0 = no).

Leadership efficacy was assessed through items asking students to rate their confidence in four areas (scaled 1 = not at all confident to 4 = very confident; e.g., leading others). Students' engagement in social change was measured through nine items assessing the frequency of students' involvement in organizations addressing societal, environmental, or community problems, taking action in communities, and so forth. These items were scaled 1 = never to 4 = very often.

Finally, the eight social change values were measured using the socially responsible leadership scale (SRLS) embedded in the MSL. This instrument includes eight separate scales, each of which measures a particular socially responsible leadership value associated with the social change model: consciousness of self (e.g., I am able to articulate my priorities), congruence (e.g., my behaviors are congruent with my beliefs), commitment (e.g., I am committed to a collective purpose in those groups to which I belong), collaboration (e.g., collaboration produces better results), common purpose (e.g., common values drive an organization), controversy with civility (e.g., greater harmony can come out of disagreement), citizenship (e.g., I volunteer my time to the community), and change (e.g., I work well in changing environments; Tyree, 1998). The SRLS contains a total of 71 items in which participants self-reported their agreement on a scale of 1 = strongly disagree to 5 = strongly agree.

Dependent variable: Self-reported grade point average

In the MSL, students were asked to report their grade point average on a scale from 1 = 1.99 or less to 5 = 3.50 to 4.00. Individual student identifiers were not retained in the data, limiting academic achievement measures to students' self-reported grade point average.

Data Analysis

I utilized factor analysis to derive factors from several survey items, including those assessing students' precollege leadership efficacy and cognitive abilities, engagement in social change, current leadership efficacy, sense of belonging, and cognitive development. These factors were computed using regression and standardized with a mean of zero and a standard deviation of one. Next, I entered the variables described above in a hierarchical multiple regression model predicting students' self-reported academic achievement. I examined assumptions of multicollinearity, homoscedasticity, linearity, and independent/normal errors and I found that the assumptions of regression were met in those areas.

RESULTS

The results of the hierarchical multiple regression model suggest that students' precollege characteristics and experiences explain a significant amount of variance in their academic achievement (R^2 = .109, F [7, 445] = 7.79, p < .001; Table 7.1). Additionally, the second block of the college environmental variables also explain a significant amount of variance in students' academic achievement above and beyond that explained by students' precollege demographics and experiences (R^2 Change = .109, F [11, 441] = 6.72, p < .001). Finally, students' leadership experiences explained a significant amount of variance in their academic achievement above and beyond that explained by students' precollege demographics, precollege experiences, and college experiences (R^2 Change = .209, F [36, 416] = 8.59, p < .001).

The results suggest that several leadership experiences are positively associated with first-generation students' academic achievement. Increases in first-generation students' participation in community service are positively associated with their self-report grade point averages. Similarly, first-generation students' involvement as leaders in on-campus student organizations was positively associated with higher self-reported grade point averages. The relationships between community service participation and involvement in on-campus student leadership positions is statistically significant (p < .05).

Furthermore, first-generation students' involvement in activities promoting social change (e.g., working with others to address social inequality, acting to raise

Table 7.1. Hierarchical Regression Analysis Predicting First-generation Students' Grade Point Average.

Predictor	B	SE	β	P
(Constant)	−.660	.658		***
Precollege Characteristics and Experiences				
Female	.047	.102	.020	
Students of Color	−.085	.109	−.032	
Precollege Leadership in School Activities	−.053	.045	−.055	
Precollege Leadership in Community Activities	−.005	.060	−.004	
Precollege Leadership Training or Education	.012	.058	.010	
Precollege Cognitive Abilities	.016	.055	.015	
Precollege Leadership Efficacy	−.007	.065	−.006	
R^2			.109	***
College Experiences				
Class Standing	−.052	.053	−.050	
Lived on Campus	.060	.128	.022	
Worked Off Campus	−.044	.097	−.019	
Biological Sciences College	.147	.184	.031	
Design College	−.023	.296	−.003	
Education and Human Development College	.041	.140	.012	
Food, Agriculture, and Natural Resources Sciences College	−.163	.164	−.040	
Business and Management College	−.039	.173	−.010	
Science and Engineering College	.060	.158	.016	
Cognitive Development	.060	.054	.052	
Sense of Belonging	.090	.052	.075	
R^2 *change*			.109	***
Leadership Experiences				
Community Service	.142	.059	.124	*
Involved in Student Organizations	−.026	.048	−.032	
Leader in On-Campus Activities	.215	.051	.263	***
Involved in Off-Campus Organizations	−.015	.049	−.017	
Leader in Off-Campus Activities	−.045	.057	−.044	
Academic Leadership Experience	.083	.054	.078	
Leadership Conference, Workshop, or Retreat	−.014	.034	−.027	
Specific Leadership Training	.020	.029	.038	
Engagement in Social Change	.151	.067	.131	*
Leadership Efficacy	−.042	.070	−.035	
Consciousness of Self	.435	.146	.193	**
Congruence	.320	.144	.143	*
Commitment	−.056	.158	−.023	
Collaboration	.392	.194	.150	*
Common Purpose	.182	.214	.069	
Controversy with Civility	−.109	.173	−.040	
Citizenship	−.094	.133	−.048	
Change	−.098	.156	−.041	
R^2 *change*			.209	***
R^2			.427	***
F			8.593	***

Note: * $p < .05$; ** $p < .01$; *** $p < .001$.

awareness about a campus, community, or global problem) was positively associated with their grade point averages. Three socially responsible leadership values were also positively and significantly associated with first-generation students' grade point averages: consciousness of self, congruence, and collaboration. None of the other leadership experiences were significant in this model.

DISCUSSION AND IMPLICATIONS

The results of this study suggest first-generation students' involvement in leadership opportunities may be important in enhancing their academic achievement. In particular, students' involvement as positional leaders in on-campus student organizations, participation in community service initiatives, and engagement in efforts to effect social change may be areas that stand to hold the most impact for students' academic outcomes. These findings are echoes of prior studies that have similarly revealed the associations between students' engagement in their communities and academic outcomes (A. Astin, Vogelsgang, Ikeda, & Yee, 2000; Fredericksen, 2000; Hart & King, 2007; Webber, Bauer Krylow, & Zhang, 2013). There are several ways in which students' involvement in leadership, community service, and social change may have contributed to their academic outcomes; for example, Baker (2008) hypothesized that students' involvement in some organizations may boost their sense of empowerment, translating to greater academic self-efficacy (Chemers, Hu, & Garcia, 2001), which in turn has been associated with students' academic achievement. Students who engage in efforts to effect social change may similarly feel empowered, thus increasing their level of self-esteem (Baker, 2008).

Furthermore, the results of this study suggest students who possess the individual social change values of consciousness of self and congruence and the group value of collaboration also report higher academic outcomes. Students who have greater self-awareness, act in accordance with their beliefs and values, and see the value in working with others to achieve goals may have greater academic achievement because they are aware of their academic abilities, strengths, or limitations and may be more likely to collaborate with their classmates on academic projects. Self-evaluation and self-monitoring are important processes associated with students' self-regulated learning (Zimmerman, 1990), which enables students to approach educational tasks with agency, diligence, and resourcefulness. Furthermore, collaborative learning is positively associated with students' academic achievement because these types of experiences enhance students' creativity in problem solving, persistence toward task completion, and intrinsic motivation (Johnson, Johnson, & Smith, 1998). These are hypotheses regarding the effects of these three socially responsible leadership values at this stage, as the extant scholarship does not examine the outcomes associated with values but instead considers the social change values to be ends, in and of themselves.

The results of this study suggest that some leadership and involvement opportunities are beneficial to first-generation students; however, against the backdrop of Soria, Huessein, and Vue's (2013) discovery that first-generation students are less likely to participate in positional leadership opportunities, higher education practitioners should examine institutional structures that may impede first-generation students from becoming involved in leadership and service. First-generation students may view co-curricular involvement opportunities as too expensive or may be prevented from engagement in leadership due to the necessity of employment to pay for tuition and college expenses (Walpole, 2003). Consequently, practitioners may wish to help first-generation students connect to paid leadership opportunities or scholarships (Soria, Hussein, & Vue, 2013). Holistically, historically underrepresented or marginalized backgrounds tend to benefit the most from supportive environments, mentorship, collaborative learning, and faculty interactions that help students to navigate academic and social challenges of campus life (Jehangir, 2010; Kuh, 2008).

LIMITATIONS AND FUTURE DIRECTIONS

Studies conducted at single institutions often produce results that are difficult to generalize to other institutions—especially if those other institutions vary considerably in their student population, size, or location. Given that this study was conducted at a large public research university, the results may be limiting to professionals working at other institutions or with a more diverse student body. The sample size was small given the large size of this institution. The measures of leadership in this study were primarily positional while the measures of leadership training were limited in that they did not cover duration or content (merely participation). It is also somewhat limiting to rely upon students' self-reported grade point averages categorized in a Likert scale instead of the more precise grade point averages collected at the institutional level. Future scholars are encouraged to continue inquiries regarding the academic outcomes of leadership experiences using institutionally derived data, more intricate measures of leadership experiences, and with a greater variety of control variables to better assess the effects of leadership experiences on college students' outcomes.

CONCLUSION

As a specific type of involvement in higher education, students' leadership experiences hold the potential to promote their academic outcomes. Among first-generation college students, these experiences may enhance students' social capital and self-confidence, which can in turn help them to achieve academic success. Practitioners are encouraged to remove potential institutional barriers first-generation students may encounter in becoming involved in leadership opportunities while in college.

REFERENCES

Astin, A. W. (1993). *What matters in college: Four critical years revisited.* San Francisco, CA: Jossey-Bass.

Astin, A. W., & Astin, H. S. (2000). *Leadership reconsidered: Engaging higher education in social change.* Battle Creek, MI: W. K. Kellogg Foundation.

Astin, A. W., & Sax, L. J. (1998). How undergraduates are affected by service participation. *Journal of College Student Development, 39*(3), 251–263.

Astin, A. W., Vogelsgang, L. J., Ikeda, E. K., & Yee, J. A. (2000). *How service learning affects students.* Los Angeles, CA: Higher Education Research Institute, University of California Los Angeles.

Astin, H. S. (1996, July–August). Leadership for social change. *About Campus,* 4–10.

Astin, H. S., & Astin, A. W. (1996). *A social change model of leadership development: Guidebook.* Los Angeles, CA: University of California Education Research Institute.

Baker, C. N. (2008). Under-represented college students and extracurricular involvement: The effects of various student organizations on academic performance. *Social Psychology of Education, 11*(3), 273–298.

Blimling, G. S. (1993). The influence of college residence halls on students. In J. C. Smart (Ed.), *Higher education: Handbook of theory and research* (Vol. 9). New York, NY: Agathon.

Broh, B. A. (2002). Linking extracurricular programming to academic achievement: Who benefits and why? *Sociology of Education, 75*(1), 69–91.

Buschlen, E., & Dvorak, R. (2011). The social change model as pedagogy: Examining undergraduate leadership growth. *Journal of Leadership Education, 10*(2), 38–56.

Buschlen, E., & Johnson, M. (2014). The effects of an introductory leadership course on socially responsible leadership, examined by age and gender. *Journal of Leadership Education, 13*(1), 31–45.

Campbell, C. M., Smith, M., Dugan, J. P., & Komives, S. R. (2012). Mentors and college student leadership outcomes: The importance of position and process. *Review of Higher Education, 35*(4), 595–625.

Chemers, M. M., Hu, L., & Garcia, B. F. (2001). Academic self-efficacy and first-year college student performance and adjustment. *Journal of Educational Psychology, 93*(1), 55–64.

Choy, S. (2001). *Students whose parents did not go to college: Postsecondary access, persistence, and attainment.* (NCES Rep. No. 2001–126). Washington, DC: National Center for Education Statistics.

Cooper, D. L., Healy, M. A., & Simpson, J. (1994). Student development through involvement: Specific changes over time. *Journal of College Student Development, 35*(2), 98–102.

Cress, C. M., Astin, H. S., Zimmerman-Oster, K., & Burkhardt, J. C. (2001). Developmental outcomes of college students' involvement in leadership activities. *Journal of College Student Development, 42*(1), 15–27.

Dugan, J. P. (2006). Involvement and leadership: A descriptive analysis of socially responsible leadership. *Journal of College Student Development, 47*(3), 335–343.

Dugan, J. P., & Komives, S. R. (2010). Influences on college students' capacity for socially responsible leadership. *Journal of College Student Development, 51*(5), 525–549.

Fredericksen, P. (2000). Does service learning make a difference in student performance? *Journal of Experiential Education, 23*(2), 64–74.

Haber, P., & Komives, S. R. (2009). Predicting the individual values of the social change model of leadership development: The role of college students' leadership and involvement experiences. *Journal of Leadership Education, 7*(3), 133–166.

Hart, S. M., & King, K. R. (2007). Service learning and literacy tutoring: Academic impact on pre-service teachers. *Teaching and Teacher Education, 23*(4), 323–338.

Horn, L., & Nunez, A. (2000). *Mapping the road to college: First-generation students' math track, planning strategies, and context of support.* Washington, DC: U.S. Department of Education, National Center for Education Statistics.

Hossler, D., Schmit, J., & Vesper, N. (1999). *Going to college: How social, economic, and educational factors influence the decisions college students make.* Baltimore, MD: Johns Hopkins University Press.

Housel, T. H., & Harvey, V. L. (2009). *The invisibility factor: Administrators and faculty reach out to first-generation college students.* Boca Raton, FL: Brown Walker.

Huang, Y., & Chang, S. (2004). Academic and co-curricular involvement: Their relationship and the best combination for student growth. *Journal of College Student Development, 45*(4), 391–406.

Hurtado, S. (2007). Linking diversity with the educational and civic missions of higher education. *Review of Higher Education, 30*(2), 185–196.

Ishitani, T. T. (2006). Studying attrition and degree completion behavior among first-generation college students in the United States. *Journal of Higher Education, 77*(5), 861–885.

Jehangir, R. R. (2009). Cultivating voice: First-generation students seek full academic citizenship in multicultural learning communities. *Innovative Higher Education, 34*(1), 33–49.

Jehangir, R. R. (2010). *Higher education and first-generation students: Cultivating community, voice, and place for the new majority.* New York, NY: Palgrave Macmillan.

Johnson, D. W., Johnson, R. T., & Smith, K. H. (1998, July–August). Cooperative learning returns to college: What evidence is there that it works? *Change,* 26–35.

Johnson, S. E., Richeson, J. A., & Finkel, E. J. (2011). Middle class and marginal? Socioeconomic status, stigma, and self-regulation at an elite university. *Journal of Personality and Social Psychology, 100*(5), 838–852.

Keup, J. R. (2011, March). *Exploring the impact of peer leadership experiences on academic development.* Paper presented at the ACPA Annual Convention, Baltimore, MD.

Kezar, A., Carducci, R., & Contreras-McGavin, M. (2006). *Rethinking the "L" word in higher education: The revolution in research on leadership.* (ASHE Higher Education Report, Vol. 31, No. 6). San Francisco, CA: Jossey-Bass.

Kezar, A. J., & Moriarty, D. (2000). Expanding our understanding of student leadership development: A study exploring gender and ethnic identity. *Journal of College Student Development, 41*(1), 55–69.

Komives, S. R., Wagner, W., & Associates. (2009). *Leadership for a better world: Understanding the social change model of leadership development.* San Francisco, CA: Jossey-Bass.

Kuh, G. D. (2008). *High-impact educational practices: What they are, who has access to them, and why they matter.* Washington, DC: Association of American Colleges & Universities.

Kuh, G. D., Kinzie, J., Schuh, J. H., & Whitt, E. J. (2005). *Student success in college: Creating conditions that matter.* San Francisco, CA: Jossey-Bass.

Logue, C. T., Hutchens, T. A., & Hector, M. A. (2005). Student leadership: A phenomenological exploration of postsecondary experiences. *Journal of College Student Development, 46*(4), 393–408.

Ostrove, J. M., & Long, S. M. (2007). Social class and belonging: Implications for college adjustment. *Review of Higher Education, 30*(4), 363–389.

Outcalt, C. L., Faris, S. K., & McMahon, K. N. (2001). *Developing non-hierarchical leadership on campus: Case studies and best practices.* Westport, CT: Greenwood.

Pascarella, E. T., Pierson, C. T., Wolniak, G. C., & Terenzini, P. T. (2004). First-generation college students: Additional evidence on college experiences and outcomes. *Journal of Higher Education, 75*(3), 249–284.

Pascarella, E. T., & Terenzini, P. T. (2005). *How college affects students: A third decade of research.* San Francisco, CA: Jossey-Bass.

Pike, G. R., & Kuh, G. D. (2005). First- and second-generation college students: A comparison of their engagement and intellectual development. *Journal of Higher Education, 76*(3), 276–300.

Roberts, D. C. (1997). The changing look of leadership programs. *Concepts & Connections: A Newsletter of Leadership Educators, 1*(3–4), 11–14.

Schuh, J. H., & Laverty, M. (1983). The perceived long-term influence of holding a significant student leadership position. *Journal of College Student Personnel, 24*(1), 28–32.

Soria, K. M., Fink, A., Lepkowski, C. C., & Snyder, L. (2013). Undergraduate student leadership and social change. *Journal of College and Character, 14*(3), 241–252.

Soria, K. M., & Gorny, L. (2012, June). *Defining first-generation students by degrees: Implications for research, policy, and practice.* Paper presented at the Association for Institutional Research Forum, New Orleans, LA.

Soria, K. M., Hussein, D., & Vue, C. (2013). Leadership for whom? Socioeconomic factors predicting undergraduate students' positional leadership participation. *Journal of Leadership Education, 13*(1), 14–30.

Soria, K. M., Nobbe, J., & Fink, A. (2013). Examining the intersections between undergraduates' engagement in community service and development of socially responsible leadership. *Journal of Leadership Education, 12*(1), 117–140.

Soria, K. M., & Stebleton, M. J. (2012). First-generation students' academic engagement and retention. *Teaching in Higher Education, 17*(6), 1–13.

Soria, K. M., Stebleton, M. J., & Huesman, R. L. (2013–2014). Class counts: Exploring differences in academic and social integration between working-class and middle/upper-class students at large, public research universities. *Journal of College Student Retention: Research, Theory, and Practice, 15*(2), 215–242.

Stebleton, M. J., & Soria, K. M. (2012). Breaking down barriers: Academic obstacles of first-generation students at research universities. *Learning Assistance Review, 17*(2), 7–19.

Stephens, N. M., Fryberg, S. A., Markus, H. R., Johnson, C., & Covarrubias, R. (2012). Unseen disadvantage: How American universities' focus on independence undermines the academic performance of first-generation college students. *Journal of Personality and Social Psychology, 102*(6), 1178–1197.

Stephens, N. M., Townsend, S. S. M., Markus, H. R., & Phillips, T. (2012). A cultural mismatch: Independent cultural norms produce greater increases in cortisol and more negative emotions among first-generation college students. *Journal of Experimental Social Psychology, 48*, 1389–1393.

Strapp, C. M., & Farr, R. J. (2009). To get involved or not: The relation among extracurricular involvement, satisfaction, and academic achievement. *Teaching of Psychology, 37*(1), 50–54.

Terenzini, P. T., Cabrera, A. F., & Bernal, E. M. (2001). *Swimming against the tide: The poor in American higher education.* Princeton, NJ: College Board.

Tyree, T. M. (1998). Designing an instrument to measure the socially responsible leadership using the social change model of leadership development. *Dissertation Abstracts International, 59*(06), 1945. (AAT 9836493)

Walpole, M. (2003). Socioeconomic status and college: How SES affects college experiences and outcomes. *Review of Higher Education, 27*(1), 45–73.

Webber, K. L., Bauer Krylow, R., & Zhang, Q. (2013). Does involvement really matter? Indicators of college student success and satisfaction. *Journal of College Student Development, 54*(6), 591–611.

Zimmerman, B. J. (1990). Self-regulated learning and academic achievement: An overview. *Educational Psychologist, 25*(1), 3–17.

Institutional Involvement

CHAPTER EIGHT

Institutional Programs TO Promote First-generation Student Involvement

Improving Academic and Social Outcomes

JARRETT GUPTON, RASHNÉ JEHANGIR AND JENNIFER TROST

On December 11, 2013, President Barack Obama invited college presidents and business leaders to a daylong summit at the White House to explore ways to make higher education more accessible to low-income students, many of whom are first in their family to attend college (Tyre, 2014). The urgency of affordability and accessibility for low-income students, while now discussed in mainstream media, is one that higher education has wrestled with for decades. While access to college has increased for first-generation and low-income students over time, the promise of the degree remains elusive and, in many ways, colleges continue to perpetuate income disparities rather than serving as pathways to upward mobility (Adelman, 2007; Engle & Tinto, 2008; Leonhardt, 2004; Mettler, 2014). Understanding the factors that impede degree completion requires careful examination of complex and intersecting issues of race, class, financial aid policies, precollegiate preparation, and aspirational opportunities for young people in the United States. The success of first-generation college students influences the collective success of the nation-state, as college graduates are more likely to have sustained employment over their lifespan, greater rates of home ownership, higher civic engagement, and better health and wellness (Baum, Ma, & Payea, 2010).

FIRST-GENERATION COLLEGE STUDENTS

First-generation students are not a homogenous group; instead, first-generation students include students of color, immigrants, and veterans (Engle & Tinto,

2008). In addition, first-generation students are more likely to be older, female, married, low-income, and have dependents than their continuing-generation peers (McCarron & Inkelas, 2006; Nuñez & Cuccaro-Alamin, 1998; Pascarella, Pierson, Wozniak, & Terenzini, 2004). First-generation students attend less-selective universities and are more likely to enroll at two-year institutions or pri-vate-for-profit institutions (Pascarella et al., 2004). First-generation students, regardless of two- or four-year enrollment, are more likely to attend part-time, live off campus, work more hours, and have lower levels of extracurricular involve-ment, athletic participation, and volunteering (Nuñez & Cuccaro-Alamin, 1998; Pascarella et al., 2004). First-generation students continue to have less involve-ment and engagement with their higher education institutions, which negatively affects persistence and success (Pike & Kuh, 2005). As these demographics sug-gest, there is a confluence of constraints related to race, class, and, increasingly, in immigrant status that influence the college trajectory of first-generation students. Clearly, to ensure success of first-generation students requires universities to con-front issues of race/ethnicity and poverty in higher education to create a more inclusive campus community.

In addition to diversity of demographics, the definition of first-generation col-lege students lacks uniformity. All definitions of first-generation students hinge on parents' educational attainment, but variations are based on how much attainment a parent has acquired. Some scholars consider first-generation students as those whose parents have a high school diploma or less (Nuñez & Cuccaro-Alamin, 1998), while others identify first-generation students as those whose parents do not have a bachelor's degree (Chen, 2005). Utilization of the second definition expands the category and increases the number of college students with first-generation status. Yet, despite this heterogeneity in their demographics, first-generation stu-dents share a common hope and expectation that a college degree will provide social mobility and financial security for them and their families.

Regardless of definition, research shows the number of first-generation stu-dents enrolled in college have increased (Chen, 2005; Lynch, 2013; Nuñez & Cuccaro-Alamin, 1998). As the demographics in the United States shift from largely White to greater numbers of people of color, groups historically under-represented in higher education, including more first-generation students, are predicted to enroll in higher education at greater rates. Lynch (2013) notes that "minority groups made up the largest demographics of students with parents that had a high school education or less, with 48.5 percent of Latino and Hispanic stu-dents and 45 percent of Black or African-American students included" (para. 3). Estimates of the number of first-generation college students range from 40% to 50% of all undergraduates (Chen, 2005; Lynch, 2013). Engle and Tinto (2008) estimate that 24% of the total college population includes both low-income and first-generation students.

Yet, despite the promise of education as the "great social class equalizer" (Langhout, Rosselli, & Feinstein, 2007, p. 146), the onus has rested on individuals to achieve upward mobility, suggesting that hard work and individual choice will determine who will or will not break through the strata that separate class lines. As evidenced by the recent summit in the White House, institutions of higher and postsecondary education, business leaders, and K–12 institutions need to actively revive opportunities to achieve college education for low-income and first-generation students as a collective and national investment. Researchers have honed in on key issues that constrain persistence toward degree completion, including financial hardships, academic preparation, isolation in the academy, lowered educational aspirations, and the adverse effects of social and cultural capital on both access and persistence in college (Coffman, 2011; Engle & O'Brien, 2007; Goldrick-Rab, 2006; Jehangir, 2010; Soria, Stebleton, & Huesman, 2013; Stebleton, Huesman, & Kuzhabekova, 2010). This chapter begins by providing an overview of issues first-generation students face. We then highlight highly effective practices at two-year and four-year institutions that might serve as templates for intentionally supporting first-generation students in higher education. This chapter examines three forms of institutional support: (1) precollege support and guidance, (2) retention and persistence programs, and (3) academic and social integration systems. In our analysis, we found several innovative examples of emerging programs, resources, and support systems that foster validation and resiliency in first-generation students and help them overcome institutional barriers to college enrollment and success; this chapter highlights some of these effective practices and programs.

FOUR-YEAR INSTITUTIONAL SUPPORTS
FOR FIRST-GENERATION STUDENTS

Cultural capital and social capital theories dominate the literature on first-generation students. Scholars suggest first-generation students lack valuable and transferable knowledge about the college process, culture, and experience—knowledge that continuing-generation students receive from college-educated parents. Without this knowledge, scholars suggest, first-generation students have a more difficult time making choices about and succeeding in college (Dumais & Ward, 2010; Pascarella et al., 2004). In addition to examining comparisons between first-generation and non-first-generation students, we approach this work from a positive psychology framework. The institutional models and strategies presented in this chapter reflect a validation (Rendón, 1994) and psychological resiliency (Garmezy, 1991; Masten 2001; Sanlo, 2004; Shield, 2004) approach to improving first-generation student outcomes. The validation and resiliency framework guided us to explore programs that actively work to support first-generation students, as opposed to requiring them to seek support from the college or university.

Precollege Academic and Social Support Programs

First-generation students disproportionately enroll in higher education institutions in comparison to their continuing-generation peers. Scholars speculate that limited family involvement, a lack of precollege experiences, financial barriers, and inadequate academic preparation are responsible for low rates of enrollment (Choy, 2001; Engle & Tinto, 2008; McCarron & Inkelas, 2006; Pascarella, Pierson, Wozniak, & Terenzini, 2003). To address the inequities in access to information, peer support, and financial support multiple publicly and privately supported programs have been developed to assist first-generation students planning to attend or attending a four-year college or university. It is critically important to support and engage first-generation college students early in their matriculation (Kuh, 2003), although institutions also need to consider how to create holistic support systems throughout their collegiate journey.

The Rutgers Future Scholars is a new social support program that began its inaugural cohort in June 2013. The Rutgers Future Scholars (RFS) program focuses on helping first-generation students become academically prepared and college ready and eliminates some financial barriers. Rutgers recruits seventh grade students from underrepresented areas in New Jersey to participate in a six-year program with the goal of high school graduation and college readiness. Through a comprehensive approach, which includes summer programming, tutors, mentors, seminars, and parent education, Rutgers helps to fill the gap in the college knowledge and academic preparation that first-generation students often exhibit. Additionally, participants who are granted admission to Rutgers will attend tuition-free (Abdul-Alim, 2013). While the Rutgers Futures Scholars program presents an interesting model, little data are available on the academic success and persistence of the RFS participants.

Another option for first-generation students looking for role models, financial assistance, and how to navigate the college process is the website I'm First. The website, targeted specifically for first-generation students, provides a forum in which students can see and hear other first-generation students, some famous, discuss their success, give advice, and create a community of first-generation students to lean on and learn from. Additionally, students have access to a database of colleges with support programs specifically targeted to first-generation students, thus eliminating the extensive research that may be necessary to find institutional fit. Last, I'm First has $2,000 renewable scholarships for those who are first in the family to attend one of I'm First's college partners. I'm First also worked with institutional partners who pay a membership fee to feature their institution on the

I'm First website. The institution can then feature specific supports they have for first-generation students on their campus and how their mission and goals might fit the needs of first-generation students.

Retention and Persistence

Overall, research has confirmed that first-generation students perform academically worse and persist at lower levels than their continuing-generation peers (Chen, 2005; Engle & Tinto, 2008). As indicated above, first-generation students begin college less academically, socially, and emotionally prepared. Thus, first-generation students achieve lower grades, accrue fewer credits, interact less with faculty, engage less in course discussion, participate more frequently in remedial courses, and are more likely to withdraw or repeat grades than continuing-generation peers (Chen, 2005; Padgett, Johnson, & Pascarella, 2012; Soria & Stebleton, 2012). The findings from previously mentioned studies reinforce Pascarella and colleagues' (2004) ideas that first-generation students experience college in a different way than their continuing-generation peers. Moreover, Chen (2005) found 43% of enrolled first-generation students leave without a degree and only 24% graduate with a bachelor's degree, which is significantly lower than the success rates of continuing-generation students.

First-generation students struggle to connect to their peers, faculty, and institutions because of a lack of the necessary social and cultural capital to navigate postsecondary education and adapt to a new environment (Dumais & Ward, 2010; McCarron & Inkelas, 2006; Padgett et al., 2012). Other important factors to the psychosocial development and positive college experience for first-generation students include feeling a sense of belonging, establishing a strong locus of control, eliminating self-doubt, and knowing the best practices for students in their situation (Stephens, Fryberg, Markus, Johnson, & Covarrubias, 2012).

Increasing the academic outcomes of first-generation students means creating immediate opportunities to build a sense of comfort, resilience, confidence, connection to the institution, and knowledge of resources necessary for success (Padgett et al., 2012). Therefore, scholars encourage institutions to build the academic confidence of first-generation students through the development of formal connections to peers and faculty outside of the classroom (Soria & Stebleton, 2012; Peabody, Hutchens, Lewis, & Deffendall, 2011). Inkelas, Daver, Vogt, and Leonard (2007) found structured activities (i.e., residential programing and faculty interaction) more influential than informal peer groups. Pascarella and colleagues (2004) also found first-generation students benefit more from structured experiences. They also note that programs linking first-generation students to peer and faculty mentors are highly regarded and yield positive results. Intentional mentoring increases the engagement and sense of belonging for first-generation students, ultimately increasing academic performance (Pascarella et al., 2004); therefore, higher education practitioners are wise to implement these types of programs.

Woosley and Shepler (2011) found students' perceptions of the campus environment and involvement on campus are major barriers to integrating to college. Therefore, the authors suggest institutions "create and foster a campus environment that enables students to feel accepted and promotes academic performance" (Woosley & Shepler, 2011, p. 711). Other researchers have found when the campus environment was described as interdependent rather than independent, first-generation students performed better academically (Stephens et al., 2012). In addition, Stephens, Hamedani, and Destin's (2014) study provided first-generation students with an opportunity during their first semester to hear stories from seasoned first-generation students who discussed how social class influenced their experience. Through this exercise, first-generation students were able to see and hear how others succeeded and learn useful strategies for their undergraduate education, resulting in increased retention and academics. Last, researchers suggest connecting students to organizations or groups with similar interests will help with integration and engagement with the campus (Miller, 2013; Woosley & Shepler, 2011).

Support programs that bridge departments or create learning communities continue to surface as necessary for the success of first-generation students (Jehangir, 2010; McCarron & Inkelas, 2006; Miller, 2013). Bridging departments, such as counseling and residence life, will create a better environment with fewer stops and contacts, which can cause roadblocks. Learning communities that link academics with a student's housing or aspects of his or her social identity (e.g., race/ethnicity, social class, sexual orientation, gender, etc.) show promise in connecting first-generation students to an institution and increasing their academic performance (Inkelas et al., 2007; Jehangir, 2010; Miller, 2013).

Academic and Social Integration Support Systems

One national program that has taken into account all of the research on first-generation students is the First Scholars program funded by the Suder Foundation (First Scholars, 2013). The Suder Foundation created a specific program that includes mentoring, scholarships, and connections to both the institutional and outside community. The tiered program includes new mentors, each year serving a different purpose. Freshmen connect with upperclassmen to create a sense of place, juniors with faculty mentors to enhance their career and community opportunities, and seniors reach out to alumni or professional mentors to help the transition into the workforce (Peabody et al., 2011). Currently, the public four-year institutions that have committed to the First Scholars (2013) program include Kansas State University, Northern Arizona University, Southern Illinois University at Carbondale, University of Alabama, University of Kentucky, University of Memphis, and Washington State University. First Scholars reports their 2011 student participants outpaced other first-generation students at three of the participating institutions (the individual universities were not identified) in terms of second-year retention and projected six-year graduation rates (91% second-year retention and 85% graduation rate). Thus, comprehensive mentoring programs directly targeted to first-generation students have the potential to increase academic success and degree completion. First Scholars appears to be the only program in the nation with this mission.

At the University of Minnesota Twin-Cities campus, the TRiO Student Support Services program has created a one-credit course specifically for first-generation students enrolled in their program. The University of Minnesota's TRiO Student Support Services (SSS, 2012) program, a federally funded college opportunity program that serves students from traditionally underrepresented groups, including low- to moderate-income and first-generation college students, has been in existence since 1976 and supports students in pursuing their educational goals through academic support, specialized advising, and leadership opportunities. The design of the class itself, as well as the curriculum, intends to engage, support, and retain first-generation students in a variety of ways. First, the curriculum design engages students in dialogue, reflection, and analysis of the college milieu through their own lived experience as well as readings and narratives that include voices of working-class, first-generation scholars. Through the course, first-year, first-generation students begin to recognize potential challenges and opportunities possible during college and use this knowledge to map out their own educational and personal journeys framed by each individual's identity and cultural lenses. Instead of faculty, the course is taught by TRiO academic advisers who have an opportunity to see their students weekly, allowing for deepening relationships with their advisees. Additionally, the structure and enrollment of the class creates a safe space to raise issues and ask questions with peers who have similar experiences coming to and adjusting to college, resulting in a cohort who serve each other as resources and peer mentors. One of the learning objectives for the course is to help students feel empowered about their identity as first-generation students and feel connected with other TRiO students, through increased engagement with Trio Student Board and other leadership activities. As such, this culturally validating context (Rendón, 1994) creates opportunities for students to begin to enhance "self-authorship" which is "the capacity to author, or invent, one's own beliefs, values, sense of self, and relationships with others" (Baxter Magolda, 2002, p. 3). This model supports previous research about the importance of spaces with a critical mass of first-generation students to cultivate voice, identity, and self-authorship in their educational journey (Jehangir, Williams, & Pete, 2011, 2012).

TWO-YEAR INSTITUTIONAL SUPPORT STRUCTURES

Where a first-generation student chooses to enroll for postsecondary education influences his or her graduation rate. Low-income, first-generation students are 1.5 times more likely to attend two-year institutions, which historically have lower graduation rates than four-year institutions. Furthermore, first-generation students are 60% less likely to enroll in private nonprofit institutions, which are known for strong support programs (Engle & Tinto, 2008; Pascarella et al., 2004). As Engle and Tinto point out, "Low-income, first-generation students were actually more than seven times more likely to earn bachelor's degrees if they started in four-year institutions, but only 25 percent of them did so" (p. 2). Furthermore, community colleges only have an 18% graduation rate over three years (Marcus, 2013) and an even worse transfer rate. Engle and Tinto (2008) found that 14% of low-income first-generation students at community colleges and for-profit institutions transferred to a four-year university within six years. Conversely, they noted that 50% of middle- and upper-income students transferred to a four-year institution during that same six years. Vulnerable students, like first-generation students, warrant specific attention from the institution to promote a climate of persistence and success.

Faculty Integration and Classroom Climate

Historically, few two-year institutions have provided direct programing to first-generation students; however, some community college institutions have increased their active involvement in first-generation students' success. The approaches have ranged from creating formal programs to specifically address the needs of first-generation students to working with faculty on creating more inclusive classroom environments. La Guardia Community College in Long Island, New York, has worked to help integrate the faculty with support services for first-generation students (Abdul-Alim, 2012; Institute of Higher Education Policy, 2012). The New Generation Scholars program helps to ease the transition to college for first-generation students, primarily adults over age 25 (Abdul-Alim, 2012). The program works to change the relationship between first-generation students and faculty. Students participate in the New Generation courses prior to transitioning into credit-based courses at La Guardia. The New Generation Scholars program includes faculty as guest instructors so that the faculty have a better understanding of the experiences of first-generation students prior to formally teaching them in a credit-based course. The experience of guest lecturers provide students a glimpse of what they can expect in a credit-bearing course; in addition, the lecture also allows the faculty member the opportunity to learn more about the students. The New Generation Scholars program helps to dispel myths and stereotypes that faculty members may have about first-generation students. The New Generation Scholars program highlights that it is the responsibility of the faculty and staff to learn about the experiences of students and adapt their curriculum, rather than the responsibility of students to justify that they are worthy to be in college.

El Camino College in Torrance, California, has focused on providing a faculty development program related to developing teaching strategies and pedagogies that are inclusive of first-generation students (Institute of Higher Education Policy, 2012). The Faculty Inquiry Partnership Program brings faculty from various departments together to work on issues of student learning and success particular to first-generation students. The faculty training helps to ensure that faculty members understand their role in creating an inclusive learning environment for their students. Further, the program helps to create peer support groups among instructors at El Camino College. This program highlights that colleges and universities need to be multifaceted in their efforts to support first-generation students. While there is a need to provide student support services, there is also a need to train faculty and instructors on campus.

Valencia Community College, in Florida, has worked to improve first-generation students' success by integrating co-curricular activities into their academic curriculum. The English for Academic Purposes program utilizes a learning community model in which students work in thematic groups, or groups based around a common theme or topic, while improving their English language proficiency. The English for Academic Purposes program helps students to build networks of support in their learning communities and makes course content more relevant and aligned to the students' interests. The English for Academic Purposes program highlights the importance of providing opportunities for first-generation students to have some level of ownership and connection to the curriculum.

Advising and Student Development Initiatives

Though not as substantive as the New Generation Scholars Program, North Hennepin Community College (NHCC) in Brooklyn Park, Minnesota, has initiated several programs aimed at improving retention rates. The goal of the new programs is to provide students with an opportunity to connect with the campus early in their college careers. One component of the new programs is that each student at NHCC is assigned an advisor. Further, the initiatives help advisors manage their caseloads as NHCC, currently, has a ratio of 500 students to 1 advisor (Williams-Wyche, 2014). As a comparison, 300 students to every advisor is considered best practice (Jones & Pirius, 2014). Of the students at NHCC 46% are from low-income backgrounds, and 59% identify as first-generation college students (Williams-Wyche, 2014). In spring semester 2012, NHCC implemented a mandatory orientation for all new students. The orientation is required for students taking traditional courses, as well as students taking online courses so that they can familiarize themselves with the campus and meet with their individual advisor.

In addition to the orientation, NHCC utilizes online software tools provided by the Hobsons Company to track students' degree progress (e.g., *AgileGrad*, *AgileAdvisor*, and *Retain*). These software packages allow students and advisors the ability to plan their program of study for the entire academic year. Moreover, the software packages allow a student to view their time to degree and how much it will cost to complete their degree. A student's course plan is automatically updated with their semester grades, including if a student withdraws from a course. The features of *AgileGrad* allow NHCC students to see their progress and make any necessary adjustments in their course plan. The Hobsons software suite does include an early warning system for students in danger of failing or withdrawing from a course. The early warning system also tracks student attendance, in addition to tracking their use of academic support services and on-campus health and wellness services. If a student is at risk of withdrawing or failing a class, they are contacted by their advisor and meet to discuss their progress (Jones & Pirius, 2014).

Mt. San Antonio College in Walnut, California, has an estimated 47% first-generation student population (Mt. San Antonio College, 2012). The college has instituted a student success program specific to first-generation students. The Achieving in College, Ensuring Success program provides a holistic approach to first-generation students' development, as it offers resources for academic support, transfer assistance, and guidance on completing an associate's degree. In addition, the Achieving in College, Ensuring Success program also provides cultural enrichment programming, financial literacy courses, and mentoring. The program is primarily targeted toward low-income students, Latina/o students, and Asian and Pacific Islander students. As Mt. San Antonio College is located in a community that is predominantly Latina/o, the college dedicated specific supports to ensure that local students have the information and resources to meet their educational goals. Programs like Achieving in College, Ensuring Success provide comprehensive academic support, in addition to social and cultural support for first-generation students. This holistic approach illustrates the need to recognize that first-generation students might be experiencing a cognitive and social transition when entering college.

Even with these supports at two-year institutions, the inconsistencies and systemic issues across sectors and between institutions continue to result in problems for first-generation students' educational attainment. Two- and four-year institutions must create seamless transfer systems for greater success of all students, not just first-generation. The need for better articulation agreements and much clearer academic pathways and rules for transfer for all students continues to be documented in the literature (Engle & Tinto, 2008; Fain, 2012; McCarron & Inkelas, 2006; Striplin, 1999). Moreover, research shows that obtaining an associate's degree increases one's likelihood of graduating with a bachelor's degree by 16% but concludes that students who take a year off between community college and four-year programs are 26% less likely to get a bachelor's degree (Marcus, 2013). Therefore, it is in the best interest of institutions and students to strongly encourage acquisition of an associate's degree, create a simplified and immediate transfer process to a four-year institution, and educate students about the process, expectations, and pitfalls of transferring (Engle & Tinto, 2008).

CONCLUSION

Although much of the research describes first-generation students' struggle to succeed in college, many first-generation students graduate and enter the labor market each year. The good news for those who persist is the differences that exist during college disappear in the labor market. First-generation graduates earn similar salaries and are employed in similar occupations as their continuing-generation peers (Ishitani, 2006; Nuñez & Cuccaro-Alamin, 1998). Although first-generation students have dedicated a great deal of financial, psychological, and emotional capital in the pursuit of a college degree, the question that remains is what might colleges and universities do to invest in the success of first-generation students.

Overall, first-generation students require more validation of their experiences and need higher self-confidence to benefit from some interventions (Inkelas et al., 2007). We offer three suggestions as key to supporting first-generation college students. First, based on our analysis of the literature and multiple programs at two-year and four-year universities, we contend that higher education institutions should use multiple strategies to improve outcomes for first-generation students. The types of strategies and approaches we identified relate to three broad categories: (1) curricular and faculty support, (2) social-integration support, and (3) academic-support partnerships. The category of curricular and faculty support relates to creating more inclusive classrooms for first-generation students through faculty training and development. The next category regards social-integration support and the ways in which colleges and universities, specifically, create programs and practices to improve the college experience for first-generation students. The final category highlights academic partnerships to support first-generation students. Examples such as holistic team advising and co-instructed courses allow faculty and student service personnel opportunities to work collaboratively to improve outcomes for first-generation students. While campuses might want to focus on one area of support, we suggest colleges and universities begin with assessment of the particular needs of first-generation students on their campuses and then work to adopt strategies from all four areas to create a holistic or systems approach to improving outcomes for first-generation students. Each of the three areas, along with corresponding strategies, is displayed in Table 8.1.

Table 8.1. Typology of Programs to Improve First-generation Student Involvement.

Programs that support curricular and faculty development	Programs that support social integration	Programs that support academic progress
Culturally relevant pedagogy and curriculum training for faculty	Campus clubs and organizations for first-generation students	Holistic academic advising
Collaborative teaching	Living learning communities	Comprehensive academic support programs
Faculty development training related to first-generation students	Summer bridge programs	Peer-mentoring support programs
Faculty mentoring programs for first-generation students	Precollege outreach and recruitment programs	First-year experience seminars

While this typology is not exhaustive, it does allow colleges and universities a means of identifying gaps in their support services as well as areas of strength. This typology might be useful as campuses form or revise their plan for improving outcomes for first-generation students.

Next, there is a need to recognize that families still play a vital role in the support of first-generation students. While familial support for first-generation students may not look the same as for those whose parents went to college, it is critical that families provide a level of social support. Rendón's (1994) work on validation theory has pointed out the important role of communities and families in serving as sources of validation for low-income students. Further, resiliency theory, or the idea that people cope with stress through individual and social support mechanisms (Garmezy, 1991; Masten, 2001; Sanlo, 2004; Shield, 2004), suggests that familial support is necessary for individuals to cope with stress. The transition to college for first-generation students can be incredibly cognitively and emotionally stressful; thus, first-generation students would benefit from some form of support and validation from their families and community. The benefit of viewing families as sources of validation and resiliency is that it helps move the conversation on first-generation students away from deficit thinking and toward a positive psychology model. Therefore, the more parties, including family, involved in supporting first-generation students the greater likelihood of success for the students.

Finally, institutions need to create a shared sense of responsibility around the issue of supporting first-generation students at two-year and four-year colleges. The institutional programs discussed in this chapter highlight the need for student services and academic affairs to work collaboratively. Clearly, the issue of first-generation students' success is related to the work of multiple areas of student services; however, first-generation student success is also clearly tied to pedagogy and curriculum. The faculty must also work to do their part to support first-generation student persistence and success. Programs that have found ways to bridge the academic and student-service communities have shown to be successful in their work with first-generation students (Institute for Higher Education Policy, 2012).

The issue of supporting first-generation college students has now become a national imperative. Ensuring that higher education remains a vehicle for social mobility is vital to the economy and to the future of higher education. If colleges and universities cannot improve outcomes for first-generation students, then they will (willingly or not) contribute to cementing economic and social inequity in the United States for first-generation students. To preserve the narrative of higher education as a means to social mobility, those most in need must be able to benefit from a college education. The present system does not allow this to happen. The programs presented in this chapter point toward strategies to foster success for first-generation students and thus enable social mobility.

REFERENCES

Abdul-Alim, J. (2012, September). New initiative helps schools cater to first-generation collegians. *Diverse Issues in Higher Education*. Retrieved from http://diverseeducation.com/article/47840/

Abdul-Alim, J. (2013). Dream big: Partnership programs make college a reality for first-generation students. *Diverse Issues in Higher Education, 30*(9), 18–19.

Adelman, C. (2007). Do we really have a college access problem? *Change, 39*(4), 48–51.

Baum, S., Ma, J., & Payee, K. (2010). *Education Pays 2010: The benefits of higher education for individuals and society*. Iowa City, IA: College Board Advocacy & Policy Center.

Baxter Magolda, M. B. (2001). *Making their own way: narratives for transforming higher education to promote self-development*. Sterling, VA: Stylus.

Baxter Magolda, M. B. (2002). Helping students make their way to adulthood: Good company for the journey. *About Campus, 6*(6), 2–9.

Chen, X. (2005). *First-generation students in postsecondary education: A look at their college transcripts*. Washington, DC: National Center for Education Statistics.

Choy, S. (2001). *Students whose parents did not go to college: Postsecondary access, persistence, and attainment*. Washington, DC: National Center for Education Statistics.

Coffman, S. (2011). A social constructionist view of issues confronting first-generation college students. *New Directions for Teaching and Learning, 2011*(127), 81–90.

Dumais, S. A., & Ward, A. (2010). Cultural capital and first-generation college success. *Poetics, 38*, 245–265.

Engle, J., & O'Brien, C. (2007). *Demography is not destiny: Increasing the graduation rates of low-income college students at large public universities.* Washington, DC: Pell Institute.

Engle, J., & Tinto, V. (2008). *Moving beyond access: College success for low-income, first-generation students.* Washington, DC: Pell Institute.

Fain, P. (2012, November 8). Graduate, transfer, graduate. *Inside Higher Education.* Retrieved from https://www.insidehighered.com/news/2012/11/08/high-graduation-rates-community-college-transfers

First Scholars. (2013). *Progress to graduation.* Retrieved from http://firstscholars.org/results/progress-to-graduation/

Garmezy, N. (1991). Resilience in children's adaptation to negative life events and stressed environments. *Pediatric Annals, 20*(9), 459–466.

Goldrick-Rab, S. (2006). Following their every move: An investigation of social-class differences in college pathways. *Sociology of Education, 79*(1), 67–79.

Howard, A., & Levine, A. (2004). Where are the poor students: A conversation about social class and college attendance. *About Campus, 9*(4), 19–22.

Inkelas, K. K., Daver, Z. E., Vogt, K. E., & Leonard, J. B. (2007). Living-learning programs and first-generation college students' academic and social transition to college. *Research in Higher Education, 48*(4), 403–434.

Institute for Higher Education Policy. (2012). Issue brief: Supporting first-generation college students through classroom-based practices. Washington, DC: Author.

Ishitani, T. T. (2006). Studying attrition and degree completion behavior among first-generation college students in the United States. *Journal of Higher Education, 77*(5), 861–885.

Jaggars, S. S., & Xu, D. (2010). *Online learning in the Virginia community college system.* New York, NY: Community College Research Center.

Jehangir, R. R. (2010). *Higher education and first-generation students: Cultivating community, voice, and place for the new majority.* New York, NY: Palgrave Macmillan.

Jehangir, R., Williams, R., & Pete, J. (2011). Multicultural learning communities: Vehicles for developing self-authorship in first-generation college students. *Journal of the First-Year Experience and Students in Transition, 23*(1), 55–76.

Jehangir, R., Williams, R., & Pete, J. (2012). The influence of multicultural learning communities on the intrapersonal development of first-generation college students. *Journal of College Student Development, 53*(2), 267–284.

Jones, D., & Pirius, L. (2014, February). *Hot topics in student success and retention.* Paper presented at the Minnesota ACT State Organization Annual Conference: Redefining Readiness, Minnetonka, MN.

Kuh, G. D. (2003). What we're learning about student engagement from NSSE: Benchmarks for effective educational practices. *Change: The Magazine of Higher Learning, 35*(2), 24–32.

Langhout, R. D., Rosselli, F., & Feinstein, J. (2007). Assessing classism in academic settings. *Review of Higher Education, 30*, 145–184.

Leonhardt, D. (2004, April 22). As wealthy fill top colleges, concerns grow over fairness. *New York Times*, p. A1.

Lynch, M. (2013, January). It's tough to trailblaze: Challenges of first-generation college students. *Diverse Issues in Higher Education.* Retrieved from http://diverseeducation.com/article/50898/

Marcus, J. (2013, August 6). New figures suggest community college grad rates higher than thought. *The Hechinger Report.* Retrieved from http://hechingerreport.org/content/new-figures-suggest-community-college-grad-rates-higher-than-thought_12824/

Masten, A. S. (2001). Ordinary magic: Resilience processes in development. *American Psychologist, 56*(3), 227–238.

McCarron, G. P., & Inkelas, K. K. (2006). The gap between educational aspirations and attainment for first-generation college students and the role of parental involvement. *Journal of College Student Development, 47*(5), 534–549.

Mettler, S. (2014, March 1). College, the great unleveler. The Great Divide Series. *New York Times*. Retrieved from http://opinionator.blogs.nytimes.com/2014/03/01/college-the-great-unleveler/

Miller, A. (2013). Institutional practices that facilitate bachelor's degree completion for transfer students. *New Directions for Higher Education, 162*, 39–50.

Mt. San Antonio College. (2012). *Building pathways to persistance and completion.* Retrieved from http://www.mtsac.edu/president/cabinet-notes/Title%20V%20HSI%20Grant%20-%20Project%20Narrative.pdf

Nuñez, A., & Cuccaro-Alamin, S. (1998). *First-generation students: Undergraduates whose parents never enrolled in postsecondary education.* Washington, DC: National Center for Education Statistics.

Padgett, R. D., Johnson, M. P., & Pascarella, E. T. (2012). First-generation undergraduate students and the impacts of the first year of college: Additional evidence. *Journal of College Student Development, 53*(2), 243–266.

Pascarella, E. T., Pierson, C. T., Wolniak, G. C., & Terenzini, P. T. (2003). Experiences and outcomes of first-generation students in community colleges. *Journal of College Student Development, 44*(3), 420–429.

Pascarella, E. T., Pierson, C. T., Wolniak, G. C., & Terenzini, P. T. (2004). First-generation college students: Additional evidence on college experiences and outcomes. *Journal of Higher Education, 75*(3), 249–284.

Peabody, M., Hutchens, N., Lewis, W., & Deffendall, M. (2011). *First-generation college students at the University of Kentucky.* Lexington, KY: Policy Analysis Center for Kentucky Education.

Pike, G. R., and Kuh, G. D. (2005). First- and second-generation college students: A comparison of their engagement and intellectual development. *Journal of Higher Education, 76*(3), 276–300.

Rendón, L. (1994). Validating culturally diverse students: Toward a new model of learning and student development. *Innovative Higher Education, 9*(1), 33–52.

Sanlo, R. (2004). Lesbian, gay, and bisexual college students: Risk, resiliency, and retention. *Journal of College Student Retention, 6*(1), 97–110.

Shield, R. W. (2004). The retention of indigenous students in higher education: Historical issues, federal policy, and indigenous resilience. *Journal of College Student Retention: Research Theory and Practice, 6*(1), 111–127.

Soria, K. M., Stebleton, M. J., & Huesman, R. L., Jr. (2013–2014). Class counts: Exploring differences in academic and social integration between working-class and middle/upper class students at large, public research universities. *Journal of College Student Retention, 15*(2), 215–242.

Soria, K. M., & Stebleton, M. J. (2012). First-generation students' academic engagement and retention. *Teaching in Higher Education, 17*(6), 673–685.

Stebleton, M. J., Huesman, R. L., Jr., & Kuzhabekova, A. (2010). *Do I belong here? Exploring immigrant college student responses on the SERU survey Sense of Belonging/Satisfaction factor* (CSHE Research and Occasional Paper Series 13.10). Berkeley: University of California, Berkeley, Center for Studies in Higher Education. Retrieved from http://cshe.berkeley.edu/publications/docs/ ROPS. Stebleton%20et%20al.ImmigrantStudents.9.14.10.pdf

Stephens, N. M., Fryberg, S. A., Markus, H. R., Johnson, C., & Covarrubias, R. (2012). Unseen disadvantage: How American universities' focus on independence undermines the academic performance of first-generation college students. *Journal of Personality and Social Psychology, 102*, 1178–1197.

Stephens, N. M., Hamedani, M. G., & Destin, M. (2014). Closing the social-class achievement gap: A difference-education intervention improves first-generation students' academic performance and all students' college transition. *Psychosocial Science, 25*, 943–953.

Striplin, J. (1999). *Facilitating transfer for first-generation community college students*. (ED430627). Los Angeles, CA: ERIC Clearinghouse for Community Colleges.

Tyre, P. (2014, February 5). Improving economic diversity at the better colleges. *New York Times, Opinion Pages*. Retrieved from http://opinionator.blogs.nytimes.com/2014/02/05/improving-economic-diversity-at-the-better-colleges/

University of Minnesota TRiO Programs. (2012). *TRiO Opportunity Programs*. Retrieved from http://www.cehd.umn.edu/trio/default.html

Williams-Wyche, S. (2014). *Intergenerational mobility and the link to postsecondary education*. Saint Paul, MN: Office of Higher Education.

Woosley, S. A., & Shepler, D. K. (2011). Understanding the early integration experiences of first-generation college students. *College Student Journal, 45*(4), 700–714.

Xu, D., & Jaggers, S. S. (2013). *Adaptability to online learning: Differences across types of students and academic subject areas* (Working Paper No. 54). New York, NY: Community College Resource Center.

CHAPTER NINE

An Antideficit Approach to Examining the Impact of Institutional Involvement on Select Academic Outcomes of Latino College Students

YOUNG K. KIM, MARLA F. FRANCO AND LIZ A. RENNICK

The college-going rate of Latinos in the United States is growing: Hispanic college student enrollment has increased 487% from 1980 to 2010 (Snyder & Dillow, 2013). The Pew Hispanic Research Center reports that, for the first time, Hispanic high school graduates surpassed their White counterparts in the rate of college enrollment (Fry & Taylor, 2013). While the increasing college-going rate of Latinos indicates improved college access for this population, Latino college students still experience observable disparities in terms of college success, including degree attainment. The terms *Hispanic* and *Latino* are used interchangeably in this chapter and defined as persons who trace their origins back to Spanish-speaking countries. In 2011, the U.S. Census Bureau documented that 13.9% of Latinos achieved a college degree or higher, whereas 30.3% of Whites, 19.8% of Blacks, and 52.4% of Asian and Pacific Islanders earned college degrees. This discrepancy between Latino students' access to higher education and their college success warrants further examination of effective institutional practices that can maximize academic outcomes for Latino college students.

Moreover, low retention and college completion rates for all college students, coupled with the racial-ethnic gap in graduation rates, have resulted in an inadequate number of U.S. citizens who have acquired the desired knowledge, skills, and competencies needed for the twenty-first century (Hussar & Bailey, 2006).

In addition, external pressure for institutional accountability of student learning (Spelling, 2006) has heightened the need to improve our understanding of empirically supported factors that influence student success in college and to be more intentional about creating educationally effective teaching and learning environments (Kinzie, Gonyea, Shoup, & Kuh, 2008). President Barack Obama set a goal of doubling the number of college graduates by the year 2020 (U.S. Department of Education, 2013). Such a goal further challenges higher education institutions to examine ways through which they facilitate the greatest learning and development among college students (Kuh, Kinzie, Schuh, Whitt, & Associates, 1991).

In this chapter, we examine ways in which institutions of higher education can enhance the academic outcomes of Latino college students. Our goal is to expand upon the antideficit achievement scholarship on Latino college student success by conducting a quantitative study using a statewide college student dataset. Particularly, we examined the relationship between students' institutional involvement and select academic outcomes among Latino college students, including grade point average (GPA), cognitive skills, and degree aspiration. In the following section, we highlight what is known about the impact of involvement on college student outcomes, both in general and among Latino college students. Then, we investigate how different types of institutional involvement impact academic outcomes (i.e., GPA, cognitive skills, and degree aspirations) of this population. Specific types of institutional involvement analyzed in this study include peer, faculty, academic, and learning involvement.

IMPACT OF INSTITUTIONAL INVOLVEMENT ON COLLEGE STUDENT OUTCOMES

Researchers, using well-established theories of involvement, have found that higher levels of campus involvement result in greater intellectual and social gains, higher degree aspirations, and increased rates of persistence and degree attainment (Astin, 1993; Tinto, 1993). Such forms of engagement, also referred to as mediating mechanisms, involve both the time and energy students invest in educationally purposeful activities, as well as the institutional effort toward integrating effective educational practices (Kuh, Kinzie, Cruce, Shoup, & Gonyea, 2007; Sax, Astin, Korn, & Mahoney, 1999). More specifically, institutional involvement and conditions found to be educationally meaningful include student-faculty interaction, relationships with peers, active learning experiences, prompt feedback, time on task, high expectations, and respect for diverse talents and ways of learning (Chickering & Gamson, 1987; Kinzie et al., 2008).

IMPACT OF INSTITUTIONAL INVOLVEMENT ON LATINO COLLEGE STUDENT OUTCOMES

Underrepresented students, including students of color and those from low-income backgrounds and first-generation students, continue to be riddled by social and educational inequity, which often creates significant barriers to pursuing and successfully completing college (González, Jovel, & Stone, 2004; Swail, Cabrera, & Lee, 2004). It is even more problematic that the underrepresentation of Latinos in higher education is not due to a lack of academic ability or lackluster goals (González et al., 2004), but due to the segregated secondary educational experiences and inequitable access to financial resources and opportunities (Saenz & Ponjuan, 2009; Valenzuela, 1999). Most models of student persistence and involvement are based on the experiences of White, middle- to upper-class college students (Fischer, 2007); hence, there is a need to develop alternative models of college student success for other types of students, particularly for those students who historically have been underserved by educational institutions. Despite this reality, it is promising that there is a proliferation of empirical studies on the impact of institutional involvement–college experiences on college outcomes among underrepresented college populations (Kuh, Kinzie, Cruce et al., 2007).

Generally speaking, students from all racial and ethnic backgrounds benefit from participating in institutional involvement that is educationally meaningful; however, some researchers have found that historically underrepresented students experience greater gains with certain types of institutional involvement compared to their majority peers (Feagin, Hernan, & Nikitah, 1996; Kim, Rennick, & Franco, 2014; Swail, Cabrera, Lee, & Williams, 2005). For example, Kim and colleagues found that Latino college students appear to benefit more from their college experiences compared to their peers of other racial groups and perceive their experiences as relevant and important to their development and achievement. Focusing on four major types of institutional involvement utilized in this study (i.e., peer, faculty, academic, and learning involvement), the next section will summarize some findings on how Latino college students uniquely experience institutional involvement and how it affects their educational outcomes.

Peer Involvement

College campuses offer interpersonal environments that influence socialization and student development and have been found to mediate institutional-level peer group effects (antonio, 2004). Such interpersonal environments exist both in and outside of the classroom. Research on supportive and collective learning environments found that peer connectedness mediated the relationships between teacher confirmation behaviors and in-class student involvement (Stuber, 2009), thus providing faculty the opportunity to be more strategic about crafting opportunities for students to develop a sense of connectedness among each other. This is especially noteworthy because making connections with other ethnic minority peers has been found to positively predict college GPA (Cerezo & Chang, 2013). Outside of the classroom, peer engagement often occurs within the setting of clubs and organizations. Estimates from the 2010 National Survey of Student Engagement indicate 53% of college students spend at least an hour or more per week participating in clubs and organizations, and 80% of students participate in at least one academically affiliated organization by the end of their senior year (Dugan & Komives, 2007). These types of involvement, which include peer and faculty engagement, have been shown to demonstrate positive influences on a range of developmental outcomes among college students (Abraham, Lujan, López, & Walker, 2002; Dugan, 2013; Pascarella & Terenzini, 2005).

Faculty Involvement

Student-faculty interaction, both in and outside of the classroom, are critical experiences found to develop college students' academic self-concept, foster their motivation to succeed, improve their likelihood of persisting in college, and produce greater gains in learning (DeFreitas & Bravo, 2012; Kim & Sax, 2009, 2011; Komarraju, Musulkin, & Bhattacharya, 2010; Lundberg & Schreiner, 2004; Tinto, 1975). In particular, student-faculty interaction has been known to be a strong positive predictor of persistence among Latino college students (Hurtado & Carter, 1997; Komarraju et al., 2010) even after controlling for background characteristics and other college experiences. Optimal conditions for producing high quality interaction between Latino college students and faculty include faculty's awareness, appreciation, and sensitivity to Latino cultures, as well as an understanding of high impact practices, Latinos' preferred learning styles, and the ability to integrate this knowledge when establishing classroom norms, environments, and expectations (Cejda & Hoover, 2010).

Academic Involvement

Pascarella and Terenzini (2005) documented various studies that link academic involvement—that is, the amount of energy and time students dedicate to academic tasks, such as writing, reading, and studying—to student development in cognitive skills, intellectual growth, and qualitative, verbal, and subject-matter competence. In particular, a seminal study by Astin (1993) found that time spent on studying was positively related to nearly all academic outcomes in the study. Compared to non-Hispanic White students, Latino college students reported higher levels of motivation and drive to achieve, which was also reflected in higher levels of academic effort during their last year of high school (Hurtado, Saenz, Santos, & Cabrera, 2008). Latino college students have also reported that a more common reason for interacting with faculty was for writing improvement (Kuh & Hu, 2001; Lundberg & Schreiner, 2004). Other research indicates that Latino college students spend more time on mental activities related to academics than their peers from other racial groups (Greene, Marti, & McClenney, 2008). Kim and colleagues (2014) found similar results: Latino students reported higher levels of critical reasoning classroom activity and elevated academic effort than their peers from other racial groups. Although these studies do not necessarily conclude higher grades as a result of this effort, Kim and colleagues did find that Latino students reported the most gains in cognitive, affective, and civic outcomes compared to their peers from other racial groups.

Learning Involvement

Ideal learning environments for Latino college students can be best characterized as ones that are culturally responsive, whereby faculty recognize the importance of integrating students' cultural identities in all aspects of learning (Ladson-Billings, 1994). Such student-centered pedagogies empower students socially, intellectually, politically, and emotionally (Ladson-Billings, 1984); hence, this type of learning environment facilitates prime conditions for Latino college students to feel comfortable asking questions, sharing ideas, contributing to class discussions, and interacting with faculty. Particularly, active learning environments enhance student engagement, knowledge, and understanding of course content among all college students, including Latinos (Anderson & Adams, 1992; Chickering & Gamson, 1987; Johnson, Johnson, & Smith, 1991). Some positive outcomes of active learning environments include students' perceived gains in knowledge, greater understanding from their course work, and the development of friendships and peer networks that facilitate the establishment of membership in social communities at their institutions (Braxton, Milem, & Sullivan, 2000). As a result, such active learning practices may not only directly influence students' social integration with peers and faculty but also indirectly affect students' institutional commitment (Braxton et al., 2000; Hurtado, Carter, & Spuler, 1996). Within such forms of learning involvement, students also experience various types of higher-order thinking activities such as critical thinking, analysis, synthesis, and evaluation mostly in conversations with their peers and faculty (Braxton et al., 2000).

METHOD

Data Source and Sample

We used the 2010 University of California Undergraduate Experience Survey (UCUES), which is administered on a biennial basis to all undergraduates across all nine campuses of the University of California (UC) system by the Office of the President. The UCUES is designed to solicit an intensive set of information about student experiences, attitudes, and engagement; and a set of core questions addresses many general aspects of peer, faculty, academic, and learning engagement among students. This study utilizes survey items collected from the set of core questions, along with institutional data on students' GPA and race/ethnicity. The response rate for the 2010 UCUES was 43% (74,410 participants).

Because we were mainly interested in the effects of involvement on college student gains or development, our sample was limited to junior and senior Latino students who had significant exposure to the college environment. The data were screened and cleaned to meet the assumptions of our analysis, and missing values were treated using list-wise deletion during the analysis. Consequently, the final analytical sample of the study was composed of 3,215 junior and senior Latino students across nine UC campuses. Within that sample, 60.5% were female, 65.3% were seniors, 48.1% were first-generation college students, 14.8% were immigrants, 49% had a language heritage that was not English, and 29.5% were transfer students. A majority (39.6%) of the participants in this study were from working-class backgrounds while 27.8% were from middle-class backgrounds, 22% were from low-income or poor backgrounds, and 10.6% were from wealthy, upper-middle, or professional class backgrounds.

Variables

Three dependent variables were utilized for this study to measure academic outcomes: (1) GPA (actual GPA supplied by the institutions), (2) cognitive skills, and (3) degree aspirations. Cognitive skills is a composite measure and consists of three individual survey items that gauge students' self-assessment on their analytical and critical thinking skills, ability to be clear and effective in writing, and ability to read and comprehend academic material. This composite measure was generated through an exploratory factor analysis and reliability estimates; the results showed that both factor loadings and reliability were well within the acceptable range. Degree aspirations was assessed by an individual survey item that asked students to identify the highest academic degree they plan to eventually earn.

The independent variables used in this study were identified based on Astin's (1993) inputs-environments-outcomes (I-E-O) model. As a methodological tool,

Astin's I-E-O model provided the framework that allowed us to more accurately estimate the unique effects of institutional involvement on college outcomes by controlling for the effects of other confounding variables related to student inputs and other college environments or experiences. Based on Astin's model, the independent variables of this study were organized into the following six major blocks: (1) pretest, (2) demographic characteristics, (3) major, (4) campus climate for diversity, (5) individual college experiences, and (6) institutional involvement (see Table 9.1). The independent variables of our main interest were included in the final block and represented four different aspects of institutional involvement: (1) peer involvement (i.e., participation in clubs or organizations, working with a group of students, helping a classmate understand material better), (2) faculty involvement (i.e., involvement in faculty research projects, academic engagement with faculty), (3) academic involvement (i.e., raising standards for acceptable effort due to high standards of a faculty member, extensively revising a paper before submitting for grade), and (4) learning involvement (i.e., active learning environments, high-order cognitive activities).

Data Analysis

We analyzed the data using IBM SPSS Statistics 22. We examined z-scores and Mahalanobis distance to detect and remove both univariate and multivariate outliers among our variables. To ensure univariate normality, we examined skewness and kurtosis and transformed variables where necessary. We also examined regression plots of standardized residuals to check homoscedasticity of our data and investigated residual probability plots and histograms to check normality. Once the assumptions of our analyses were satisfied, a series of hierarchical multiple regression analyses were conducted to examine the types of institutional involvement that predicted GPA, cognitive skills, and degree aspirations among Latino college students.

RESULTS AND DISCUSSION

The purpose of our study was to examine which forms of institutional involvement were best at predicting select academic outcomes (i.e., GPA, cognitive skills, and degree aspirations) of Latino college students. In lieu of exacerbating Latino college student failure by framing research, analysis, and practice using a deficit-achievement framework (Harper, 2010), more critical attention was given to examining the conditions necessary to produce academic success among Latino college students. Within this context, our findings revealed that institutional involvement mattered to Latino college students and worked in unique ways to produce positive outcomes.

Predictors of Latino College Student Success

Numerous studies report that Latino students who become more involved in various aspects of campus life are more likely to persist and graduate from college and perform better academically (Arbona & Nora, 2007; Cerna, Pérez, & Saenz, 2009; Crisp, Taggart, & Nora, 2012; Fischer, 2007). Our study further clarifies that the type of involvement matters for Latino college students, revealing some patterns of institutional involvement as they relate to select academic outcomes. Overall, faculty involvement and certain types of academic involvement appear to have positive effects across all outcomes (i.e., GPA, cognitive skills, degree aspirations). However, peer involvement is restricted to its effect (both positive and negative) on degree aspirations, while learning involvement is restricted to its effect (both positive and negative) on GPA and cognitive skills. These findings are displayed in Table 9.1 and discussed here in more detail.

Peer involvement

Peer involvement appears to have an impact on degree aspirations for Latino students, but with mixed results. Both participating in clubs and organizations and helping fellow classmates understand the material better positively impacted degree aspirations. However, working with a group of students outside of class appears to have a negative impact on degree aspirations. Previously, Cole (2008) found that, for Latino students in STEM fields, studying with other students was negatively correlated with GPA. These findings could be related to the personality, political, and power dynamics of working with a group of students with whom the student does not relate well. It could be that the difference between working with a group of students outside of class and participating in clubs or organizations has to do with choice in the matter. Students typically have no choice or limited choice when it comes to which group of students they find themselves working with on projects outside of class, but students do have the choice to associate with other students in clubs or organizations with whom they have much in common.

Faculty involvement

Faculty involvement was revealed to have a positive impact on all measured outcomes in our study, which confirms existing literature on the positive impact of student-faculty interaction for Latino college students on an array of college outcomes, including GPA (Cole, 2008, 2010; Kim, 2010; Kim & Sax, 2009), cognitive skills (Einarson & Clarkberg, 2010; Kim & Sax, 2009; Lundberg, 2010), and degree aspirations (Ceja & Rivas, 2010; Kim, 2010; Kim & Sax, 2009; McKay & Estrella, 2008). From our findings, we can also discern two specific types of faculty involvement that meaningfully contribute to academic outcomes among Latino college students.

Table 9.1. Results of the Regression Analysis on the Impact of Institutional Involvement on Academic Outcomes Among Latino College Students (Standardized regression coefficients).

	GPA (n = 2,188)	Cognitive Skills (n = 3,214)	Degree Aspirations (n =3,179)
Block 1: Pretest			
Pretest Variable	.322***	.504***	.301***
Block 2: Demographic			
Socioeconomic Status	.063**		−.039*
Parent(s) education level (AA degree or more)	.082***		
Immigrant Status			−.061***
Language Heritage (English)	.083***		
Transfer Status		−.113***	
Block 3: Major (Ref=Arts and Humanities)			
Engineering and Computer Sciences	−.136***	−.082***	−.053**
Physical and Biological Sciences	−.156***	−.088***	.140***
Social Sciences	−.075***		.049*
Professional Schools			−.066***
Block 4: Climate for Diversity			
Freedom to express political beliefs		.077***	
Block 5: Individual College Experiences			
Time Spent with Family	−.058**		
Psychological Well-being†	.097***	.140***	
Symptomatic Academic Barriers†	−.136***		
Block 6: Institutional Involvement			
Peer Involvement			
Participated in clubs or organizations			.078***
Worked with group of students outside of class			−.086***
Helped classmate understand material better			.073**
Faculty Involvement			
Involved in faculty research projects	.076***	.037**	.072***
Academic engagement with faculty†	.117***	.066***	.090***
Academic Involvement			
Raised standard for acceptable effort due to high standards of a faculty member		.039**	
Extensively revised a paper at least once before submitting for grade	.048*	.063***	.065***
Learning Involvement			
Active Learning Environments†	.062*	.164***	
Higher-order Cognitive Activities†	−.089***	.144***	
Adjusted R^2	.25	.50	.20

†Denotes scale items. Factor loadings and reliability estimates available from the first author upon request.
*$p < .05$, **$p < .01$, ***$p < .001$.

First, involvement in faculty research appears to have a positive impact on the academic outcomes of Latino students, confirming prior research in this area about its positive effects on GPA and cognitive skills (Kim et al., 2014; Kim & Sax, 2009). However, auxiliary statistics of this study indicate that only 30% of Latino students in our sample participated in faculty research, indicating an area in need of greater attention. Prior research also indicates low levels of student involvement in faculty research in general (Kim & Sax, 2009) and among Latino college students in particular (Webber, Nelson Laird, & BrckaLorenz, 2013). Low levels of student involvement in faculty research indicate that higher education institutions may be overlooking the benefits of undergraduate research as an effective form of student-faculty interaction that has wide-reaching and tangible benefits, especially for Latino students. Rogers, Kranz, and Ferguson (2013) acknowledge the potential benefits of Latino students' involvement in research; however, they also recognize some barriers of the involvement such as the lack of time among Latino college students and the considerable strain on workload and resources for faculty to increase student participation in research. The results of this study, along with previous research with similar findings, are a clarion call for higher educational professionals to look toward ways of increasing Latino students' involvement in faculty research.

Second, students appear to benefit from their academic interactions with faculty, such as communicating outside of the class about course material or working with faculty on projects other than coursework. We found that such interactions positively impact all three academic outcomes of this study (i.e., GPA, cognitive skills, degree aspirations). However, the levels of students' participation in this type of faculty involvement were not high (this involvement was measured by a factor scale using a 6-point Likert scale, ranging from 1—never to 6—very often; mean score of the factor scale was 2.65). In other words, few students indicated that they often or very often had academic interactions with faculty, indicating another area of missed opportunity for Latino student development.

Academic involvement

Our study also revealed some interesting findings regarding academic involvement when it relates to academic outcomes of Latino college students. We found that Latino students who extensively revise papers prior to submitting them for a grade were also more likely to have a higher GPA, greater gains in cognitive skills, and higher degree aspirations. In addition, results show that students who raise their standard for acceptable effort due to the high standards of faculty were also more likely to report higher levels of cognitive skills development. Findings from this and other studies (e.g., Lundberg & Schreiner, 2004) suggest the positive effect of keeping high standards and a high level of expectations on academic outcomes for Latino students. These findings also confirm the positive effects of an antideficit approach on Latino students' gains and development. Latino students are typically thought of as the minority group that is the least prepared for college and the most at risk for leaving college, but these characterizations should not preclude faculty from expecting Latino students to perform well academically. Steele (1997) has shown how affiliation with a certain stereotype can cause a negative psychological reaction that induces lower academic performance, a phenomenon he defined as *stereotype threat*. Latino students, fearing that faculty are reducing them to their worst stereotypes, may underperform as a result of a negative psychological reaction to notions that they are not well prepared for college. Steele further argues that remediation can reinforce stereotypes about Latino students' abilities that further undermine their performance, adding that "giving challenging work to students conveys respect for their potential and thus shows them that they are not regarded through the lens of an ability-demeaning stereotype" (p. 625). Thus, it is appropriate for faculty to believe in their students to achieve, regardless of their background characteristics. In order to maximize their educational benefits, Latino students should be appropriately challenged as well as supported in their academic endeavors.

Learning involvement

Learning involvement was also shown to have an impact on GPA and cognitive skills among Latino college students. Our results show that Latino students who indicated that they were more involved in active learning environments (i.e., actively participating in classroom discussions, finding a course so interesting that the student does more work than is required, making class presentations, having faculty who know the student's name) were also more likely to have a higher GPA and greater gains in cognitive skills development. Some of the most effective teachers reject the idea of power within the classroom and create learning atmospheres that are based on trust, that don't belittle or embarrass, and that encourage students to feel free to be expressive in their learning without fear of making mistakes (Bain, 2004). Faculty should be encouraged to adopt a more relational form of teaching where Latino students, in their pursuit of knowledge, are comfortable enough to ask important questions and engage in dialogue. On the other hand, we found some mixed results in terms of the impact of high-order cognitive activities on Latino students' academic outcomes. Results of this study indicate that high-order cognitive activities were associated with lower GPA and greater gains in cognitive skills among Latino college students. One possible explanation for this finding is that it may be related to the level of difficulty or challenge in certain majors and at selective research institutions, where data from our study were collected. As Kim and colleagues (2014) found in a previous study, we also found that GPA appeared to drop from high school to the junior or senior year for all students, including Latinos. They also found that critical reasoning classroom activity, a factor scale conceptually related to high-order cognitive skills, was a negative predictor of GPA for Latino students. Another possible explanation is that perhaps students attribute the more challenging aspects of the academic experience (i.e., high-order cognitive activities) to lower GPA rather than the more pleasurable, exciting, or stimulating aspects of the academic experience (i.e., active learning environments).

FOSTERING SUCCESS AMONG LATINO COLLEGE STUDENTS

This study suggests that Latino college students (particularly those attending selective research universities) experience positive outcomes specific to their GPA, cognitive skills, and degree aspirations when involved in select forms of peer, faculty, academic, and learning engagement. The findings of this study and others provide empirical direction for institutional interventions to facilitate Latino students' success and development during their college years and demonstrate areas in need of improvement. Based on our findings, best practices for fostering Latino college student success through institutional involvement may be summarized as follows:

- Find ways to encourage the creation of more opportunities for students to participate in faculty research, and find ways to increase student participation in this area.
- Find ways to increase student-faculty interactions that personalize the academic experience.
- Create an antideficit learning environment that focuses less on student risk factors associated with negative stereotypes about Latino student achievement. This can be achieved by providing academically challenging environments for students while also providing appropriate levels of support.
- Faculty should be encouraged to adopt a more relational form of teaching where Latino students, in their pursuit of knowledge, are comfortable enough to ask important questions and engage in dialogue.
- Encourage positive peer interactions among Latino students through clubs and organizations to help foster their sense of belonging and create a more positive academic self-concept.

The rationale for fostering success among Latino college students does require the recognition of educational disparities and the unique challenges that put Latino college students at risk; however, as we have shown in this chapter, it is at least equally important to take the antideficit perspective that focuses on the factors that contribute to success if we are to make a continuous effort at addressing the educational achievement gap between Latinos and other races/ethnicities. Additionally, improved compositional diversity among college students must not represent the extent of institutional effort to meet the needs of an increasingly diverse college student population. Latino college student outcomes must be measured, tracked over time, disaggregated, and used to make empirically supported decisions. The nature of this type of student data that institutions transparently share is an indication of what an institution values and comes with an obligation to affirm good practice and make empirically supported decisions that support Latino college student success.

REFERENCES

Abraham, J. P., Lujan, S. S., López, E. E., & Walker, M. T. (2002). Graduating students' perceptions of outcomes of college experiences at a predominantly Hispanic university. *Journal of Hispanic Higher Education, 1*(3), 267–276.

Anderson, J. A., & Adams, M. (1992). Acknowledging the learning styles of diverse student populations: Implications for instructional design. *New Directions for Teaching and Learning, 1992*(49), 19–33.

antonio, a. l. (2004). The influence of friendship groups on intellectual self-confidence and educational aspirations in college. *Journal of Higher Education, 75*(4), 446–471.

Arbona, C., & Nora, A. (2007). The influence of academic and environmental factors on Hispanic college degree attainment. *Review of Higher Education, 30*(3), 247–269.

Astin, A. W. (1993). *What matters in college? Four critical years revisited.* San Francisco, CA: Jossey-Bass.

Bain, K. (2004). *What the best college teachers do.* Cambridge, MA: Harvard University Press.

Braxton, J. M., Milem, J. F., & Sullivan, A. S. (2000). The influence of active learning on the college student departure process: Toward a revision of Tinto's theory. *Journal of Higher Education, 71*(5), 569–590.

Ceja, M., & Rivas, M. (2010). Faculty-student interactions and Chicana PhD aspirations. *Journal of the Professoriate, 3*(2), 75–100.

Cejda, B. D., & Hoover, R. E. (2010). Perceived educational barriers, cultural congruity, coping responses, and psychological well-being of Latina undergraduates. *Hispanic Journal of Behavioral Sciences, 27*(2), 161–183.

Cerezo, A., & Chang, T. (2013). Latina/o achievement at predominantly White universities: The importance of culture and ethnic community. *Journal of Hispanic Higher Education, 12*(1), 72–85.

Cerna, O. S., Perez, P. A., & Saenz, V. (2009). Examining the precollege attributes and values of Latina/o bachelor's degree attainers. *Journal of Hispanic Higher Education, 8*(2), 130–157.

Chickering, A. W., & Gamson, Z. F. (1987). *Seven principles of good practice for undergraduate education.* Retrieved from http://teaching.uncc.edu/sites/teaching.uncc.edu/ files/media/files/file/InstructionalMethods/SevenPrinciples.pdf

Cole, D. (2007). Do interracial interactions matter? An examination of student-faculty contact and intellectual self-concept. *Journal of Higher Education, 78*(3), 248–272.

Cole, D. (2008). Constructive criticism: The role of student-faculty interactions on African American and Hispanic students' educational gains. *Journal of College Student Development, 49*(6), 587–605.

Cole, D. (2010). The effects of student-faculty interactions on minority students' college grades: Differences between aggregated and disaggregated data. *Journal of the Professoriate, 3*(2), 137–160.

Crisp, G., Taggart, A., & Nora, A. (2012). *Undergraduate Hispanic students: A systematic review of research identifying factors contributing to academic success outcomes.* Paper presented at the Annual Meeting of the Association of the Study of Higher Education, Las Vegas, NV.

DeFreitas, S. C., & Bravo, A. (2012). The influence of involvement with faculty and mentoring on the self-efficacy and academic achievement of African American and Latino college students. *Journal of the Scholarship of Teaching and Learning, 12*(4), 1–11.

Dugan, J. P. (2013). Patterns in group involvement experiences during college: Identifying a taxonomy. *Journal of College Student Development, 54*(3), 229–246.

Dugan, J. P., & Komives, S. R. (2007). *Developing leadership capacity in college students: Findings from a national study.* A Report from the Multi-Institutional Study of Leadership. College Park, MD: National Clearinghouse for Leadership Programs.

Einarson, M. K., & Clarkberg, M. E. (2010). Race differences in the impact of students' out-of-class interactions with faculty. *Journal of the Professoriate, 3*(2), 101–136.

Feagin, J. R., Hernan, V., & Nikitah, I. (1996). *The agony of education: Black students at White colleges and universities.* New York, NY: Routledge.

Fischer, M. J. (2007). Settling into campus life: Differences by race/ethnicity in college involvement and outcomes. *Journal of Higher Education, 78*(2), 125–161.

Fry, R., & Taylor, P. (2013). Hispanic high school graduates pass Whites in rate of college enrollment. Washington, DC: Pew Hispanic Research Center.

Gandara, P. C., & Contreras, F. (2009). *The Latino education crisis: The consequences of failed social policies.* Cambridge, MA: Harvard University Press.

González, K. P., Jovel, J. E., & Stone, C. (2004). Latinas: The new Latino majority in college. *New Directions for Student Services, 2004*(105), 17–27.

Greene, T. G., Marti, C. N., & McClenney, K. (2008). The effort-outcome gap: Differences for African American and Hispanic community college students in student engagement and academic achievement. *Journal of Higher Education, 79*(5), 513–539.

Harper, S. R. (2010). An anti-deficit achievement framework for research on students of color in STEM. *New Directions for Institutional Research, 2010*(148), 63–74.

Hurtado, S., & Carter, D. F. (1997). Effects of college transition and perceptions of the campus racial climate on Latino college students' sense of belonging. *Sociology of Education, 70*(4), 324–345.

Hurtado, S., Carter, D. F., & Spuler, A. (1996). Latino student transition to college: Assessing difficulties and factors in successful college adjustment. *Research in Higher Education, 37*(2), 135–157.

Hurtado, S., Saenz, V. B., Santos, J. L., & Cabrera, N. L. (2008). *Advancing in higher education: A portrait of Latina/o college freshmen at four-year institutions, 1975–2006.* Los Angeles: University of California Los Angeles, Higher Education Research Institute.

Hussar, W. J., & Bailey, T. M. (2006). *Projections of education statistics to 2015.* Washington, DC: U.S. Department of Education, NCES 2006–084.

Johnson, D. W., Johnson, R. T., & Smith, K. A. (1991). *Cooperative learning: Increasing college faculty instructional productivity.* Washington, DC: School of Education & Human Development, George Washington University.

Kim, Y. K. (2010). Racially different patterns of student-faculty interaction in college: A focus on levels, effects, and causal directions. *Journal of the Professoriate, 3*(2), 161–189.

Kim, Y. K., Rennick, L. A., & Franco, M. (2014). Latino college students at highly selective institutions: A comparison of their college experiences and outcomes to other racial groups. *Journal of Hispanic Higher Education, 13*(4), 245–268.

Kim, Y. K., & Sax, L. J. (2009). Student-faculty interaction in research universities: Differences by student gender, race, social class, and first-generation status. *Research in Higher Education, 50*(5), 437–459.

Kim, Y. K., & Sax, L. (2011). Are the effects of student-faculty interaction dependent on academic major? An examination using multilevel modeling. *Research in Higher Education, 52*(6), 589–615

Kinzie, J., Gonyea, R., Shoup, R., & Kuh, G. D. (2008). Promoting persistence and success of under-represented students: Lessons for teaching and learning. *New Directions for Teaching and Learning, 2008*(115), 21–38.

Komarraju, M., Musulkin, S., & Bhattacharya, G. (2010). Role of student-faculty interactions in developing college students' academic self-concept, motivation, and achievement. *Journal of College Student Development, 51*(3), 332–342.

Kuh, G. D., & Hu, S. (2001). The effects of student-faculty interaction in the 1990s. *Review of Higher Education, 24*(3), 309–32.

Kuh, G. D., Kinzie, J., Cruce, T., Shoup, R., & Gonyea, R. M. (2007). *Connecting the dots: Multi-faceted analyses of the relationships between student engagement results from the NSSE, and the institutional practices and conditions that foster student success.* Final report prepared for Lumina Foundation for Education. Bloomington: Indiana University, Center for Postsecondary Research.

Kuh, G. D., Kinzie, J., Schuh, J. H., Whitt, E. J., & Associates. (1991). *Student success through effective educational practice: Lessons from the field.* San Francisco, CA: Jossey-Bass & American Association for Higher Education.

Ladson-Billings, G. (1994). *The dreamkeepers: Successful teachers of African American children.* San Francisco, CA: Jossey-Bass.

Lundberg, C. A. (2010). Institutional commitment to diversity, college involvement, and faculty relationships as predictors of learning for students of color. *Journal of the Professoriate, 3*(2), 50–74.

Lundberg, C. A., & Schreiner, L. A. (2004). Quality and frequency of faculty-student interaction as predictors of learning: An analysis by student race/ethnicity. *Journal of College Student Development, 45*(5), 549–565.

McKay, V. C., & Estrella, J. (2008). First-generation student success: The role of faculty interaction in service learning courses. *Communication Education, 57*(3), 356–372.

Nora, A., & Crisp, G. (2009). Hispanics and higher education: An overview of research, theory, and practice. *Higher Education: Handbook of Theory and Research, 2009*(24), 321–358.

Pascarella, E. T., Pierson, C. T., Wolniak, G. C., & Terenzini, P. T. (2004). First-generation college students: Additional evidence on college experiences and outcomes. *Journal of Higher Education, 75*(3), 249–284.

Pascarella, E. T., & Terenzini, P. T. (2005). *How college affects students.* San Francisco, CA: Jossey-Bass.

Rogers, D. L., Kranz, P. L., & Ferguson, C. J. (2013). The embedded researcher method for involving undergraduates in research new data and observations. *Journal of Hispanic Higher Education, 12*(3), 225–236.

Saenz, V. B., & Ponjuan, L. (2009). The vanishing Latino male in higher education. *Journal of Hispanic Higher Education, 54*(8), 54–89.

Sax, L. J., Astin, A. W., Korn, W. S., & Mahoney, K. M. (1999). *The American freshman: National norms for fall 1999.* Los Angeles: University of California Los Angeles, Cooperative Institutional Research Program.

Schwartz, S. J., Kim, S. Y., Whitbourne, S. K., Zamboanga, B. L., Weisskirch, R. L., Forthun, L. F., Vazsonyi, A. T., Beyers, W., & Luyckx, K. (2013). Converging identities: Dimensions of acculturation and personal identity status among immigrant college students. *Cultural Diversity and Ethnic Minority Psychology, 19*(2), 155–165.

Snyder, T. D., & Dillow, S. A. (2013). *Digest of education statistics, 2012.* Washington, DC: National Center for Education Statistics.

Spelling, M. (2006). *A test of leadership: Charting the future of U.S. higher education.* Washington, DC: U.S. Department of Education.

Steele, C. M. (1997). A threat in the air: How stereotypes shape intellectual identity and performance. *American Psychologist, 52*(6), 613–629.

Stuart, M., Lido, C., Morgan, J., Solomon, L., & May, S. (2011). The impact of engagement with extracurricular activities on the student experience and graduate outcomes for widening the participation populations. *Active Learning in Higher Education, 12*(3), 203–215.

Stuber, J. M. (2009). Class, culture, and participation in the collegiate extra-curriculum. *Sociological Forum, 24*(4), 877–900.

Swail, W. S., Cabrera, A. F., & Lee, C. (2004). *Latino youth and the pathway to college.* Washington, DC: Pew Hispanic Center.

Swail, W. S., Cabrera, A. F., Lee, C., & Williams, A. (2005). *Part III: Pathways to the bachelor's degree for Latino students.* Washington, DC: Educational Policy Institute.

Tinto, V. (1975). Dropout from higher education: A theoretical synthesis of recent research. *Review of Educational Research, 45*(1), 89–125.

Tinto, V. (1993). *Leaving college: Rethinking the causes and cures of student attrition* (2nd ed.). Chicago, IL: University of Chicago Press.

Webber, K. L., Nelson Laird, T. F., & BrckaLorenz, A. M. (2013). Student and faculty member engagement in undergraduate research. *Research in Higher Education, 54*(2), 227–249.

U.S. Census Bureau. (2011). *2010 census shows nation's Hispanic population grew four times faster than total U.S. population.* Washington, DC: Author.

U.S. Department of Education, National Center for Education Statistics. (2013). *The condition of education 2013* (NCES 2013–037). Washington, DC: Author.

Valenzuela, A. (1999). *Subtractive schooling: U.S.-Mexican youth and the politics of caring.* New York: State University of New York Press.

Villenas, S., & Deyhle, D. (1999). Critical race theory and ethnographies challenging the stereotypes: Latino families, schooling, resilience and resistance. *Curriculum Inquiry, 29*(4), 413–445.

Employment

College Employment AND Academic Outcomes FOR African American Students ON Elite Campuses

MARY J. FISCHER AND DERONTA SPENCER

Many college students are employed in a variety of capacities over the course of their academic careers. While the reasons for working during college are multifold, the rising costs of college tuition and related expenses are a clear driving force behind the decision to work for many students. For instance, from 2000–2001 to 2010–2011 the average cost of full-time college enrollment rose 35.4% (U.S. Department of Education, 2012), while average salaries remained stagnant. Furthermore, the demographics of higher education have been changing with growing numbers of low-income students now attending, some of whom are also from racial/ethnic minority groups and many of whom are first-generation college students. Not surprisingly, in addition to greater dependence on financial aid of various forms to attend college, students are increasingly likely to work to help offset some of their college expenses. Perna (2010) reports that two-thirds of students at four-year institutions are employed; however, African American students are particularly likely to be engaged in formal employment while in school, with nearly 75% of African American undergraduates in 2004–2005 reporting full- or part-time employment (Flowers, 2010). Also, African American students have lower GPAs and four-year graduation rates than Whites. For instance, in 2007–2008 more than 40% of White students had a GPA of 3.5 or higher while only 19.5% of Blacks had a GPA of 3.5 or higher (Woo, Green, & Matthews, 2012). In 2013 the college graduation rates for Blacks was 20% while the college graduation rate was 40% for Whites (U.S.

Department of Education, 2012). To what extent does working while in college contribute to these academic struggles?

On the one hand, working during college clearly takes time that could be used on academic pursuits. However, there is some research evidence that working, particularly in on-campus jobs, can help to integrate students into campus life. This integration is a key element in student retention, academic achievement, and eventual graduation (Tinto, 1993). Prior research has suggested that academic and social integration into campus life may be particularly critical for minority students (Fischer, 2007). Furthermore, holding down a job either on or off campus requires the development of skills (e.g., time management, responsibility, communication) that are instrumental to academic success. While formal employment was not part of the early models of student attachment and retention, it is becoming a growing area of research interest and policy relevance. The purpose of this chapter is to contribute to student employment literature by examining the impact of college employment on the academic success of African American students at elite colleges and universities.

THE EFFECTS OF EMPLOYMENT ON GPA

Prior research has mixed findings on the effect of employment on college students' academic achievement. There are several scholars who have found no significant difference in grades between student workers and nonworkers (Gleason, 1993; Henry, 1967; Kaiser & Bergen, 1968; Mounsey & Diekhoff, 2012; Nonis & Hudson, 2006). In a few of these earlier studies, scholars only examined students who worked no more than 15 hours a week (Henry, 1967; Kaiser & Bergen, 1968). There have also been some studies in which researchers have found a negative relationship between working and grades (Callender, 2008; Dadgar, 2011; Hunt, Lincoln, & Walker, 2004). These studies examined students who worked a range of hours, which as we will see below is central to how work impacts students academically. Other researchers have found that student workers had better grades and GPAs than nonworkers (Hammes & Haller, 1983), but this positive finding was often contingent upon students working a lower threshold of hours. Hammes and Haller (1983) also specifically focused on graduating seniors, which could have biased their results since students who persist to the senior year are more likely to have developed strategies to enable them to balance studying with work, while students who are less able to manage this balance may have been more likely to have left prior to attaining senior-year status.

One of the most obvious ways in which work may be detrimental to college students' academic achievement is that the time spent in paid employment may come at the expense of time that could be devoted to studying. This trade-off between hours spent working and studying theoretically becomes more salient the more hours that are devoted to working. Nevertheless, paid employment and academic efforts can be complementary (Beeson & Wessel, 2002; Curtis & Williams, 2002). Beeson and Wessel (2002), for instance, found that student workers persist and have higher six-year graduation rates than their peers who are not employed. Students who work on campus in particular may find that their employment helps them to establish linkages to others in their institutions and thus aid integration into campus life (Curtis & Shani, 2010). This integration, in turn, is positively associated with academic achievement. The act of holding a paid position also fosters skills such as time management, responsibility, and communication (Curtis & Shani, 2010), skills important for academic success. Working while in school forces students to structure their time more effectively because they have more limited time to devote to studies; however, the ability to balance work and studies hinges at least in part on how many hours students are working.

There is widespread agreement in the literature on the deleterious effects of high numbers of hours worked on student achievement (Callendar, 2008; Derousa & Ryan, 2008; Furr & Elling, 2000; McCormick, Moore, & Kuh, 2010). Greater number of hours worked also is associated with heighted financial worries and stress (Furr & Elling, 2000). Leppel (2002) found that hours worked have a negative effect on the persistence of both men and women, while Lammers, Onwuegbuzie, and Slate (2001) found GPA to be negatively impacted by more hours spent working. Callender (2008) found that the negative effects of working on grades and degree completion increase as the number of hours worked increase. Derousa and Ryan (2008) found that there is a significant negative relationship between time spent in employment and study attitudes, but there are also positive effects of working dependent upon job demands and autonomy. For instance, working had a positive effect on study attitudes when high work hours were combined with a high motivation to perform the duties of the job or high working hours were combined with low job demand. The findings with respect to hours worked are not universal; however, a few studies have found no significant impact of hours worked on academic performance (Henke, Lyons, & Krachenberg, 1993; Nonis & Hudson, 2006), but these studies also both focused on business students who may be different on average than the general student population.

Studies have examined specific hourly thresholds to try to discern the point at which working becomes detrimental to academic outcomes. A few studies found that students who work 15 hours a week or less are more likely to persist (Horn & Berktold, 1998; Horn & Malizio, 1996). These students are also less likely to report that work limits their class choices, their class schedules, the number of classes they could take, and their access to the library than students who worked full time (35 or more hours). Also, students who work fewer than 15 hours a week are more likely to have high GPAs than students who work 15 or more hours (National Center for Education Statistics, 1994).

Other studies have pointed to a slightly higher threshold of 20 hours or more a week as the critical tipping point for work negatively impacting studies. Pike, Kuh, and Massa-McKinley (2008) found a negative relationship between working 20 hours a week or more and grades, even after controlling for student characteristics and engagements. By contrast, students who worked fewer than 20 hours stated that working did not affect their study time or hurt their grades (General Accounting Office, 1995). Similarly, Umbach, Padgett, and Pascarella (2010) found higher levels of interaction with faculty among first-year students who work less than 20 hours per week compared to those working more than 20 hours a week or not working at all; however, the 20-hour threshold was not uniformly found to be the tipping point for negative outcomes. Contrary to most other studies, McCormick, Moore, and Kuh (2010) discovered that working more than 20 hours a week is strongly positively related to student engagement among their senior and freshman respondents from the National Survey of Student Engagement; however, they also found this high level of employment has a negative impact on grades for both groups (McCormick, Moore, & Kuh, 2010).

Furr and Elling (2000) considered the even higher hourly threshold per week of 30 hours and found that these students are, unsurprisingly, more likely to report that financial worries affect their academic studies and that their work schedule negatively affects their academic progress. Furthermore, students working 30 or more hours a week reported less participation in campus activities (Furr & Elling, 2000). Similarly, Lammers and colleagues (2001) found that students who worked between 23 and 60 hours a week are less likely to review material frequently, concentrate less on studying, report more sleep deprivation, and are more likely to skip class.

THE EFFECTS OF EMPLOYMENT ON GRADUATION

The prior research shows mixed results with respect to the effect of work on grades, but how does work impact the ultimate likelihood of graduating from college? The research findings suggest working can impact both the attainment of the degree and the time it takes to do so (Beeson & Wessel, 2002; Callender, 2008; Ehrenberg & Sherman, 1987; Gleason, 1993). Ehrenberg and Sherman (1987) found that hours of work have a negative effect on the probability of a student persisting to the next year and reduce the probability of graduating on time for those who did persist to the next year. Gleason (1993) found that students who work constantly throughout college took 9.2 semesters to graduate, while students who have at least one semester without a job took only 8.9 semesters to graduate.

These findings suggest that persistent working can have a small negative impact on progression to graduation; however, Beeson and Wessel (2002), in their longitudinal study of over three thousands students in a Midwestern public university, found that the students who work consistently have higher rates of persistence and are more likely to graduate within six years than students who do not work. On the whole, these findings do not suggest that working while in college has a strongly deleterious impact on progression to graduation and student workers may even be more likely to graduate (Beeson & Wessel, 2002).

THE EFFECTS OF EMPLOYMENT FOR AFRICAN AMERICAN STUDENTS

Although African American students are more likely to work than students from other groups, there is very little research that looks specifically at how employment impacts their academic success. An exception to this is Flowers (2010), who examined African American students' employment using data from the 2004 National Postsecondary Student Aid Study. Flowers found differences by type of institution, as well as by family background. Black students at public universities are more likely to work part-time than Black students at elite universities. Additionally, Black students from low-income homes or who are first-generation college students are more likely to work full-time than the children of college-educated parents from high-income homes. Working, however, has a positive impact on Black students' engagement; furthermore, student engagement increases as the amount of time working on campus increases (Flowers, 2010).

Looking at students at elite colleges and universities, Charles, Fischer, Mooney, and Massey (2009) found Black students are more likely to work and more likely to work more hours than Latino, Asian, and White students. They also found that feeling the need to work was more salient for Black students than other students. For instance, 66% of Black students felt that they needed to work and about 63% held a paying job during their freshman year. Whereas, 57% of Whites, 53% of Asians, and 69% of Latinos felt that they needed to work; however, only 46% of White and Asians and 61% of Latinos held a paying job during their freshman year (Charles et al., 2009).

In this chapter, we provide a longitudinal examination of African American students' employment during college for a cohort of students from 28 elite colleges and universities. We will first provide a descriptive overview of how many of these students work each year of college, how much they work, and whether this employment is part of their financial aid package (e.g., work-study program). We then examine the average characteristics of African American students who worked at least one year during college compared to students who never worked.

Our multivariate analysis then builds on this contrast, examining the cumulative GPA and graduation rates for Black students who worked during college versus those who did not.

METHOD

We drew on data from the National Longitudinal Survey of Freshmen (NLSF, n.d.), a probability sample of students who entered selective U.S. colleges and universities as freshmen in the fall of 1999. Students at 28 selective private and public institutions were interviewed over the course of their college careers, including a baseline survey that gathered extensive information about respondents prior to their entering college. All students in the NSLF were between 18 and 19 years of age at the time of the first survey. A detailed description of the sampling methodology, including the institutions and their characteristics, is contained in Massey and colleagues (2003). For the purposes of this chapter, we will be examining only the African American students in the study, who were oversampled in order to obtain a sufficiently sized population to be able to make within group comparisons.

Table 10.1 summarizes the employment histories of our sample during college. These accounts of employment come from the yearly spring surveys, in which students were asked, "At any time during the current academic year, have you worked for pay?" Consistent with prior studies (Charles et al., 2009; Flowers, 2010), we found that African American students were heavily engaged in paid

Table 10.1. African American Students' Paid Employment and Time Usage by Year.

	Freshman	Sophomore	Junior	Senior	Average*
Work Required for Aid	39.20	33.50	29.20	33.80	33.93
Felt Need to Work	66.10	66.80	69.80	68.70	67.85
Held Paying Job	62.50	73.00	75.50	79.30	85.63
For Those Who Worked					
Work Contributions	$641.02	$857.98	$902.66		800.55
Mean hrs worked per week	8.38	12.77	16.29	22.35	14.95
Mean hrs studying per week	27.08	22.98	19.23		23.09
Ratio of work to study hours	0.44	0.72	0.80		0.65

Source: National Longitudinal Survey of Freshmen, n.d.

*For held paying job, this is the percent reporting paid work any year. For the other figures, it is an average for the relevant years worked (or for which data are available).

employment. Of the African American students in the NLSF, 85% reported being employed during the school year at least one of their years in college and nearly 50% were employed at least three of their four years. Unfortunately, we cannot differentiate between on- and off-campus employment, or the specific nature of employment during the school term. In a different part of the survey, students were asked to estimate how many hours they spent in a typical week engaged in various activities, including work for pay. We drew on these estimates to calculate the number of hours worked in each academic year. The average hours worked for these students was low, particularly in the first year, with an average of less than 10 hours of work per week (9.01 hours). As students progressed through college, the average number of hours worked also increased, while the hours spent studying decreased. Thus, the ratio of work to study hours went up steadily, from .34 in the freshman year to .85 in the junior year. Students were not asked about their hours spent studying in the senior year.

This chapter is centrally concerned with examining the relationship between working in college and academic achievement for African American students. Thus, our primary outcome variables are cumulative GPA and graduation rates. We show the values of these variables by year and employment status in the first panel of Table 10.2. Not surprisingly, students who are employed during college are different in significant ways from students who are not employed. Overall, the profile of African American employed students in the NLSF is somewhat more disadvantaged compared to their nonemployed counterparts, with a slightly higher percentage being first-generation college students, a slightly lower percent being from two-parent households, and on average taking on a greater amount of loan debt. This is consistent with prior research findings about the demographics of student workers (Hunt, Lincoln, & Walker, 2004); however, this is not the case in terms of academic preparation for college. On average, those who never worked for pay during college took 2.2 AP courses in high school compared to an average of 2.7 AP courses in high school for students who were employed. The high school GPA of students who were employed during college was also slightly higher than those who did not work during college (3.534 versus 3.421).

Once in college, the Black students who worked for pay reported significantly more average hours devoted to academics per week than their nonworking counterparts (69 hours per week versus 56 hours per week). This greater amount of time spent studying appears to have paid off, with Black students who worked during school reporting significantly higher GPAs (3.066 versus 2.951) and being more likely to graduate in four years. On average, these students spent nearly 17.73 hours a week working in paid employment; however, there was a great deal of variation in the amount of time that students devoted to work during school. We looked more specifically at a breakdown of average hours worked using thresholds that were found to be significant in previous studies. We found that only 24%

Table 10.2. Means for African American Students by Work Status.

	No Paid Employment		Paid Employment	
	Mean	SD	Mean	SD
Outcomes				
Cumulative GPA	2.951	0.460	3.066	0.422**
Grad 4 years	0.532	0.501	0.587	0.493
Grad 6 years	0.790	0.409	0.801	0.400
College Work and Study				
Average Hours Studying~	56.234	33.574	69.278	33.666***
Average Hours Worked			17.730	8.473
Hours <10			0.235	0.425
Hours 10–15			0.188	0.391
Hours 15–20			0.203	0.402
Hours >20			0.374	0.484
Freq of Visits to Fin Aid Office	2.815	3.247	4.262	3.829***
Freq of Aid Problems	4.290	5.173	7.887	6.149***
Loans~	$3,502	$7,583	$9,191	$10,476***
Grants~	$6,453	$10,706	$7,191	$9,621
Family and Ind. Background				
Male	0.565	0.498	0.315	0.465***
Parent SES				
No College	0.274	0.448	0.312	0.463
Family Structure				
Two Parent	0.581	0.495	0.497	0.500
College Preparation				
AP Classes	2.194	1.945	2.666	1.938**
High School GPA	3.429	0.462	3.534	0.408**
Self-rated Prep for College	6.492	3.075	6.342	3.015
N =	124		879	

~Average of first year years of college (questions not asked in last year survey).
~p < .10, *p < 0.05, **p < 0.01, ***p < 0.001.

of our working students worked the more conservative recommended threshold of 10 hours or less per week. On the other hand, 37% worked 20 hours or more a week, which has been shown in several studies to be detrimental to students' academic development. Not surprisingly, students who worked were also more likely to report more frequent visits to the financial aid office and problems with their financial aid, both of which can cause stress for students and undermine their academic success.

In the analyses that follow, we will examine the impact of working in general and the number of hours worked in particular on academic performance as measured by GPA and college graduation. The models predicting GPA will be estimated using ordinary least square (OLS), while the models predicting four and six graduation rates will be estimated using multinomial logistic regression due to the binary and dependent nature of the outcome variables. All models include controls for gender, parents' educational background, marital status, college preparation, and the degree to which the student reported difficulties with financial aid.

RESULTS

We first estimated the impact of working each year of college on that year's cumulative GPA, but for none of the individual years was there a significant relationship between working or hours worked on GPA. Thus, we only show the models predicting cumulative GPA. Table 10.3 estimates the impact of employment and hours worked on the cumulative GPA for Black students in the NLSF using ordinary least squares (OLS) regression. The first model shows the effect of cumulative work experience, average hours worked, and self-reported financial aid difficulties on cumulative GPA across the five waves of data collection. Working during college had a significant positive association with cumulative GPA, with each additional year of work increasing GPA by an estimated .05 points. Employment, particularly on campus, can serve to integrate students into campus life. Furthermore, holding a job, especially while in school, requires many of the skills (time management, responsibility, etc.) that would also be useful for cultivating good study habits. Thus, we are not surprised to see that working experience is positively related to GPA. However, students working a higher average number of hours obtained slighted lower GPAs: for each additional hour worked, the estimated impact on GPA was −.005. Reports of financial aid difficulties were also associated with a lower cumulative GPA (B = −0.004).

The second model in Table 10.3 adds parental and individual characteristics, which move the impact of financial aid problems to nonsignificance; however, cumulative work experience and hours worked remain significant with these additional controls. The final model adds college preparatory experiences, which are all strongly and positively related to African American student's cumulative GPA. With the addition of college preparatory experiences, the effect of hours worked on GPA is no longer statistically significant, but the positive impact of working still remains positively related to grades. The final column of Model 3 shows the standardized beta regression coefficients. As can be seen,

Table 10.3. Effects of Work on Cumulative GPA for African American Students.

	Model 1			Model 2			Model 3		
	B	SE	Beta	B	SE	Beta	B	SE	Beta
College Factors									
Cumulative Work Experience	0.050	0.012***	0.156	0.042	0.012**	0.130	0.024	0.011*	0.074
Avg. hrs. working	-0.005	0.003+	-0.067	-0.004	0.002+	-0.064	-0.002	0.002	-0.030
Financial aid problems	-0.004	0.002+	-0.054	-0.002	0.002	-0.034	0.000	0.002	0.001
Individual and Family Background									
Male				-0.152	0.028***	-0.168	-0.121	0.026***	-0.135
First-generation College				-0.104	0.029***	-0.112	-0.047	0.027+	-0.051
Two-parent Household				0.084	0.027**	0.098	0.051	0.025*	0.060
College Preparation									
AP Courses							0.033	0.007***	0.152
HS GPA							0.277	0.030***	0.269
Self-rated preparation							0.028	0.004***	0.200
Constant	3.002	0.030		3.051	0.038***		1.802	0.116***	
R-squared	0.017			0.071			0.2158		
N	1003			1003			1003		

+p < .10, *p < 0.05, **p < 0.01, ***p < 0.001.

cumulative work experience is the strongest predictor of GPA among the college-based inputs. As we will see in the next set of models, grades are not only an important indicator of academic growth but are strongly linked to graduation outcomes.

Controlling for cumulative GPA, we examine the impact of work experience, individual and family background, and college preparation on four- and six-year graduation rates. Table 10.4 shows the multinomial logistic regression model estimating four-year graduation rates for the African American students in the NLSF. Cumulative GPA is strongly related to the timely completion of college with each one-point increase in GPA being associated with a fourfold increase in the odds of graduating in four years compared to not graduating within six years. Cumulative GPA continued to exert a moderate impact on the odds of graduating in six years (conditional on having not already graduated in four years). Net of cumulative GPA, preparation for college in terms of AP courses taken, and high school GPA are significantly and positively related to the likelihood of four-year graduation. However, after controlling for the likelihood of graduating from college in four years, high school preparation was not significantly related to the odds of graduating in six years. Finally, Black males were less likely to graduate from college in four years, but there is not a significant difference by gender in six-year graduation rates.

Work experience is also significantly related to the likelihood of graduation. For each additional year of paid employment during the school year, there is a 44.5% increase in the odds of four-year graduation and a 32.9% increase in the odds of six-year graduation. Just as we saw in the models predicting GPA, however, higher numbers of hours worked have a negative impact on graduation rates. For each additional average hour worked, there is a 7.3% decrease in the odds of graduating in four years and a 5.9% decrease in the odds of graduating in six years (for those who did not graduate in four years). We estimated an additional set of models not shown here using the hourly thresholds examined in prior research, but none were significantly related to graduation rates. Thus, the linear representation of hours appears to fit our model best. In summary, across both the GPA and graduation outcomes we find strong evidence that working per se is positively related to both grades and the likelihood of graduating from college, but that working more hours reduces the likelihood of college completion for African American students.

We estimated models with different thresholds of average hours worked on GPA by dividing work hours into categories based on the prior literature: working fewer than 10 hours, working between 10–15 hours, working between 15–20 hours, and working more than 20 hours per week on average; however, since none of these were significant net of controls for family background, we did not include these models for presentation.

Table 10.4. Multinomial Logit Regression of Work on Four- and Six-year Graduation Rates.

	4-Year Grad Vs. No Grad			6-Year Grad Vs. No Grad		
	B	SE	EXP(B)	B	SE	EXP(B)
College Factors						
Cumulative Work Experience	0.546	0.089***	1.727	0.313	0.096**	1.367
Avg. hrs. working	−0.087	0.017***	0.917	−0.029	0.017⁺	0.971
Financial aid problems	−0.012	0.015	0.988	−0.040	0.017*	0.961
Cumulative GPA	1.466	0.235***	4.333	0.492	0.243*	1.635
Individual and Family Background						
Male	−0.501	0.189*	0.606	−0.143	0.209	0.867
First-generation College	−0.304	0.196	0.738	−0.139	0.214	0.870
Two-parent Household	0.394	0.186*	1.482	0.016	0.207	1.017
College Preparation						
AP Courses	0.080	0.051	1.083	−0.042	0.058	0.959
HS GPA	0.531	0.228*	1.700	0.032	0.242	1.032
Self-rated preparation	0.031	0.031	1.032	0.002	0.034	1.002
Constant	−5.881	0.969***		−1.356	0.984	
Pseudo R-squared	0.108					
N	1003					

⁺p < .10, *p < 0.05, **p < 0.01, ***p < 0.001.

CONCLUSIONS

In this chapter, we explored the impact of working on grades and graduation rates for African American students attending 28 selective colleges and universities. We found that work itself is not negatively related to student outcomes; in fact, the total number of years in which students were employed during college was positively associated with cumulative GPA. This suggests that employment as a form of involvement may be positively associated with African American students' academic achievements. Work may help students forge connections to others on campus, which facilitates the social integration that has been found to be particularly important for African American college students (Fischer, 2007). Holding a job while being a student also requires students to structure their time more effectively, which can help students to be more focused in their studying with their more limited time to do so; however, consistent with prior research, we also find that students' ability to balance work and studies hinges at least in part on how many hours students are working. Students who worked more hours on average during their college career had lower cumulative GPAs (though this effect became nonsignificant after controlling for high school preparation) and were less likely to persist to graduation (see Tables 10.3 and 10.4).

Although it does not appear that working in college affects African American students differently than other students, the issue of working while in college remains salient because African American students are both more likely to work and are more likely to work higher numbers of hours. Working high numbers of hours per week can cut into study time, as well as time students could spend in college-related activities that could serve to integrate them more fully into the academic and social realms of college life. High numbers of hours of work may also signal more severe financial situations and more generalized stress. The progress of such students should be monitored closely and, if possible, additional resources such as specialized financial and academic counseling should be devoted to helping them successfully complete their schooling.

REFERENCES

Beeson, M. J., & Wessel, R. D. (2002). The impact of working on campus on the academic persistence of freshmen. *Journal of Student Financial Aid, 32*(2), 37–45.

Callender, C. (2008). The impact of term-time employment on higher education students' academic attainment and achievement. *Journal of Education Policy, 23*(4), 359–377.

Charles, C. Z., Fischer, M. J., Mooney, M. A., & Massey, D. S. (2009). *Taming the river: Negotiating the academic, financial, and social currents in selective colleges and universities.* Princeton, NJ: Princeton University Press.

Curtis, S., & Shani, N. (2010). The effect of taking paid employment during term-time on students' academic studies. *Journal of Further and Higher Education, 26*(2), 129–138.

Curtis, S., & Williams, J. (2002). The reluctant workforce: Undergraduates' part-time employment. *Education and Training, 44*(1), 5–10.

Dadgar, M. (2011, March). *To work or not to work? Understanding the academic consequences of community college students' employment while enrolled* (CCRC Working Paper No. 48). Paper presented to the Association for Education Finance and Policy (AEFP) Annual Conference, Seattle, WA.

Derousa, E., & Ryan, A. M. (2008). When earning is beneficial for learning: The relation. *Journal of Vocational Behavior, 73*, 118–131.

Ehrenberg, R. G., and Sherman, D. R. (1987). While in college, academic achievement, and post-college outcomes: A summary of results. *Journal of Human Resources, 22*(1), 1–23.

Fischer, M. J. (2007). Settling into campus life: Differences by race/ethnicity in college involvement and outcomes. *Journal of Higher Education, 78*(2), 125–161.

Flowers, L. A. (2010). The effects of work on African American college students' engagement. In L. W. Perna (Ed.), *Understanding the working college student: New research and its implications for policy and practice* (pp. 213–233). Sterling, VA: Stylus.

Furr, S. R., & Elling, T. W. (2000). The influence of work on college student development. *NASPA Journal, 37*(2), 454–470.

General Accounting Office. (1995). *Restructuring student aid could reduce low-income student dropout rate.* Washington, DC: Author.

Gleason, P. M. (1993). College student employment academic progress, and post-college labor market success. *Journal of Student Financial Aid, 23*(2), 5–14.

Hammes, J. F., & Haller, E. J. (1983). Making ends meet: Some of the consequences of part-time work for college students. *Journal of College Student Personnel, 24*(6), 529–535.

Henke, J. W., Jr., Lyons, T. F., & Krachenberg, A. R. (1993). Knowing your market: How working students balance work, grades, and course load. *Journal of Marketing for Higher Education, 4*(1–2), 191–203.

Henry, J. B. (1967). Part-time employment and academic performance of freshmen. *Journal of College Student Personnel, 8*(4), 257–260.

Horn, L. J., & Berktold, J. (1998). *Profile of undergraduates in US postsecondary education institutions: 1995–96* (NCES 98–084). Washington, DC: U.S. Department of Education, National Center for Education Statistics.

Horn, L. J., & Malizio, A. J. (1996). *Undergraduates who work: National postsecondary student aid study 1996* (NCES 98–137). Washington, DC: U.S. Department of Education, National Center for Education Statistics.

Hunt, A., Lincoln, I., & Walker, A. (2004). Term-time employment and academic attainment: Evidence from a large-scale survey of undergraduates at Northumbria University. *Journal of Further and Higher Education, 28*(1), 3–18.

Kaiser, H. E., & Bergen, G. (1968). Shall college freshmen work? *Journal of College Student Personnel, 9*, 384–385.

Lammers, W. J., Onwuegbuzie, A. J., & Slate, J. R. (2001). Academic success as a function of the gender, class, age, study habits, and employment of college students. *Research in the Schools, 8*(2), 71–81.

Leppel, K. (2002). Similarities and differences in the college persistence of men and women. *Review of Higher Education, 25*(4), 433–450.

Massey, D. S., Charles, C. Z., Lundy, G. F., & Fischer, M. J. (2003). *The Source of the river: The social origins of freshmen at America's selective colleges and universities.* Princeton, NJ: Princeton University Press.

McCormick, A. C., Moore, J. V., III, & Kuh, G. D. (2010). Working during college: Its relationship to student engagement and education outcomes. In L. W. Perna (Ed.), *Understanding the working college student: New research and its implications for policy and practice* (pp. 179–212). Sterling, VA: Stylus.

Mounsey, R., & Diekhoff, G. M. (2012). Working and non-working university students: Anxiety, depression, and grade point average. *College Student Journal, 47*(2), 379–389.

National Center for Education Statistics. (1994). *Undergraduates who work while enrolled in postsecondary education: 1989–1990.* NCES Statistical Analysis Report 94–311. Washington, DC: U.S. Department of Education.

National Longitudinal Survey of Freshmen (n.d.). *Public data.* Retrieved from http://nlsf.princeton.edu/data.htm

Nonis, S. A., & Hudson, G. I. (2006). Academic performance of college students: Influence of time spent studying and working. *Journal of Education for Business, 81*(3), 151–159.

Perna, L. W. (2010). Understanding the working college student: New research and its implications for policy and practice. Sterling, VA: Stylus.

Pike, G. R., Kuh, G. D., & Massa-McKinley, R. (2008). First year students' employment, engagement, and academic achievement: Untangling the relationship between work and grades. *NASPA Journal, 45*(4), 560–582.

Tinto, V. (1993). *Leaving College: Rethinking the causes and cures of student attrition.* Chicago, IL: University of Chicago Press.

Umbach, P. D., Padgett, R. D., & Pascarella, E. T. (2010). The impact of working on undergraduate students' interactions with faculty. In L. W. Perna (Ed.), *Understanding the meaning of "work" for today's undergraduates* (pp. 234–257). Sterling, VA: Stylus.

U.S. Department of Education. (2012). Table 385: Full-time, first-time degree/certificate-seeking undergraduate students enrolled in degree-granting institutions, by participation and average amount awarded in financial aid programs, and control and level of institution: 2000–01 through 2010–11. *Digest of Education Statistics, 2012.* Retrieved from http://nces.ed.gov/programs/digest/d12/tables/dt12_387.asp

U.S. Department of Education. (2013). Figure 3: Percentage of 25- to 29-year-olds who completed a bachelor's or higher degree, by race/ethnicity: Selected years, 1990–2013. *Digest of Education Statistics, 2013.* Retrieved from http://nces.ed.gov/programs/coe/indicator_caa.asp

Woo, J., Green, C., & Matthews, C. (2012). *Web Tables—Profile of 2007–08 First-Time Bachelor's Degree Recipients in 2009, Table 2.3: Percentage distribution of 2007–08 first-time bachelor's degree recipients' cumulative undergraduate grade point average, by selected individual and institutional characteristics: 2009.* U.S. Department of Education NCES 2013–150. Washington, DC. Retrieved from http://nces.ed.gov/pubs2013/2013150.pdf

Working TO Learn OR Working TO Live? Exploring THE Impact OF Employment ON College Outcomes FOR Low-income AND First-generation Students

GEORGIANNA L. MARTIN AND MELANDIE MCGEE

Working during college has become a common phenomenon among students in American higher education. Whereas the "typical" college student was once characterized as enrolling in college directly after high school, relying on parents for financial need, and refraining from working or working limited hours during a semester (Mounsey, Vandehey, & Diekhoff, 2013), at present an overwhelming number of college and university students are juggling the demands of working either part-time or full-time and managing the many responsibilities associated with obtaining a college degree. Employment plays a major role in the lives of many college students despite the different experiences that students bring with them to college (Billson & Terry, 1982). Consequently, time that students allocate toward work responsibilities may detract from time that could be devoted to coursework or other key educational experiences (e.g., research with a faculty member, involvement in co-curricular activities, or study abroad).

Stern and Nakata (1991) explain that the number of U.S. college students who work for pay during the academic year grew steadily between the 1960s and the mid-1980s. According to the Bureau of Labor Statistics (2002), the overall employment rate was 52.6% for traditionally aged students (18–24 years old) enrolled in college. In this age group, 62.4% of students at two-year institutions were employed and 48.9% of four-year college students were employed. More recent national data indicates that 68% of all college students work for pay during the academic year and one-third of these students work more than 20 hours per week (Pike, Kuh, & Massa-McKinley, 2008).

As the cost of college tuition continues to increase, it is likely that more college students will find it necessary to work during college. This will be particularly true for those students from low-income backgrounds and for those who are the first in their family to attend college. Taking into account the prevalence and potential impending increase of students who work and attend college, it is important to consider the extent to which being employed while in college interferes with students' academic performance and development of key college outcomes. The possibility that working while in college can result in negative student outcomes, such as poor grades and attrition, has received some attention among colleges, universities, and researchers. For instance, Tinto (1993) cautions that employment in college limits not only the time students can give to their academic work but also the time they can give to engaging with their peers and faculty, resulting in a decreased sense of social integration.

Twenty years later, educators have yet to fully acknowledge or address the impact, both positive and negative, employment has on student success, particularly for low-income, first-generation college students. Scholars have consistently found that first-generation college students work significantly more hours per week than their peers whose parents completed postsecondary education (Pascarella, Pierson, & Wolniak, 2004; Terenzini, Springer, Yaeger, Pascarella, & Nora, 1996). Martinez, Sher, Krull, and Wood (2009) not only found that first-generation students are more likely than their peers to work in college but also report that first-generation students are more likely to work part-time jobs at all times during college, and they are even more likely to have full-time jobs. Further, Pike and colleagues (2008) indicate that first-generation students are significantly more likely to work 20 hours or less on-campus and work more than 20 hours a week on- or off-campus. Similar patterns exist for students from low-income backgrounds and researchers suggest there is much overlap between first-generation student status and low-income student status (Paulsen & St. John, 2002; Walpole, 2007). It is not surprising that students from low socioeconomic status (SES) backgrounds work more while in college: low SES students likely work in order to support themselves, finance their education, and, in some cases, help support their family members. When compared to their high SES peers, there are fewer low SES students who report not working at all while in college, and more low SES students who report working more than 16 hours per week or working full-time (Walpole, 2003). More specifically, over half of the low SES students (52%) report either working 16 or more hours per week or working full-time (40 hours a week or more), compared to 37% of the students from higher SES backgrounds.

Consequently, low SES students who spend a considerable amount of time working while in college have less time to devote to other activities such as studying or being involved in student clubs or groups. Interestingly, while scholars and educators readily acknowledge that first-generation and low-income college students spend more time working in college than their economically advantaged peers—and the literature suggests that increased time spent working has some negative influences on college outcomes—relatively little research has specifically explored the impact of work for first-generation, low-income college students. Many readers may find this news surprising given what educators know about the impact of work on students and the barriers present for first-generation, low-income students. In the following sections, we provide a review of the literature on the influences of employment on college students' educational and developmental outcomes, with a specific focus on the experiences of low-income, first-generation students. We end with suggestions for educators invested in improving the college experiences and outcomes for first-generation and low-income students.

EFFECTS OF WORK ON STUDENT RETENTION

One major goal of any college or university is to retain and graduate a high proportion of its students. Interestingly, much of the literature on the effects of work on student persistence does not disaggregate data to explore the unique experiences of low-income, first-generation students. In other words, a lot of what educators know about the impact of work on college persistence is based on all students, not an isolated sample of students from low-income, first-generation backgrounds. To further complicate this limitation in the research, it is important to note that scholars have overwhelmingly cited first-generation and low-income college students as significantly less likely to persist in college as their socioeconomically advantaged peers (Ishitani, 2003; Martinez et al., 2009; Walpole, 2003). Taken together, it becomes important for educators to consider the ways in which working during college might have a compounding effect for students from marginalized groups.

Research has shown that increased time spent working while in college can impact a student's ability to persist throughout college and ultimately graduate. The National Center for Education Statistics found that students working 35 or more hours per week experience the highest risk of nonpersistence (Horn & Malizio, 1998); however, students who worked 1–15 hours per week had the lowest risk for enrollment interruption, even when compared with students working 16–34 hours per week and students who did not work. According to Cuccaro-Alamin (1997), students who work full-time and attend school part-time have lower levels of persistence and college attainment. Students who work on-campus are more likely to graduate and attend graduate school than students who work off-campus

(Ehrenberg & Sherman, 1987). Furthermore, first- and second-year students, whether at two-year or four-year institutions, are more likely to withdraw if they work more (Ehrenberg & Sherman, 1987). Finally, Canabal (1998) reports that the time one devotes to employment may actually increase the time required to graduate. Given the precarious financial position that many low-income, first-generation students find themselves in during college, extending the time to graduate is likely a barrier for these students.

Other studies specifically focused on the college persistence of first-generation students. Ishitani (2006) reports that campus-based employment, such as work-study, has positive effects on first- and second-year retention among first-generation students. First-generation students who held work-study jobs were 41% less likely to depart in their first year than students who received no aid. Furthermore, Ishitani reports that work-study recipients were 43% less likely to depart in the second year. Finally, being employed on-campus via work-study also has a positive impact on fourth-year graduation behavior. Ishitani indicates that work-study students are 81% more likely to graduate within four years than were those who were not work-study recipients in their first year of college. From this study, it appears that participation in work-study may play an important role in first-generation students' likelihood of persisting in college; however, although first-generation status is often used as a proxy for socioeconomic status, it is important to note that this study did not specifically consider the intersection of low-income status with first-generation student status. In other words, the extent to which this positive impact of work-study on first-generation students' retention holds true for students from low-income backgrounds is yet to be determined.

EFFECTS OF WORK ON ACADEMIC ACHIEVEMENT

Research on the relationship between work and grades has been inconsistent (Riggert, Boyle, Petrosko, Ash, & Rude-Parkins, 2006; Stern & Nakata, 1991). Some researchers have found that working while in college negatively affects students' grades. Astin (1993) states that working a full-time and part-time job off-campus is associated with outcomes that are uniformly negative. Some of the outcomes that are negatively related with working full-time or part-time off-campus include completion of a bachelor's degree, grade point average (GPA), graduating with honors, and enrollment in graduate or professional school (Astin, 1993). Further, Astin also reports that full-time and part-time student employment on-campus is associated with lower GPA. In a study of 300 undergraduate social work majors, Hawkins, Smith, and Hawkins (2005) found that overall GPA is inversely related to the number of hours worked. That is, the average number of hours worked were significant negative predictors of self-reported overall grade point average. Conversely, other researchers did not find a negative relationship between student employment and academic performance. In a study by Hammes and Haller (1983), students who worked are found to have significantly higher GPAs than students who do not work. Other studies have found similar results (Canabal, 1998; Stern & Nakata, 1991). However, a limitation in all of these studies is that they did not consider whether or not a student was low-income or of the first generation in their family to attend college.

Differences also exist for the relationship between grades, level of work a student engages in, whether the work is performed on- or off-campus, and whether the student lives on- or off-campus. Some research suggests that work does not adversely affect students' grades if they work less than 25 hours per week (Ehrenberg & Sherman, 1987). Similarly, Pike and colleagues (2008) found that students who worked more than 20 hours per week on- or off-campus had substantially lower grades than students who did not work and students who worked 20 hours or fewer per week on- or off-campus. To add nuance to the effects of work on student outcomes, Lang (2012) found that students who worked on-campus had slightly higher grades than students who worked off-campus. However, educators have yet to fully consider how to create meaningful experiences for students in their on-campus employment positions. Alfano and Eduljee (2013) explored the residential context of students and found no significant differences between the GPA of working students who lived off-campus and working students who lived on-campus. Mounsey and colleagues (2013) also found no significant differences in the grade point averages of working versus non-working students. Specifically focusing on first-generation college students, Pascarella, Pierson and colleagues (2004) concluded that the added work responsibilities of first-generation students may in part explain the fact that, despite a lighter academic load, first-generation students in his study had significantly lower cumulative grades than similar students whose parents were both college graduates.

Cognitive development is another construct that assists educators in measuring students' academic achievement. In terms of assessing cognitive development among students who work, Pascarella, Edison, Nora, Hagedorn, and Terenzini (1998) examined the impact of on- and off-campus work during the first three years of college on standardized measures of cognitive development (reading comprehension, mathematics, critical thinking, writing skills, and science reasoning). The authors found modest and inconsistent evidence to suggest that neither on-campus nor off-campus work seriously inhibits students' learning or cognitive development; however, there was at least some evidence in the third year of the study to suggest that reasonable amounts of part-time on- or off-campus work may actually facilitate learning. For instance, working part-time (10–15 hours per week) on-campus and working part-time (16–20 hours per week) off-campus has a positive impact on third-year cognitive development; however, working more than 10–15 hours per week on campus or 16–20 hours a week off-campus was reported to inhibit cognitive development.

Terenzini and colleagues (1996) examined whether there are any differences in cognitive development among first-generation students and continuing-generation students who worked. It is interesting that results indicated that hours worked off-campus promote reading gains among first-generation students while it reduces reading gains among continuing-generation students. This finding is in contrast to much of the literature that suggests working off-campus, particularly for first-generation students, has detrimental effects. In a follow-up study, Pascarella, Pierson and colleagues (2004) found that, when compared to their peers, first-generation students' work responsibilities tend to have stronger negative implications for their college experiences including critical thinking, internal locus of control in relation to college success, and preference for cognitive tasks that engage higher order thinking skills.

EFFECTS OF WORK ON OUT-OF-CLASS OPPORTUNITIES

Along with the impact of student employment on educational outcomes, colleges and universities should also be concerned with how working influences the college-going experience of students. In terms of student involvement, Lang (2012) reports that working students tend to be less engaged in social activities than nonworking students; however, students who work on-campus spend more time engaging in co-curricular activities and social activities than students who work off-campus. Students who work 30 or more hours per week were less involved with campus activities than students who are not employed or are employed fewer than 30 hours (Furr & Elling, 2000). The authors also found that students who did not work report more frequent interactions with faculty. Similarly, Pike and colleagues (2008) report a positive relationship between student-faculty interaction and students who work 20 hours or less per week either on-campus or off-campus. In terms of leadership development, Salisbury, Pascarella, Padgett, and Blaich (2012) discovered first-year students who work on campus 10 hours or more per week, and particularly students who work off-campus more than 20 hours per week, are more likely to experience leadership development. However, similar to other research findings, off-campus work commitments in excess of 20 hours per week are found to inhibit first-year students' interactions with peers and co-curricular involvement (Salisbury et al., 2012). It is important to note that this study controlled for first-generation student status rather than considering any unique effects it might have for the students in the study.

In terms of well-being, working students exhibit more anxiety symptoms than students who do not work (Mounsey et al., 2013). Students who work produce scores within the mild anxiety range and nonworking students produce scores within the minimal anxiety range. Finally, working students report experiencing more stress and fewer buffers than their nonworking counterparts. Although Mounsey and colleagues' (2013) study did not specifically consider the impact of work on well-being for first-generation, low-income students, given the high number of hours this unique population of students tends to work during college, it is likely that the magnitude of the effects found in this study might be greater for students from first-generation, low-income backgrounds.

Pascarella, Pierson, and Wolniak (2004) concluded that greater work responsibility is likely one of many factors that contributed substantially to the tendency for first-generation college students to have significantly lower levels of extracurricular involvement, athletic participation, and volunteer work than other students in the second year of college and significantly lower levels of non-course-related interactions with peers in the third year of college. In a qualitative study of low-income, first-generation students' experiences, Martin (in press) found that the large number of hours most students in her study spent working precludes them from involvement in a host of out-of-class opportunities, including involvement in student organizations, participation in career-center events, serving as resident assistants or orientation leaders, conducting research with a faculty member, and studying abroad, to name a few. Using quantitative methods, additional scholars also have found that low-income and first-generation students work with faculty on research projects less often and have fewer interactions overall with faculty outside of the classroom than their socioeconomically advantaged peers (e.g., Kim & Sax, 2009). In a study examining how low SES affects college experiences and outcomes among African American students, Walpole (2008) found that low SES students work more hours than their peers and cited it as part of the reason why they study less and spend less time in student organizations. Particularly, 42% of low SES students indicate that they spend more than 16 hours per week working, while 40% of high SES students, and 39% of all students report working between 3 and 15 hours per week. Participants in Martin's (2012) research expressed frustration and in some cases anger and resentment toward their higher SES peers who do not have to work the long hours that their low SES background necessitated they work. It was clear to the low-SES students in this study that they were receiving a completely different and less desirable college experience, in nearly every way, than their higher SES peers.

Furthermore, the students in Martin's (2012) study express feeling socially isolated from their peers in college both because of the amount of time they spend working instead of being involved on campus or partying with their peers and due to the social class differences present between them and their higher socioeconomic status peers. This finding is consistent with Rubin's (2012) meta-analysis, which offers the clearest evidence to date that students from lower SES backgrounds are less socially integrated in college than their peers from socioeconomically advantaged backgrounds.

RECOMMENDATIONS FOR EDUCATORS

In this section, we offer recommendations for educators invested in improving the college experiences and educational outcomes for first-generation and low-income students. From the literature on employment during college and the literature on this unique population of students, it is clear that long hours spent working during college results in less time engaged in academic and extracurricular opportunities. Further, as we have illustrated in this chapter, these long hours spent working seem to make the social class differences experienced by first-generation and low-income students more pronounced. Yet, with a lack of substantial increase in need-based grant funding and an increased dependence on student loans, it is unlikely that the necessity of work for first-generation, low-income students will decline in the coming years. This reality requires that educators act intentionally to meet the needs of these students. With this in mind, we offer several recommendations here for improved college experiences for first-generation, low-income students.

Increase Opportunities for Social Integration of Low-income, First-generation College Students

Scholars have identified a lack of social integration as a concern for students from low SES backgrounds (e.g., Armstrong & Hamilton, 2013; Martin, 2012; Rubin, 2012; Soria & Stebleton, 2013; Soria, Stebleton, & Huesman, 2013–2014), and yet few higher education institutions have seriously considered this aspect of the college experience for these students. In their ethnographic study on social class in college, Armstrong and Hamilton (2013) highlight the intense social isolation that the low-income students in their study experience. This isolation became an important factor in these students' decisions to leave college. It appears that outlets for social connection and support among this population of students are rare in higher education, furthering the need for increased attention by educators to this aspect of the student experience.

Provide Meaningful Employment Opportunities on Campus

The research is inconsistent on the impact of work specifically for low-income, first-generation students; however, it is unlikely the need for these students to work while in college will dissipate in the near future. Given the positive relationship between working on campus and student retention, it may be prudent for educators to create meaningful student employment opportunities on campus for first-generation, low-income college students. While some work-study positions offer opportunities for students to gain skills and develop in their field, other positions are little more than secretarial. An intentional approach to developing meaningful work-study positions for these students would require a concerted effort by higher education professionals to know which students on campus are from low SES backgrounds, learn the interests and career goals of these students, identify work-study experiences that offer more than secretarial or administrative skill sets, and intentionally connect students with work-study opportunities on-campus and in the community that will provide them with an opportunity to learn in an area of interest and build crucial professional networks. The often invisible nature of social class in higher education (Duffy, 2007) makes it difficult for higher education professionals to identify the students who might benefit most from this type of practice.

Expand Programs to Assist Low-income, First-generation Students to Transition and Navigate College

If colleges and universities are to move beyond simply providing access to higher education for low-income, first-generation students to working more actively to ensure students' success, then educators must attend to what happens to these students once they matriculate to college. Armstrong and Hamilton (2013) describe a process they call *creaming* whereby only the highest achieving students from low SES backgrounds are selected for programs designed to assist underrepresented students' transition to college. This, they explain, is a prevalent practice in higher education. Sadly, educators do a grave disservice to the low SES students who are not among the "cream of the crop" by not offering opportunities for them to gain the capital needed to be successful in higher education. Consequently, higher education practitioners should create additional programs and resources for low SES students who are not among the top 10% of their high school graduating class to give these students an opportunity to develop the skills and knowledge needed to be successful in higher education. Higher education professionals must begin to expand transition programs and other college navigation resources to include low SES students who are not deemed high achieving upon high school graduation.

Develop Intentional Mentoring Opportunities with Faculty and Staff for First-generation, Low-Income College Students

The benefits of mentoring are well documented in the higher education literature (e.g., Crisp & Cruz, 2009); however, the often invisible nature of social class may make it difficult for educators to seek out first-generation and low-income students for mentoring opportunities. In spite of this reality, students in Martin's (2012) study express a lack of mentorship during college and a deep desire to have mentors. The students in her study not only want an opportunity to be mentored by faculty or staff but also by other students from low SES backgrounds who are juniors or seniors in college. These mentoring opportunities should provide students with important information such as time management skills, seeking out faculty during office hours or for other out-of-class interactions such as research opportunities, and the possibilities of graduate or professional education. Mentoring opportunities between students could focus on balancing the demands of working for pay with academic coursework and building a social network.

Create Space and Place for Low-income, First-generation Students On-campus

Low-income and first-generation college students need opportunities to connect with peers from similar backgrounds. Some authors have suggested that the taboo nature of discussing social class in society as a whole has prevented us from making class-based experiences visible in the United States and in higher education (e.g., hooks, 2000; Soria, 2012). Students from low SES backgrounds may need the help of higher education professionals to identify other students from similar backgrounds. Developing a student organization or a living-learning community that provides camaraderie and support for first-generation and low-income students not only offers a place for these students to find peers who may share some of their experiences, but it also may serve to de-stigmatize conversations about social class in college. First-generation and low-income students' social class identities will likely remain a hidden aspect of themselves as long as they do not see themselves represented among faculty, staff, and their peers in higher education.

REFERENCES

Alfano, H. J., & Eduljee, N. B. (2013). Differences in work, levels of involvement and academic performance between residential and commuter students. *College Student Journal, 47*(2), 334–342.

Armstrong, E. A., & Hamilton, L. T. (2013). *Paying for the party: How college maintains inequality.* Cambridge, MA: Harvard University Press.

Astin, A. (1993). *What matters in college: Four critical years revisited.* San Francisco, CA: Jossey-Bass.

Billson, J., & Terry, M. (1982, January). *In search of the silken purse: Factors in attrition among first-generation students.* Paper presented at the Annual Meeting of the Association of American Colleges, Denver, CO.

Bureau of Labor Statistics. (2002). *College enrollment and work activity of 2002 high school graduates* (USDL 03–330). Washington, DC: Author.

Canabal, M. E. (1998). College student degree of participation in the labor force: Determinants and relationship to school performance. *College Student Journal, 32*(4), 597.

Cuccaro-Alamin, S. (1997). *Findings from the condition of education, 1997: Postsecondary persistence and attainment* (NCES No. 97–984). Washington, DC: U.S. Government Printing Office.

Crisp, G., & Cruz, I. (2009). Mentoring college students: A critical review of the literature between 1990 and 2007. *Research in Higher Education, 50*(6), 525–545.

Duffy, J. O. (2007). Invisibility at risk: Low-income students in a middle- and upper-class world. *About Campus, 12*(2), 18–25.

Ehrenberg, R. G., & Sherman, D. R. (1987). Employment while in college, academic achievements, and postcollege outcomes. *Journal of Human Resources, 22*(1), 1–23.

Furr, S. R., & Elling, T. W. (2000). The influence of work on college student development. *NASPA Journal, 37*(2), 454–70.

Hammes, J. F., & Haller, E. J. (1983). Making ends meet: Some of the consequences of part-time work for college students. *Journal of College Student Personnel, 24*(6), 529–535.

Hawkins, C. A., Smith, M. L., & Hawkins, R. (2005). The relationships among hours employed, perceived work interference, and grades as reported by undergraduate social work students. *Journal of Social Work Education, 41*(1), 13–27.

hooks, b. (2000). *Where we stand: Class matters*. New York, NY: Routledge.

Horn, L. J., & Malizio, A. (1998). Undergraduates who work: National postsecondary student aid study, 1996 (National Center for Education Statistics, U.S. Department of Education, Office of Educational Research and Improvement Publication No. NCES 98–137). Washington, DC: U.S. Government Printing Office.

Ishitani, T. (2003). A longitudinal approach to assessing attrition behavior among first-generation students: Time-varying effects of pre-college characteristics. *Research in Higher Education, 44*(4), 433–449.

Ishitani, T. T. (2006). Studying attrition and degree completion behavior among first-generation college students in the United States. *Journal of Higher Education, 77*(5), 861–885.

Kim, Y. K., & Sax, L. J. (2009). Student-faculty interaction in research universities: Differences by student gender, race, social class, and first-generation status. *Research in Higher Education, 50*(5), 437–459.

Lang, K. (2012). The similarities and differences between working and non-working students at a mid-sized American public university. *College Student Journal, 46*(2), 243–255.

Martin, G. L. (2012). *Getting out, missing out, and surviving: The social class experiences of White, low-income, first-generation college students* (Unpublished doctoral dissertation). University of Iowa, Iowa City.

Martin, G. L. (in press). "Always in my face": An exploration of social class consciousness, salience, and values. *Journal of College Student Development.*

Martinez, J., Sher, K., Krull, J., & Wood, P. (2009). Blue-collar scholars? Mediators and moderators of university attrition in first-generation college students. *Journal of College Student Development, 50*(1), 87–103.

Mounsey, R., Vandehey, M., & Diekhoff, G. (2013). Working and non-working university students: Anxiety, depression and grade point average. *College Student Journal, 47*(2), 379–389.

Pascarella, E. T., Edison, M. I., Nora, A., Hagedorn, L., & Terenzini, P. T. (1998). Does work inhibit cognitive development during college? *Educational Evaluation and Policy Analysis, 20*(2), 75–93.

Pascarella, E. T., Pierson, C. T., & Wolniak, G. C. (2004). First-generation college students: Additional evidence on college experiences and outcomes. *Journal of Higher Education, 75*(3), 249–284.

Paulsen, M. B., & St. John, E. P. (2002). Social class and college costs: Examining the financial nexus between college choice and persistence. *Journal of Higher Education, 73*(2), 189–236.

Pike, G., Kuh, G., & Massa-McKinley, R. (2008). First-year students' employment, engagement, and academic achievement: Untangling the relationship between work and grades. *NASPA Journal, 45*(4), 560–582.

Riggert, S. C., Boyle, M., Petrosko, J. M., Ash, D., & Rude-Parkins, C. (2006). Student employment and higher education: Empiricism and contradiction. *Review of Educational Research, 76*(1), 63–92.

Rubin, M. (2012). Social class differences in social integration among students in higher education: A meta-analysis and recommendations for future research. *Journal of Diversity in Higher Education, 5*(1), 22–38.

Salisbury, M. H., Pascarella, E. T., Padgett, R. D., & Blaich, C. (2012). The effects of work on leadership development among first-year college students. *Journal of College Student Development, 53*(2), 300–324.

Soria, K. M. (2012). Creating a successful transition for working-class first-year students. *Journal of College Orientation and Transition, 20*(1), 44–55.

Soria, K. M., & Stebleton, M. J. (2013). Social capital, academic engagement, and sense of belonging among working-class college students. *College Student Affairs Journal, 31*(2), 139–153.

Soria, K. M., Stebleton, M. J., & Huesman, R. L. (2013–2014). Class counts: Exploring differences in academic and social integration between working-class and middle/upper-class students at large, public research universities. *Journal of College Student Retention: Research, Theory, and Practice, 15*(2), 215–242.

Stern, D. S., & Nakata, Y. (1991). Paid employment among U.S. college students: Trends, effects, and possible causes. *Journal of Higher Education, 62*(1), 25–43.

Terenzini, P., Springer, L., Yaeger, P., Pascarella, E., & Nora, A. (1996). First-generation college students: Characteristics, experiences, and cognitive development. *Research in Higher Education, 37*(1), 1–22.

Tinto, V. (1993). *Leaving college: Rethinking the causes and cures of student attrition.* Chicago, IL: University of Chicago Press.

Walpole, M. (2003). Socioeconomic status and college: How SES affects college experiences and outcomes. *Review of Higher Education, 27*(1), 45–73.

Walpole, M. (2007). Economically and educationally challenged students in higher education. *ASHE Higher Education Report, 33*(3).

Walpole, M. (2008). Emerging from the pipeline: African American students, socioeconomic status, and college experiences and outcomes. *Research in Higher Education, 49*(3), 237–255.

CHAPTER TWELVE

Mexicano Male Students' Engagement WITH Faculty IN THE Community College

ANGELICA M. G. PALACIOS, J. LUKE WOOD AND FRANK HARRIS III

In the past 10 years, research relevant to men of color in postsecondary education has explored factors influencing their success in college (Bush & Bush, 2010; Flowers, 2006; Mason, 1998; Wood, 2012). In particular, scholars have found that men of color who are more academically engaged in college environments tend to perform better than those who are not academically engaged, specifically within academic achievement and persistence (Ingram & Gonzalez-Matthews, 2013; Sutherland, 2011). One important type of engagement often examined in research is that of faculty-student engagement. Faculty-student engagement refers to key interactions inside and outside of the class that students have with faculty regarding academic and nonacademic matters (Wood & Ireland, 2014); however, students' engagement in any academic environment can be hindered by the nexus of numerous factors.

In this chapter, we examine key engagement experience for Mexicano men in community colleges. Due to the nature of this study that has differentiated Latino subgroups as in other comprehensive studies (Navarro, 2005), *Mexicano* was operationalized to refer to men of Mexican, Mexican American, and Chicano identity in order to distinguish students of Mexican descent from other Latino subgroups, that is, *Guatemalteco, Salvadoreño, Hondureño, Costarriqueño, Panameño, Colombiano, Venezolano, Brasileño, Argentino, Cubano, Puertorriqueño*, and so forth. To provide context to this study, we interviewed several Mexicano men who had previous experience as community college students. We use examples from one of these men to illuminate experiences and perceptions that are interwoven throughout this manuscript. The following quote from a Mexicano male community college student named Juan González (a pseudonym) illustrates this point:

> When I was at [a community college], I took an anthropology class and almost the first half of the semester I had an "F" in that class and [professor of color] pulled me to the side and he's like, "Dude, what are you doing? Do you want to actually go to school? What is your problem, why are you doing bad?" And I told him, "I am working, I have work, and I am trying to do everything, and it's just tough." See, he pulled me out in the hall … not even after class, this was passing by, I was getting lunch and he pulled me to the side … and he's like, "You know what? When I was your age, I already had my degree. I'm not trying to brag …" And I was like, "Look …" I stopped him right there … "You don't know what it means to be me. You don't know what my family is." And I told him, "You were probably someone that didn't have a job and stuff." And we were getting into it. And [professor says], "Look man …" He pulled out something that kind of put me in shock, and it's like to not judge a book by its cover … he pulled out his contractor's license and he told me, "Look man, I know where you've been, cause I've done the same thing." He was a painter; he was all of those things … he would mow grass and do what he can to pay his tuition, and he didn't have the programs they have now … he wanted it so bad, that he got it … and he's like, "You know what? You need to make your decision, do you want to make money now, or do you want to make money later?" And that put me in a position because I never really thought about it. So, I started doing all of my course work, and I ended the course with an "A" … And that's one thing that I feel that there is not a lot of teachers that do things like that. He did that to me … that was probably one of the best semesters I had and I ended up with higher than a 3.0. I think there needs to be a lot more professors that actually care about their students, because me personally that's where my discouragement derives from because I see teachers that don't want to help.

Juan discussed the important effect that employment can have on student success, particularly for men of color, and stressed the challenge of having an outside commitment to working while simultaneously attending to the high demands of his academics. Juan additionally noted that his grades suffered at the start of the semester, but rose by the end of the semester based on a breakthrough encounter with a faculty member. Embodied within this discussion of the significance of employment are the confluence key concepts explored in this chapter, including degree utility and the masculine ideal or pressure to be the family's breadwinner. In this chapter, we explore the effect of employment on Mexicano males' faculty-student engagement. We also investigate whether perceptions of degree utility and masculine identity in four domains (i.e., breadwinner orientation, help-seeking behavior, school as a feminine domain, and competitive ethos) has a moderating effect on the relationship between students' employment and faculty-student engagement.

Researchers investigating the experiences of men of color in community colleges have found that degree utility—students' perceptions of the worthwhileness of their collegiate endeavors—serves as a critical linchpin for student success. Specifically, Mason (1998) examined persistence factors for urban African American male community college students in Illinois and found that degree utility serves as a strong positive predictor of first-semester persistence for these men. In the case of Juan, the faculty member intentionally provoked ideas relative to the student's current life, such as "Do you want to make money now, or do you want to make money later?" This comment caused Juan to reassess his commitment to school in light of his external commitments to work; consequently, Juan placed greater value on the importance of college and embraced the notion of delayed gratification.

Also evident within these same words is the faculty member's appeal to Juan's masculinity. Many men are socialized to serve as primary breadwinners, referred to as a breadwinner orientation. This orientation often suggests that providing for oneself and one's family is more important for men than women. When taken to extreme, men may in some cases devalue school and place greater importance on work for fear of not fulfilling their masculine duties of providing. Coupled with the expectation of getting a job, financial family obligations, and the desire for financial prosperity (Bean & Metzner, 1985; Harris & Wood, 2013; Palmer & Dubord, 2013; Sáenz, Bukoski, Lu, & Rodriguez, 2013; Wood & Palmer, 2013a, 2013b; Wood, Hilton, & Lewis, 2011), men are often encouraged at home to embrace breadwinning (Harris & Harper, 2008, Sáenz et al., 2013). As a result, more than 70% of Latino men who are enrolled in higher education are employed and attend school part-time (NCES, 2012); however, a breadwinner orientation is not the only masculine ideal influencing outcomes for men of color. In addition, men may perceive school as a feminine domain, have perceptions of competition associated with masculinity, and may be fearful in seeking out help from faculty and staff, as they may believe doing so will illustrate traits of weakness. Take help-seeking as an example: for Juan, despite his awareness of his failing grade in anthropology, there was no indication of initiated discourse from him to seek out assistance from faculty. Juan was discouraged from help-seeking as a result of negative faculty behaviors, which is an important consideration given that avoidance of help-seeking has been linked to attributes related to traditional masculine socialization reinforced through norms and expectations of gender behaviors (Harris & Harper, 2008).

Furthermore, working male Mexicanos face additional challenges of fulfilling socialized masculine roles to work as soon as they reach adulthood. Comprehending the effect that gender roles have on males' success in college is essential for facilitating the success of men of color. Certainly it is no surprise that the majority of two-year college students hold some form of employment while in school (Pascarella & Terenzini, 2005). Recent data notes that more than 65% of students work a minimum of 26 hours or more while in school (NPSAS, 2012). For Latino men, research has shown that approximately 66% work a minimum of 26 hours or more while attending a public two-year college, and 42.5% of Latino males work a minimum 40 hours or more (NPSAS, 2012). Nonetheless, the majority of Latino men begin their academic careers at a community college (College Board, 2011; Hagedorn, Maxwell, & Hampton, 2001–2002; Perrakis, 2008; Sáenz et al., 2013; Strayhorn, 2012); consequently, it is important to better understand Mexicano male students' experiences in this institutional context given their numbers.

In providing additional context to this study, in the next section, we examine select background characteristics of Latino men in community colleges, which does not differentiate between Mexicano and Latino men. In addition, the following sections address key concepts explored in this study. The authors have employed insights from the interview with Juan and prior research to help contextualize the experiences of Mexicano men. That being said, as mentioned, much of the research on these men do not delineate between Mexicano men and Latino men (in general). Thus, what follows is inclusive of literature more broadly contextualized as referring to Latino men and, in some cases, men of color as a whole.

By shedding light on the counternarratives of men of color, we begin to understand the inner workings of the socialization that takes place within this group. Specifically, in this chapter, we explore the effect of employment on faculty-student engagement and investigate whether perceptions of degree utility and masculine identity in four domains—breadwinner orientation, help-seeking behavior, school as a feminine domain, and competitive ethos—have a moderating effect on the relationship between employment and faculty-student engagement.

Excerpts on Latino Men

Reinforcement of gender behavior has been linked to direct or indirect observations of gendered acts learned through one's childhood, particularly through parents and familial influences (MacNaughton, 2006). As such, from early on, boys begin to associate masculinity as a representation of physical rigor, strength, and power (Harris & Harper, 2008). Harris and Harper (2008) have discussed how masculine identities can conflict with success in college, noting that ideations of manhood are developed at early stages of childhood. The socialization of one's masculinity is reinforced through "manhood messages" endorsed by family, male peers, and schools; for example, key influences within the home have been reported to reinforce socializations of gender behavior throughout their expected domestic duties (Harris & Harper, 2008). In addition, the father-son interaction plays a critical role to the development in shaping males' understanding of their own masculinity. For instance, socialized activities ranging from the kinds of toys bought for boys to the enrollment in sports popular among boys affect the internalization of socialized masculine gender roles (Harris & Harper, 2008).

Help-seeking

As noted earlier, some men avoid seeking out help from faculty and staff. They do so because help-seeking can be erroneously associated with weakness and femininity. Such internalization of these traditional masculine notions has led to conflicts between men's identities and successful practices in college. For instance, men's perceptions of help-seeking influences whether or not they will engage in academic matters directly related to their success (e.g., accessing campus resources, centers, tutoring services, talking with faculty). For example, two students interviewed in Gardenhire-Crooks, Collado, Martin, Castro, Brock, and Orr's (2010) study noted the following: "I paid for school, out of my pocket. I pay for my books … I ain't ask nobody to help me, you know, I ain't need no help, that's the type of person I am" (p. 46).

Similarly, Juan reported:

> I feel that one thing that I've learned from my father and it's not like bad, I love everything that my father taught me. He's taught me a lot about pride and it's something that I have a lot of sense of pride … with that I feel that because of the culture that I have, it's a lot of that *machismo* which is the *masculinity* of not asking for help, of being a man, showing people you're strong and you can do it. And it's something that I do have, and it's something that I know I don't want to be a part of, but at the same time I don't regret because it's something that defines who I am … when I do graduate, hopefully this semester, to me it's going to be one of the happiest things in my life because I did it by myself. Not because I asked somebody to help me, not because it was handed to me, but the fact that I did it myself.

Nonetheless, the message behind the usage of phrases such as "I did it by myself" and "I ain't ask nobody to help me" clearly solidifies their identities as products of socialized gender roles; yet, the frustrations of failure in school permeate a male-gendered identity conflict from the students noted above. Some males are aware of their frustrations in college; however, sometimes males have trouble expressing their need for help among peers, more so with faculty when feelings of faculty disconnect are high. As an example, Juan further demonstrated his own frustrations with help seeking from faculty:

> I don't want people to know that I want help. And I do ask my friends for help and they are the same way, "Dude, it's easy, I didn't even study for that class and I passed" and I feel so discouraged that I want to ask for help but don't because it's kind of embarrassing. And when you finally do ask for help or ask teachers for assistance, the teacher is a gamble whether they want to help you or not if you're taking their time.

Similarly, another student interviewed by Gardenhire-Crooks and colleagues (2010) expressed his attitude about faculty in community college: "If they don't care about how I do, neither do I" (p. 25). Akin to what Juan underscored within his passage, both students seem to have emphasized individualized self-determination. As such, more researchers are turning their attention to factors associated with college success, including socialized gender traits that shape or restrict social skills of men while in college (Ludeman, 2004).

Breadwinner Orientation

In addition to school and work, some Latino men are also responsible for fulfilling family obligations (e.g., caring for dependents, providing financially). Past research indicates that having family obligations is related to lower completion rates and dropping out of higher education institutions (Bean & Metzner, 1985; Harris & Wood, 2013; Wood, 2012). Coupling one's internalization of masculinity with cultural and familial expectations of getting a job can lead to even further pressures for a student. One male student interviewed by Sáenz and colleagues (2013) expressed his unease over pressures of obtaining a job in order to contribute to the household, while still understanding his responsibilities as a student:

> [Mother] keeps reminding me, "When are you going to get a job? You have to help us with the income …" And then my mind's like, "I'm taking all these classes and I have a full course load and everything so I can't do it." It's not like easy classes, they're pretty difficult classes so … I mean I've gotten to understand it, but she always used to remind me, "When are you going to get a job? When are you going to help out?" (p. 14)

Similarly, Harris and Harper (2008) noted that a student in their study

> had to reduce his work hours by half to make time for classes and studying. Consequently, his girlfriend took a part-time job to supplement their income. Adam recently asked a friend, "What kind of man has two kids and quits working so he can go and read poetry at some damn college?" (p. 31).

Working off-campus and having family responsibilities are some factors that could negatively impact student engagement and success (Freeman & Huggans, 2009; Harris & Wood, 2013; Mason, 1998). Take for instance, similar experiences echoed by another Latino male student interviewed by Gardenhire-Crooks and colleagues (2010):

> It's like, as a man, I still got to support … She's not working at the moment. She goes to school. So, I still have to come up with money to help my father pay the rent, pay my car insurance, pay my gas, fix my car and still send money to [her] so I can at least help her out with her cell phone bills, clothes and stuff like that. Even though she lives with her parents, but still, me, as a man, like [I can't say] "Yeah, live off your father." That's not me, you know what I mean? (p. 42)

These students clearly displayed a clear sense of gender- and identity-related challenges and the pressure of contributing at home as well as supporting a significant other posed a significant challenge. These influences from home are the stresses noted in the literature as the "expectation to contribute to family life" (Sáenz et al., 2013, p. 14). Additionally, as mentioned in Harris and Harper, characteristics from this narrative also suggest that these students embody the socialization to embrace the breadwinner role at home, which further suggest the maintenance of traditional male behavior (O'Neil, 1981). In pursuit of fulfilling this role, some men pursue a college degree to fulfill this expectation of acquiring higher paying jobs (Harris & Harper, 2008), adding to the perception among men as breadwinners.

Competitive Ethos

Another integral masculine concept that can influence success is competitive ethos. The competitive ethos subconstruct refers to men's dispositions and perceptions around competition with other men. Successful competition with others can provide men with a sense of control and power over their own lives and an enhanced sense of pride (Sáenz et al., 2013). Boys learn early on from other men (e.g., fathers, brothers, uncles) that their worth as men is tied to successful competition with other men (Harris & Harper, 2008); for example, many young boys are engaged in sports by their fathers and socialized to perceive sports as a domain that is key to their success as men. Socialized messages around competition continue throughout life and can also be reinforced via faculty. This is exemplified by a message that Juan received from his male professor:

> Something he had told me that I never really forgot was "nobody in your life is ever going to hand you things and when you see a lot of, everything like today, you're similar to what America wants with your credit score. If you don't have credit you're nothing." And a lot of the times I feel that's what [professor] was trying to tell me was that if you don't have your degree, you're nothing. You're in competition with everyone else in the world, and you having a degree, is one step above them.

Competition among men is evident in many domains, including "sexual relationships with women, status within exclusively male peer groups, and the accumulation of material possessions" (Harris & Harper, 2008, p. 30). Competitive ethos can be a critical linchpin to success in college for those whom college is a domain where they exert their competitive efforts. That being said, an excessive focus on competition can also be unhealthy, especially when one perceives that their success in academic matters is tied to their self-worth. Competition can also occur as it relates to college: when men do not succeed in school in relation to other men, they may feel a sense of being lesser than their masculine peers (O'Neil, 1981). As a result, men can withdraw their interest in school and place it in other domains of competition (e.g., sports, women) where they may experience greater levels of success.

School as a Feminine Domain

Men may also perceive school as a feminine domain (Weaver-Hightower, 2003). Specifically, boys of color attend schools where the vast majority of teachers are of White ethnicity and female. Thus, due to the structural composition of school as a White-feminine domain, when boys engage in schools, they also experience a conflict with their masculine identities (Gilbert & Gilbert, 1998; Weaver-Hightower, 2003). Thus, boys who excel in school are often referred to (by peers) as being a wuss, sissy, punk, b**ch, or other names that suggest feminization. This notion of school as a feminine domain is typified by the following quote:

> Erik decided to enroll in community college to pursue a vocational certificate and an associate degree. His friends from high school offered a perspective on his decision: "School is for girls and sissies. If you need to support your family, be a man and go out and get a real job." (Harris & Harper, 2008, p. 32)

As evidenced by this quote, school is widely viewed as a domain for women. As noted by Gilbert and Gilbert (1998), "If commitment to schoolwork is characteristic of girls, and if to be masculine requires being different from girls, then boys' commitment to schoolwork becomes a challenge to their masculinity" (p. 140).

Moreover, school can also be perceived as a White domain as well: young children of color (regardless of gender) are socialized to perceive school as being structured for people other than themselves (Ogbu, 2004). Thus, a student of color who engages in school may feel a conflict with academic success and their identity as a person of color, which is typified by Ogbu's (2004) notion of *acting White*. In this notion, students of color are socialized to perceive school as a White domain and, thus, students of color who excel in school are teased for acting outside of the normal expectation of their race (Ogbu, 2004). The confluence of these two concepts, acting White and being feminine, further socialize boys of color to see school as a domain that is not suited for them (Harris & Wood, 2014). While this section has provided contextual support for this chapter in overviewing research on Latino men and masculinities, the next section will describe the methods employed in this study.

METHOD

Data from this study were derived from the Community College Survey of Men (CCSM). The CCSM is an institutional-level needs assessment tool used by community colleges to better understand factors that influence success for historically underrepresented and underserved men (Wood & Harris, 2013). In the past two years, the CCSM has been employed at nearly 40 community colleges in eight states (i.e., California, Arizona, Arkansas, Illinois, Maryland, Pennsylvania, Minnesota, and Texas). In total, nearly 6,000 men have been surveyed via this instrument. Colleges participating in the CCSM receive comprehension reports on between-racial/ethnic group differences and summaries identifying factors most predictive of student success. Institutional agents use the data derived from the CCSM for establishing benchmarks, monitoring student progress, and identifying areas in need of intervention. The CCSM was designed based on findings from extant research on men of color in community college, community college student success, and racial and masculine identity (Flowers, 2006; Freeman & Huggans, 2009; Glenn, 2003; Hagedorn, Maxwell, & Hampton, 2001–2002; Mason, 1998; Vasquez-Urias, 2012; Wood & Williams, 2013). Prior research has shown that the instrument has strong psychometric properties (Wood & Harris, 2013). Specifically Wood and Harris (2013) found that the instrument has strong internal consistency and reliability across racial/ethnic populations.

Data employed in this study were derived from the final pilot phase of the instrument. This phase was conducted in fall 2013 with 17 participating community colleges. These colleges spanned four states, including Arizona, California, Maryland, and Illinois. A total of 3,781 men participated in the survey. The ethnic breakdown of the sample was as follows: 40% White, 5.2% Asian (excluding Southeast Asian), 2.7% Southeast Asian (e.g., Hmong, Cambodian, Vietnamese, Laotian), 0.6% South Asian (Indian, Pakistani, Sri-Lankan), 0.8% Pacific Islander, 2.8% Filipino, 10.0% Black, 18.4% Mexican/Mexican American, 8.9% Hispanic (excluding Mexican/Mexican American descent), 2.1% American Indian, 1.1% Middle Eastern, 2.2% other, and 4.8% Multiethnic. Analyses employed in this analysis were restricted to men identifying as Mexican/Mexican American (n = 337). The next section identifies the variables employed from the CCSM that were used in this study.

Measures and Analysis

The primary outcome employed in this study was faculty-student engagement, which was operationalized in this study to refer to the degree to which students were engaged inside and outside of the classroom in academic and nonacademic matters with faculty. Faculty-student engagement was a composite variable composed of students' responses to four statements. Students were asked to indicate the frequency of their engagement with faculty (e.g., never, once this semester, once a month, a few times a month, once a week, several times a week) on the following four areas: "talk with professors about academic matters inside of class," "talk with professors about academic matters outside of class," "talk with professors about non-academic matters (e.g., personal, family, current events) outside of class," and "talk with professors about course grade(s)."

The analysis controlled for four potential variables, including respondents' age, total number of dependents, full-time or part-time enrollment, and stressful life events. Respondents' age was collected via class intervals on the following scale: Under 18, 18 to 24 years old, 25 to 31 years old, 32 to 38 years old, 39 to 45 years old, 46 to 52 years told, 53 to 59 years old, 60 to 66 years old, and 67 years and older. Stressful life events identified the total number of stressful life circumstances that the student had experienced in the last two years (e.g., divorce, death in family, eviction, relationship breakup, health concerns, and incarceration).

The primary predictor variable employed in this study was hours worked per week. This variable was collected on the following scale: none, 1 to 5 hours, 6 to 10 hours, 11 to 15 hours, 16 to 20 hours, 21 to 25 hours, 26 to 30 hours, 31 to 35 hours, 36 to 40 hours, and 41 or more hours. In addition to examining hours worked per week as a predictor of faculty-student engagement, in this study we also examined whether degree utility and four masculine domains had a moderating effect on the relationship between work and the outcome. As noted, degree utility refers to students' perceptions of the worthwhileness of their collegiate endeavors. The four masculine domains examined in this study included school as a feminine domain, breadwinner orientation, competitive ethos, and help-seeking. These composite variables assessed men's healthy conceptions of masculinities in the areas mentioned above.

Data in this study were analyzed using multiple linear regression. Specifically, the researchers examined the association between hours worked in employment with faculty-student engagement (with controls). The model also explored the interactions of work with degree utility and the four masculine domains on the outcome. Effect sizes were examined using R-squared (R^2) and the adjusted R-squared (adjR^2). Data are presented in the next section using the unstandardized and standardized coefficients.

RESULTS

The first model examined the relationships between hours worked in employment and faculty-student engagement for Mexicano men. This model was significantly predictive of the outcome $F = 6.511, p < .001$. The full model accounted for 14.2% of the variance in the outcome ($R^2 = .142$, adj$R^2 = .120$). As previously discussed, this study employed four primary control variables, age, total number of dependents, stressful life events, and time status. Age was not found to have a significant effect on the outcome ($B = -.239$, p = .271). The total number of dependents had a slight positive effect on the outcome, suggesting that more dependents was associated with greater levels of faculty-student engagement ($B = .353$, p < .05). Stressful life event was found to have a positive effect on the outcome ($B = .407$, p < .001). Interestingly, this finding suggests that students with greater numbers of stressful life events (e.g., eviction, divorce, death in family, incarceration) were more likely to report higher levels of engagement with faculty members. Time status had a negative effect on the outcome. Given that full-time status was the reference category, this result indicated that part-time students reported lower levels of faculty-student engagement than their full-time peers ($B = -1.337, p < .01$). Table 12.1 summarizes the findings.

Table 12.1. Regression Coefficients for Predictors of Faculty-Student Engagement.

	Unstandardized Coefficients		Standardized Coefficients	
	B	Std. Error	Beta	t
(Constant)	10.083***	.948		10.638
Age	−.239	.217	−.056	−1.101
Dependents	.353*	.166	.108	2.124
Time Status	−1.337**	.478	−.142	−2.795
Stressful Life Events	.407***	.106	.183	3.847
Working for Pay	−2.930**	1.020	−.627	−2.873
Work*Degree Utility	.722	.753	.154	.960
Work*Feminine	−.880	1.033	−.188	−.851
Work*Breadwinning	1.727**	.623	.368	2.773
Work*Competitive Ethos	−1.768***	.489	−.377	−3.619
Work*Help-seeking	3.173***	.754	.680	4.209

Note: *< .05, **< .01, ***< .001.

The primary predictor variable employed in this study was hours worked per week off-campus. As hypothesized, this variable was negatively predictive of faculty-student engagement. As a result, the more hours a Mexicano male student worked per week, the less likely he was to have engaging experiences with faculty members ($B = -.2.930, p < .01$). Another important element of this study was examining the effect of several moderating variables on the relationship between hours worked per week and faculty-student engagement. These moderating variables included degree utility and four measures of masculine identity (e.g., school as a feminine domain, breadwinner orientation, competitive ethos, and help-seeking). Of the potential moderators examined, two did not have a significant effect on the relationship between hours worked per week and the outcome. Perceptions of school as a feminine domain was not found to have a moderating effect in this study ($B = -.880$, p = .395). Moreover, degree utility also did not have a significant moderating effect (B = .722, p = .338).

Breadwinner orientation was also found to have a significant moderating effect in this study ($B = .1.727$, p < .01). This suggests that healthy conceptions of breadwinning mitigated (or diminished) the negative effect of hours worked per week on faculty-student engagement. In contrast, competitive ethos had a differential moderating effect in this study. The negative relationship between hours worked per week and faculty-student engagement was intensified (i.e., made worse) for men with more healthy conceptions of competitive ethos ($B = -1.768$, p < .001). As such, men who perceived that being successful in academic competition—that is, in reference to the subconstruct, competitive ethos—was core to their self-worth (in an excessive manner) benefited from this unhealthy disposition. The last moderator examined was perceptions of help-seeking behaviors. As with degree utility and breadwinner orientation, this variable lessened the negative effect between hours worked per week and faculty-student engagement ($B = .3.173$, p < .001). Thus, when men in the sample had healthier perceptions about their ability to seek out help, the negative effect of work on engagement lessened.

IMPLICATIONS FOR PRACTICE

We set out to examine the relationship between work and faculty-student engagement with a focus on how degree utility and four domains of masculinity can influence that relationship. Four salient findings emerged from this study. First, increased hours working per week have a negative association with faculty-student engagement. As such, the more a Mexicano male student works, the less likely he is to engage with faculty. Possibly, working impedes the time that a student has available to have engaging experiences with faculty. Given that many Mexicano men work while attending school, this finding is disappointing and could explain (in part) disparate outcomes experienced by these men in college. With respect to practice, during the admissions process (e.g., initial advising appointment, orientation) college personnel could engage working students to limit the amount of time they will be working to a point that will allow them to effectively balance both their work and school commitments. Moreover, given that research has shown that the negative association between work and school is mitigated when students' employment is tied to their academics (Wood, Hilton, & Lewis, 2011), personnel should also encourage working students to find work that is related to their academic pursuits. One strategy that could be employed is to identify working students during initial advising and counseling sessions that could be referred to career services for counseling on how to find a job directly in their field of interest.

Second, healthy conceptions of breadwinner orientation mitigated (or diminished) the negative association between hours worked per week and faculty-student engagement. Thus, working while attending college was not as detrimental on students' engagement with faculty for men who perceived that breadwinning was a responsibility that could be shared by men and women. With respect to practice, faculty could be encouraged to convey positive messages about breadwinning as it relates to the academic success of male Mexicano students. Specifically, faculty should convey the importance of attaining a college degree as a long-term strategy for successfully providing for oneself and one's family. Third, healthy perceptions of competition among men served to worsen the negative effect that hours worked per week had on faculty-student engagement. As a result, men who focused excessively on competing with others and tied that competition to their self-worth actually benefitted from that unhealthy conception of masculinity. For these men, unhealthy dispositions around competition reduced the negative relationship between work and faculty-student engagement.

Finally, healthy perceptions of help-seeking reduced the negative effect of hours worked on engagement. As such, men felt comfortable seeking out help from faculty and believed that asking for help did not threaten their manhood. However, faculty should initiate engagement in the classroom in order to ensure that students, regardless of their perception of help-seeking, are being provided with the help that they need. Faculty should engage in "intrusive instruction," ensuring that interactions with students (in and out of class) are built in as a component of the course; for example, faculty could make attending office hours a mandatory part of the course. This could ensure that students, regardless of disposition, are getting necessary feedback on their progress in the course.

CONCLUSION

Examining the four key bodies of masculinity in this particular study has surely contributed to the understanding of factors influencing college success for Mexicano men. While we understand that the role each subconstruct (i.e., help-seeking, breadwinning, competitive ethos, and school as a feminine domain) plays for Mexicano men is very different from one another, practitioners could take note to how these four domains could influence engagement differently. As mentioned earlier on in this chapter, Mexicano men are likely to attend a public two-year college, while more than 60% are both working and attending school. In fact, more men struggle than women when it comes to completion rates. Thus, more than ever, faculty are needed who can help engage men within their academics while conveying the importance of completing and attaining a degree. With this support, perhaps more men of color will feel empowered throughout their educational pursuits to succeed academically.

REFERENCES

Bean, J. P., & Metzner, B. S. (1985). A conceptual model of nontraditional undergraduate student attrition. *Review of Educational Research, 55*(4), 485–540.

Bush, E. C., & Bush, V. L. (2010). Calling out the elephant: An examination of African American male achievement in community colleges. *Journal of African American Males in Education, 1*(1), 40–62.

Cejda, B., & Rhodes, J. (2004). Through the pipeline: The role of faculty in promoting associate degree completion among Hispanic students. *Community College Journal of Research and Practice, 28*(3), 249–262.

College Board. (2011). *The educational experience of young men of color: Capturing the student voice.* New York, NY: Author.

Flowers, L. A. (2006). Effects of attending a 2-year institution on African American males' academic and social integration in the first year of college. *Teachers College Record, 108*(2), 267–286.

Freeman, T. L., & Huggans, M. A. (2009). Persistence of African-American male community college students in engineering. In H. T. Frierson, W. Pearson Jr., & J. H. Wyche (Eds.), *Black American males in higher education: Diminishing proportions* (pp. 229–251). Bingley, UK: Emerald.

Gardenhire-Crooks, A., Collado, H., Martin, K., Castro, A., Brock, T., & Orr, G. (2010). *Terms of engagement: Men of color discuss their experiences in community college.* New York, NY: MDRC.

Gilbert, R., & Gilbert, P. (1998). *Masculinity goes to school.* New York, NY: Routledge.

Glenn, F. S. (2003). The retention of Black male students in Texas public community colleges. *Journal of College Student Retention, 5*(2), 115–133.

Hagedorn, L. S., Maxwell, W., & Hampton, P. (2001–2002). Correlates of retention for African-American males in community colleges. *Journal of College Student Retention, 3*(3), 243–263.

Harris, F., III, & Harper, S. R. (2008). Masculinities go to community college: Understanding male identity socialization and gender role conflict. *New Directions for Community Colleges, 2008*(142), 25–35.

Harris, F., III, & Wood, J. L. (2013). Student success for men of color in community college: A review of published literature and research, 1998–2012. *Journal of Diversity in Higher Education, 6*(3), 174–185.

Harris, F., III, & Wood, J. L. (2014, April). Student development theories in the community college: The socio-ecological outcomes (SEO) model. Paper presented at the annual meeting of the Council for the Study of Community Colleges, Washington, DC.

Ingram, T. N., & Gonzalez-Matthews, M. (2013). Moving towards engagement: Promoting persistence among Latino male undergraduates at an urban community college. *Community College Journal of Research and Practice, 37*, 636–648.

Ludeman, R. B. (2004). Arrested emotional development: Connecting college men, emotions, and misconduct. *New Directions for Student Services, 2004*(107), 75–86.

MacNaughton, G. (2006). Constructing gender in early-years education. In C. Skelton, B. Francis, & L. Smulyan (Eds.), *The Sage handbook of gender and education* (pp. 127–138). Thousand Oaks, CA: Sage.

Mason, H. P. (1998). A persistence model for African American male urban community college students. *Community College Journal of Research and Practice, 22*(8), 751–760.

National Center for Education Statistics (NCES). (2011). *Postsecondary education* (chap. 3). Washington, DC: U.S. Department of Education.

Navarro, A. (2005). *Mexicano political experience in occupied Aztlán: Struggles and change.* New York, NY: AltaMira.

NPSAS. (2012). *Hours worked per week by ethnic group. National Postsecondary Student Aid Study. Computed using POWERSTATS.* Washington, DC: National Center for Education Statistics.

Ogbu, J. (2004). Collective identity and the burden of "acting White" in Black history, community, and education. *Urban Review, 36*(1), 1–35.

O'Neil, J. M. (1981). Patterns of gender role conflict and strain: Sexism and fear of femininity in men's lives. *Personnel and Guidance Journal, 60*, 203–210.

Palmer, R. T., & Dubord, Z. (2013). Achieving success: A model of success for Black men in STEM at community colleges. In R. T. Palmer & J. L. Wood (Eds.), *Community colleges and STEM: Examining underrepresented racial and ethnic minorities* (pp. 193–208). New York, NY: Routledge.

Pascarella, E. T., & Terenzini, P. T. (2005). *How college affects students: A third decade of research* (Vol. 2). San Francisco, CA: Jossey-Bass.

Perrakis, A. I. (2008). Factors promoting academic success among African American and White male community college students. *New Directions for Community Colleges, 2008*(142), 15–23.

Sáenz, V. B., Bukoski, B. E., Lu, C., & Rodriguez, S. (2013). Latino males in Texas community colleges: A phenomenological study of masculinity constructs and their effect on college experiences. *Journal of African American Males in Education, 4*(2), 82–102.

Strayhorn, T. L. (2012). Satisfaction and retention among African American men at two-year community colleges. *Community College Journal of Research and Practice, 36*(5), 358–375.

Sutherland, J. A. (2011). Building an academic nation through social networks: Black immigrant men in community colleges. *Community College Journal of Research and Practice, 35*, 267–279.

Swain, J. (2005). Masculinities in education. In M. Kimmel, J. Hearn, & R. W. Connell (Eds.), *Handbook of studies on men and masculinities.* Thousand Oaks, CA: Sage.

Vasquez-Urias, M. (2012). The impact of institutional characteristics on Latino male graduation rates in community colleges. *Annuals of the Next Generation, 3*(1), 1–12.

Weaver-Hightower, M. (2003). The "boy turn" in research on gender and education. *Review of Educational Research, 73*(4), 471–498.

Wood, J. L. (2011). Falling through the cracks: An early warning system can help keep Black males on the community college campus. *Diverse Issues in Higher Education, 28*(18), 24.

Wood, J. L. (2012). Leaving the 2-year college: Predictors of Black male collegian departure. *Journal of Black Studies, 43*(3), 303–326.

Wood, J. L., & Harris, F. (2013). The community college survey of men: An initial validation of the instrument's non-cognitive outcomes construct. *Community College Journal of Research and Practice, 37*(4), 333–338.

Wood, J. L., Hilton, A. A., & Lewis, C. W. (2011). Black male collegians in public two-year colleges: Student perspectives on the effect of employment on academic success. *NASAP Journal, 14*(1), 97–110.

Wood, J. L., Hilton, A. A., & Hicks, T. (2014). Motivational factors for academic success: Perspectives of African American males in the community college. *National Journal of Urban Education & Practice, 7*(3), 247–265.

Wood, J. L., & Ireland, S. M. (2014). Supporting Black male community college success: Determinants of faculty-student engagement. *Community College Journal of Research and Practice, 38,* 154–165.

Wood, J. L., & Palmer, R. T. (2013a). Understanding the personal goals of Black male community college students: Facilitating academic and psychosocial development. *Journal of African American Studies, 17*(2), 222–241.

Wood, J. L., & Palmer, R. T. (2013b). The likelihood of transfer for Black males in community colleges: Examining the effects of engagement using multilevel, multinomial modeling. *Journal of Negro Education, 82*(3), 272–287.

Wood, J. L., & Williams, R. C. (2013). Persistence factors for Black males in the community college: An examination of background, academic, social, and environmental variables. *Spectrum, 1*(2), 1–28.

Family and Friends

CHAPTER THIRTEEN

Native American Student Connections TO Community AND Family

Impacts on Academic Outcomes

ROBIN MINTHORN

Native American students' enrollment in higher education has slowly increased over the last several decades, ranging from 0.7% to 1.0% of total enrollments between 1976 and 2007 (National Center for Education Statistics [NCES], 2009). Native American students benefit from support services, development programs, and safe places as essential pieces of their lived campus experiences, particularly at non-Native colleges and universities (NNCUs; Shotton, Lowe, & Waterman, 2013). A vital aspect of these programs and services is the inclusion of culturally relevant perspectives incorporating families and communities (Martin & Thunder, 2013). Building a strong community on campus away from home holds the potential to positively benefit Native American college students' academic outcomes.

The presence of Native American college students requires an increasing level of advocacy and promotion of Native students' cultural values and perspectives in the services and programs offered at NNCUs—practices that require researchers and practitioners to better understand not only the views of Native students, but also how cultural values impact academic outcomes through the influence of tribal values, families, and home communities. The purpose of this study was to explore the meanings and perspectives of current Native American college student leaders and how the roles of cultural values, family, and community impact academic outcomes.

LITERATURE REVIEW

Native American students are slowly becoming more visible in higher education and receiving more bachelor's and graduate degrees than ever before (DeVoe, Darling-Churchill, & Synder, 2008). In 1998, 7,903 Native American students received a bachelor's degree, and by 2008 the number rose to 11,509 (U.S. Department of Education, 2011). With increased enrollment of Native American students, their need for student services accordingly increases, as does the need for institutions to incorporate Native voices and perspectives.

Values and Cultural Norms of Native American Students

Recent studies have identified factors that impact the success of Native American students in higher education. These findings have allowed mainstream institutions and practitioners to understand the unique values and cultures that Native American students bring with them to campus (Belgarde, 1992; Larimore & McClellan, 2005; Lin, LaCounte, & Eder, 1988). Conversely, at NNCUs the culture of the institution is often reflective of the dominant population (Tierney, 1992). The differences between the values and cultural norms of Native students and those exhibited at NNCUs contribute to some of the difficulties Native students encounter within the academy while attending NNCUs (Locust, 1988; Mihesuah & Wilson, 2004). Some aspects of Native American cultures and values sharply contrast with those of the mainstream culture; for example, in Native culture there is an emphasis on the group more than on the individual. Many of the Native students attending NNCUs are raised in homes where the values of sharing, generosity, and cooperation are taught (Deyhle & Swisher, 1997). Consequently, definitions for success and achievement differ for Native Americans who are not raised with the individualistic perspective of mainstream American culture, which automatically creates a cultural conflict between the student and the institution (Lin et al., 1988; Pottinger, 1989; Scott, 1986). These cultural mismatches negatively impact students' successful transition during the first years of attendance, an important time when students must learn to navigate the institution and understand its cultural values (Swisher & Deyhle, 1989; Wright & Tierney, 1991).

Another factor that may impact the success of Native American students in higher education at NNCUs is the underrepresentation of Native American students in retention theories and student development models (Tierney, 1992). The dominant current theories are grounded in research based on Western cultural values, which neither include students who are representative of Native perspectives nor address the specific and unique needs of Native American students (Huffman, 2003).

A limited number of theoretical frameworks on retention issues faced by Native students are beginning to emerge (e.g., Heavyrunner & DeCelles, 2002; Heavyrunner & Morris, 1997) and may inform practices for working with Native students to ensure their success. These retention models are reflective of Native cultural values in which family and support systems such as peer, faculty, staff, and community are tied to the success of Native students (Pavel & Padilla, 1993). Including the academic, social, cultural, and psychological needs of Native students in the support networks and services can facilitate the successful transition of Native students from high school or tribal colleges to predominantly White institutions (PWIs; Wright, 1985). For many Native students, the motivation to complete an academic degree is based on—and reflects—the cultural values of the sharing of knowledge, collaboration, and giving back to the community (Guillory & Wolverton, 2008).

At a minimum, differing cultural and societal values, norms, and identities between Native American and non-Native American students may impede Native American students' success in higher education. Native American culture is particularly and deeply connected to human relationships and to a meaningful relationship to place (Deloria & Wildcat, 2001). Consequently, building relationships with other students, staff, and faculty, as well as with the campus itself, is essential for Native American students to feel accepted, welcomed, and engaged. When the institution demonstrates a commitment to being supportive and honoring Native students' cultural values as strengths, the relationship to the institution is deeply connected and aligned with Native student tribal and cultural values (Huffman, 2001).

Academic Persistence

Multiple studies have examined factors that contribute to the success and academic persistence of Native American students in higher education. Identified factors include confidence and self-perception as possible predictors of academic persistence among Native American students (Brown & Robinson Kurpius, 1997). Jackson, Smith, and Hill (2003) also found that confidence and self-efficacy are related to academic persistence. Other studies found that self-efficacy is critical for helping students to overcome obstacles (Coffman & Gilligan, 2002–2003; Kalsner, 1992). Consequently, as Native students transition from high school to college, nurturing their confidence and positive self-perception is important. In addition, scholars have identified other factors that are important for Native students' academic persistence, including precollege academic preparation, family support, faculty involvement and support, institutional commitment to students and community, financial support, and institutional and individual support for students to stay connected to home communities while at college (Astin, 1982; Brown &

Robinson Kurpius, 1997; Falk & Aitken, 1984). Generally, if Native students aspire to attend college, receive support to attend college, and prepare for college while in high school, they are more likely to persist academically (Benjamin, Chambers, & Reiterman, 1993).

Native and non-Native faculty play a critical role in Native students' academic persistence, particularly when they seek to understand the concerns and issues that Native students face and demonstrate their support for and connection with Native students (Brown & Robinson Kurpius, 1997). Scholars consistently indicate that positive interactions between faculty members and Native American students are critical for fostering persistence and academic achievement (Jackson et al., 2003). Positive faculty and staff interaction, coupled with an institutional commitment to support Native American students through services and an inclusive campus climate, also increases students' persistence (Garrod & Larimore, 1997). Similarly, an inclusive campus climate is conducive for institutions to assist incoming and returning college students with information regarding financial resources, scholarships, and financial management (Almeida, 1999; Dodd, Garcia, Meccage, & Nelson, 1995; Falk & Aitken, 1994).

Families and support networks also are critical. Many students draw their strength and motivation to persist from families, which often includes the desire to make life better for their families and even the goal of not letting their families down (Guillory & Wolverton, 2008). The home or tribal community of Native college students helps them persist because they receive emotional, spiritual, and financial support that encourages them to achieve their higher education goals (Bowker, 1992; Heavyrunner & DeCelles, 2002). As PWIs acknowledge the important roles that family, community, and support networks play with regard to academic persistence, they enhance the likelihood that Native students will maintain cultural ties to their community and benefit from a social support system while away (Guillory & Wolverton, 2008).

In summation, as mainstream higher education institutions increasingly recognize the needs of various student populations, the inclusion of the voice and needs of Native American students is essential. Incorporating broad definitions of families, empowering students, facilitating relationships between students and their home communities, building Native retention theories and student development models, and recognizing the culture and values that each student brings to campus are all important factors associated with enhancing Native students' success in higher education (Jackson & Smith, 2001; Jenkins, 1999; Tippeconnic Fox, Lowe, & McClellan, 2005).

This study was guided by the following research questions:

1. How does the role of student leadership in a Native American student organization impact academic outcomes?

2. How does the role of student leadership in a Native American student organization impact perceptions of family and community?

The research questions provided insight on Native American college students from a Native American student leader perspective in relation to academic outcomes and the role of family and community. Native student leaders were chosen because of their level of involvement on campus, connection to the broader community, and acknowledging the likelihood of persisting to graduation.

METHOD

To ensure that the voices of the participants—current Native American college students—are shared, this study utilized qualitative methodology. Focus groups and one-on-one interviews were conducted among current Native American student leaders at five NNCUs that are four-year institutions. To increase credibility the qualitative research process may include member checking by soliciting feedback from participants regarding findings and interpretations of the data (Lincoln & Guba, 1985). In this study, I asked student participants to member check the transcriptions of the focus groups and one-on-one interviews. Another way of increasing the credibility of the study is to use external peer review or to provide an external check of the qualitative research process (Creswell, 1998; Lincoln & Guba, 1985). In this study, a colleague experienced in qualitative research helped me to conduct the external peer review of the codes, data analysis, and findings.

Participants

I deemed it important that the student participants had leadership experience in the Native American organizations on the NNCU; this enabled them to provide their perspectives of how these roles impact their perceptions of leadership, role of family and community, and ultimately how those factors impact academic outcomes. Each NNCU was located in a distinct geographic region of the United States that represented diverse tribal nations from which student leaders originated. In addition to focus groups, one-on-one interviews were conducted with Native American student leaders at each institution to provide a narrative of his or her experience as a campus leader and his or her lived experiences. Participants were chosen using purposive sampling through identification by Native American student affairs professionals at the five NNCUs. Four participants were selected at four institutions and at one NNCU five participants were selected, representing a total of twenty-one participants. Table 13.1 lists more information about the Native student leaders who participated in this study.

Table 13.1. Native Student Leader Participant Demographics.

Participant	Tribal Affiliation	Major	# Yrs. at University	Type of Community	# Yrs. Participated
Good	Seneca Cayuga (En), Wyandotte, Papako	NAS, minor in History	2	Tribal Rural	1
Lillian	Osage (En), Seminole, Creek	Adult and Higher Education	5	Small Urban	5
Leonard	Muscogee Creek (En), Kiowa, Wichita, Pawnee	NAS and Political Science	3	Urban	3
Walter	United Keetoowah Band of Cherokees	NAS	3	Tribal Rural	3
Art Pino	Laguna Pueblo	Mechanical Engineering	3	Urban	3
Cloud Hehaka Sapa	Oglala Lakota	NAS	7	Urban	3
Phillip	Washoe, Anishina	NAS	4	Rural Reservation	2
Sydney	Navajo	Master's Public Admin	2 (in grad program)	Urban	$2\frac{1}{2}$
Wilma	Blackfeet	Actuarial Science	1 (transfer)	Reservation	1
Winona	Shoshone Bannock	Anthropology	1	Reservation and Urban	1
Ben	Okanagan	Child Development, minor in drug and alcohol addictions	5	Reservation	5
Russell	Navajo	Electrical Engineering	3	Reservation	3

(To be continued)

Participant	Tribal Affiliation	Major	# Yrs. at University	Type of Community	# Yrs. Participated
Kateri	Nez Perce	Anthropology, minor AIS, Fisheries, Natural Resources, Art	2	Reservation	2
Clark	Pawnee	Law student	3	Reservation, Rural, and Urban	3
Vera	Hopi	PhD in History of Art, minor in AIS	3	Urban	3
Charlie	Tuscarora	Development Sociology, minor AIS	3	Reservation	2
Nathan	Oneida Wisconsin	Applied and Engineering Physics	4	Urban	4
Scott	Lumbee	Technology Design and Engineering Education	3	Rural	3
Chad	Lumbee	Psychology	4	Rural	4
Big Country	Lumbee	Graphic Communications	4	Rural	4
Joy	Haliwa Saponi	Environmental Technology and Management	3	Tribal Rural	3

Data Analysis

I used the phenomenological data analysis approach, which provides a basis for researchers to explore meaning-making in human experiences (Polkinghorne, 1989). I took into account the "epoch" (or gaining awareness of one's own experience and removing oneself from judgment) of the participants' meaning-making (Patton, 2002). The second step of the phenomenological data analysis process was for me to bracket out my own experiences and biases, allowing the topic or responses of the participants to be seen in their own terms. I examined student participants' responses per individual institution and then overall to determine if there were any relationships between regions or meaning made across the regions represented. I put them into meaningful clusters. From the clusters, I developed emergent themes to gain the meanings of the various Native American college students' perspectives on student involvement and academic outcomes.

FINDINGS

In this findings section, there are two overarching areas that are discussed on the value of family and community for Native college students and the impact of Native student involvement. Within the value of family and community for Native college students, two areas are discussed in more detail around the importance of community and family and culture. These two subareas highlight the important and unique values that are attributed to many Native students and what they bring with them to campus. In the impact on Native student involvement, one area of focus is the motivation to pursue a degree. Under the motivation to pursue a degree, four subareas are highlighted in connection to Native student leaders' involvement and academic outcomes; they include (1) awareness of issues affecting Native people, (2) quality of life, (3) support, and (4) motivation to continue persisting. These findings help provide a better understanding of how culture, family, community, and Native student involvement impact the academic outcomes and successes of this specific student population.

The Value of Family and Community for Native College Students' Community

The Native students spoke about the importance of community, how they were interconnected, and how community is a construct that should be inherently understood as an indigenous leader and student (Minthorn, 2014). The Native student leaders are individuals who came from a community, whether that community is urban, reservation, tribal, or rural. In addition, as Native students on campus they sought to build a community for themselves and other Native students. It is important to understand how Native students comprehend the concept of community. One of the students, Cloud Hehaka Sapa, described community as an important factor in pursuing a higher education:

> Community first and foremost because I think in any Indigenous perspective one of the main differences from Western is the concept of "I" and "I am nothing without my community." Whether that be here in the urban setting or if it's back home in South Dakota then, you know, "I am only because they are." So I think that's one thing that motivates me. The whole reason I'm doing this is for my community, not for me.

The drive and motivation to accomplish personal goals and to succeed for these Native college students are for the good of the community. Phillip captured this well; his comments are more about the efforts to help the tribal community and to do so with the best of intentions:

> The entire idea of an Indigenous leader is someone who comes from the community and it's not someone who is there to lead the community and change them. They are there to maintain and keep the community healthy and safe and do their best as a leader, do their best by their people. It's never an individual thing, even though the individual is only allowable through the community, without a community there is no individual.

The Native students understood the concept of community; this is seen in their words and their descriptions of the role of a Native leader and as a Native college student within the community. As an Indigenous researcher and practitioner, I viewed the epistemology and understanding of the concept of community as the same, as a shared idea and lived experience as an Indigenous person and Native American college student.

Family and Culture

The Native student leaders also described how family and culture impact them by contributing to support and development (Minthorn, 2014). Walter spoke about the broadness of the term *family* and how it can refer to various individuals who are not biologically related but are who he knows as his family:

> That term *family* doesn't mean your mom, your dad, your sisters, and your brothers, and that's your grandma too. At least to me it does, again this is just how I was raised, you know, the teachings I had growing up. To me when someone says *family* it means your aunts, your uncles, your friends, people your [sic] around, your community, your environment, you know, everything is your family, any person that you call friend … Then culture that's from my personal perspective [be]cause I know I wouldn't be able to do the things that I do here leadership-wise without the ties to the culture that I have. Without being able to lean on that when I need it for support, being able to lean on what I was taught when I'm in a bind on what to do to help me, to help the people around me.

This Native student's understanding of community, family, and culture are tied together: because, in his perception of them, one cannot exist without the other. Recognizing the role that family played in the development of an Indigenous leader and as Native American college student, Kateri states:

> So your family plays in [contributes] because your family is who made you who you are. No matter what you say. They are the people that helped you on this journey all the way to where you are. They help supported you when you were in high school, when you were a baby, you know. Because of them that's where you are and think that like no matter what in all the way until you're like in grandma status you're still going to have your family and that's still going to be a part of your leadership. And number two, your education as being Native American and not just, like, I say education but, like, not just books or anything you know like your tribal ways, your customs, your heritage. Like all the experiences that you had your education is like coming from your family or from your tribe.

Kateri indicates that family, culture, and values are the foundation for Indigenous leadership and as a person. The upbringing of the individual—through the values instilled through family and culture—consequently impacts the type of leader they become and their success as a Native college student.

IMPACT OF NATIVE STUDENT INVOLVEMENT

In order to understand the impact of Native student involvement on campus and connections to academic outcomes, it was necessary to ask the participants if their involvement motivated them to continue pursuing their degree. Through the voices of these Native student leaders a better understanding emerged of the impact that Native student involvement has on perceptions of academic outcomes.

Motivation to Pursue a Degree

One of the focus group questions posed to the Native student leaders is whether participating on campus impacts their motivation to continue pursuing a degree. Analysis of the student responses reveals different ways their involvement contributed to their motivation. It is also important to note that through each Native college student's involvement on campus they built a community and support system equivalent to family support while away from home. The findings are that their involvement contributed by increased awareness of issues affecting Native people, contributed to their quality of life, provided support, and impacted their motivation to continue pursuing a degree. In the following sections each of these different contributions is examined.

Awareness of issues affecting Native people

A theme that emerged was connected to the increased awareness that took place through Native student involvement. Phillip offered, "It just kind of helps reaffirm that there's a lot of issues in Indigenous communities all over that need support and they need people to kind of step up and do it." Charlie added that involvement "definitely influenced some of the questions that I have about Indigenous communities generally and peoples and so it was more of an influence rather than a motivation." Native student leaders who participated not only became more aware of what happened on campus within the Native community but also learned about the issues that their home communities face. This provided an increased motivation to pursue their degrees in the realization of the pertinent issues facing their communities, which displays the influence of community on persistence in their degrees.

Quality of life

Participation in building community on campus is also related to student quality of life while on campus. Clark stated, "A quality of life is a big thing but showing up in my first year and seeing the people who sort of balance this." His comment is in reference to how his connection to the Native law student association and other programs helped him by providing a balance during his first year of law school at Cornell, building that community on campus. Vera added: "I think it's more of a quality of life. It adds to the quality of life being a student, having some sort of cohort. It's sort of different; it's more social than related to my degree." Clark and Vera recognize that participation provides both a life balance and the social support they would not otherwise receive on their campuses, which is essential to Native student success. For some of the Native students, involvement not only adds quality of life but also provides a greater purpose while on campus. Nathan stated, "Time, I mean it definitely, sort of, helped give me more purpose while I'm here." Although the Native students may not specifically use the word *motivation*, their words reveal that participation contributed to quality of life, added purpose, and even encouragement to persist and work toward their respective degrees.

Support

Another theme associated with participation in a Native student organization is the concept of support. Wilma stated, "Before there wasn't a Native student center here and now this is here to support me." This affirmation resonated throughout the Native student leaders at the university. Ben added, "It has helped me in knowing there is help and support here. There wasn't a Native student center here before." Similarly, Scott talked about how being around other Native students facilitates becoming a family, by saying, "Motivation, yes, because we had, like, people that we could relate with, you know, that we could talk [to] if we needed something, help with anything, and they were just there like family members." For Native students, serving and being involved on campus by participating in a Native student organization (NSO), or simply enjoying a Native student center on campus, provides additional support that increases the motivation to pursue a degree, to which we now turn.

Motivation to continue persisting

Increased motivation to persist is evident in the multiple voices of the current Native student leaders. Scott, in reference to student involvement and building community on campus, stated, "It helps me as in motivation, in staying in school, just not pursuing a certain degree but, you know, pursuing a degree to get here." Leonard added:

> I'm involved with our larger American Indian student group to be more sociable to get to know other students from tribes across the state, across the country. Then for more intellectual-wise I'm in council of fire so we look into current issues in Indian country and talk about them. That's how I balance that and it helps keep me motivated towards my overall major goals.

In this regard Leonard's involvement in the NSO encourages his overall goals of pursuing a degree. Another example of the impact of involvement and building community on campus is found in the words of Big Country:

> It's more of a motivation because I met a lot of people in the program and out of the program, but all of it came through NASA [Native American student association]. So it's a lot of motivation and also a lot of networking for me so it's helped me in a lot of different ways, but all together it motivated me.

Walter added, "In that way it's kind of motivated me to get my degree, get out, and go home." In addition, seeing other previously involved students encouraged the Native students to achieve their own degree, as Art stated:

> To see what people do after they obtain a bachelor's of science, you know, engineering or other science degrees. So it's pretty hard to complete my program. Seeing people who have already finished and what they're doing, that gave me a lot of motivation.

Similarly, the students who participated and had become student leaders and advocates on campus felt a responsibility to go out and help encourage Native youth to go to college and pursue a degree. Joy emphasized this in her words:

> Participating in a Native American student organization did motivate me to continue, because we're such a small group. All of us are leaders so it motivated me to want to pursue my degree and go off and influence other generations after me to pursue it as well.

Joy talked about her own campus experiences and the influence they had for her to go home and encourage younger generations to pursue a degree. The connection to involvement and building a community on campus to academic outcomes is apparent.

These Native student narratives verify the deep connection to building a community on campus and the impact of motivation and ultimately the academic outcomes of receiving a college degree. These experiences encourage Native students to understand that they, in turn, can influence other Native students to go to college.

IMPLICATIONS FOR RESEARCH AND PRACTICE

The implication for this study on research and practice is apparent in better understanding the cultural values that students bring with them to campus, the impact of student involvement, and building campus community have on academic outcomes. I hope this study will encourage future researchers and graduate students to understand the lived experiences of diverse college students and their need for a strong campus community and space to increase their academic success on campus. There is an increasing need to acknowledge the missing voices in dominant research paradigms and models in higher education through continued research and redefining the values and relevancy they hold to diverse students, especially Native American college students. The implication for practice is for administrators, student affairs professionals, and faculty to better understand the values that Native American college students place on family and community and how this is directly tied to academic outcomes. To bring to light the voices of this student population, who are often left out of the consciousness in planning, recruitment, and student services, is paramount in creating safe and welcoming spaces on campus for Native American college students.

CONCLUSION

In this chapter, I offer a better understanding, including literature and lived experiences, of the current state of Native American college students that ties the importance of family and community to academic outcomes and motivation to pursue a degree. This is a starting point, highlighting the voices of Native American college students and the values they bring to campus, as well as the importance of community and creating family-type support systems on campus to increase academic success. Native American college students bring their cultural values and desire to give back to campus. It is up to each university and college to nurture and honor these values so they can see Native American college students flourish and become leaders on campus and within their respective communities.

REFERENCES

Almeida, D. A. (1999). *Postsecondary financial aid for American Indians and Alaska Natives.* Charleston, WV: ERIC Clearinghouse on Rural Education & Small Schools.

Astin, A. W. (1982). *Minorities in higher education.* San Francisco, CA: Jossey-Bass.

Belgarde, M. J. (1992). The performance and persistence of American Indian undergraduate students at Stanford University (Doctoral dissertation, Stanford University). *Dissertation Abstracts International,* 53, 05A.

Benjamin, D., Chambers, S., & Reiterman, G. (1993). A focus on American Indian college persistence. *Journal of American Indian Education, 32*(2), 24–39.

Bowker, A. (1992). The American Indian female dropout. *Journal of American Indian Education, 31*(3), 3–21.

Brown, L. L., & Robinson Kurpius, S. E. (1997). Psychosocial factors influencing academic persistence of American Indian college students. *Journal of College Student Development, 38*(1), 3–12.

Coffman, D. L., & Gilligan, T. D. (2002–2003). Social support, stress, and self-efficacy: Effects on students' satisfaction. *Journal of College Student Retention: Research, Theory, and Practice, 4*(1), 53–66.

Creswell, J. W. (1998). *Qualitative inquiry and research design: Choosing among five traditions.* Thousand Oaks, CA: Sage.

Deloria, V., & Wildcat, D. (2001). *Power and place: Indian education in America.* Golden, CO: Fulcrum.

DeVoe, J., Darling-Churchill, K., & Snyder, T. (2008). *Status and trends in the education of American Indians and Alaska Natives: 2008.* Report to the U.S. Department of Education, NCES 2008–084.

Deyhle, D., & Swisher, K. G. (1997). Research in American Indian and Alaska Native education: From assimilation to self-determination. *Review of Research in Education, 22*(1), 113–194.

Dodd, J. M., Garcia, F. M., Meccage, C., & Nelson, J. R. (1995). American Indian student retention. *Journal of the National Association of Student Personnel Administrators, 33*(1), 72–78.

Falk, D. R., & Aitken, L. P. (1984). Promoting retention among American Indian college students. *Journal of American Indian Education, 23*(2), 24–31.

Garrod, A., & Larimore, C. (1997). *First person, first peoples: Native American college graduates tell their life stories.* Ithaca, NY: Cornell University Press.

Guillory, R., & Wolverton, M. (2008). It's about family: Native American student persistence in higher education. *Journal of Higher Education, 79*(1), 58–87.

Heavyrunner, I., & DeCelles, R. (2002). Family education model: Meeting the student retention challenge. *Journal of American Indian Higher Education, 41*(2), 29–37.

Heavyrunner, I., & Morris, J. S. (1997). Traditional Native culture and resilience. *Research & Practice, 5*(1), 1–6.

Huffman, T. E. (2001). Resistance theory and the transculturation hypothesis as explanations of college attrition and persistence among culturally traditional American Indian students. *Journal of American Indian Education, 40*(3), 1–23.

Huffman, T. E. (2003). A comparison of personal assessments of the college experience among reservation and nonreservation American Indian students. *Journal of American Indian Education, 42*(2), 1–16.

Jackson, A. P., & Smith, S. A. (2001). Postsecondary transitions among Navajo students. *Journal of American Indian Education, 40*(2), 28–47.

Jackson, A. P., Smith, S. A., & Hill, C. L. (2003). Academic persistence among Native American college students. *Journal of College Student Development, 44*(4), 548–565.

Jenkins, M. (1999). Factors which influence the success or failure of American Indian/Native American college students. *Research and Teaching in Developmental Education, 15*(20), 49–52.

Kalsner, L. (1992). The influence of developmental and emotional factors on success in college. *Higher Education Extension Service Review, 3*(2), 3–13.

Larimore, J., & McClellan, G. (2005). Native American student retention in U.S. postsecondary education. In M. Fox, S. Lowe, & G. McClellan (Eds.), *Serving Native American students* (pp. 17–29). San Francisco, CA: Jossey-Bass.

Lin, R., LaCounte, D., & Eder, J. (1988). A study of Native American students in a predominantly white college. *Journal of American Indian Education, 27*(3), 8–15.

Lincoln, Y., & Guba, E. (1985). *Naturalistic inquiry.* Newbury Park, CA: Sage.

Locust, C. (1988). Wounding the spirit: Discrimination and traditional American Indian belief systems. *Harvard Educational Review, 58*(3), 315–330.

Martin, S., & Thunder, A. (2013). Incorporating Native Culture into student affairs. In H. Shotton, S. Lowe, & S. Waterman (Eds.), *Understanding Native students in higher education* (pp. 39–51). Sterling, VA: Stylus.

Mihesuah, D., & Wilson, A. (2004). *Indigenizing the academy: Transforming scholarship and empowering communities.* Lincoln: University of Nebraska Press.

Minthorn, R. (2014). Perspectives and values of leadership for Native American college students in non-Native colleges and universities. *Journal of Leadership Education, 13*(2), 67–95.

National Center for Education Statistics (NCES). (2010). *Condition of education 2010,* Table A-23-2 (NCES 2010–028).

Patton, M. (2002). *Qualitative research & evaluation methods* (3rd ed.). Thousand Oaks, CA: Sage.

Pavel, D. M., & Padilla, R. V. (1993). American Indian and Alaska Native postsecondary departure: An example of assessing a mainstream model using national longitudinal data. *Journal of American Indian Education, 32*(2), 1–23.

Polkinghorne, D. E. (1989). Phenomenological research methods. In R. S. Valle & S. Hailing (Eds.), *Existential-phenomenological perspectives in psychology: Exploring the breadth of human experience* (pp. 41–60). New York, NY: Plenum.

Pottinger, R. (1989). Disjunction to higher education: American Indian students in the southwest. *Anthropology & Education Quarterly, 20*(4), 326–344.

Scott, W. F. (1986). Attachment to Indian culture and "difficult situation": A study of American Indian college students. *Youth and Society, 17*(4), 381–395.

Shotton, H. J., Lowe, S. C., & Waterman, S. J. (Eds.). (2013). *Beyond the asterisk: Understanding Native students in higher education.* Sterling, VA: Stylus.

Swisher, K., & Deyhle, D. (1989, August). The styles of learning are different, but the teaching is just the same: Suggestions for teachers of American Indian youth, *Journal of American Indian Education* [Special issue], 1–14.

Tierney, W. G. (1992). *Official encouragement, institutional discouragement: Minorities in academe—The Native American experience.* Norwood, NJ: Ablex.

Tippeconnic Fox, M. J., Lowe, S. C., & McClellan, G. S. (2005). From discussion to action. In M. J. Tippeconnic Fox, S. C. Lowe, & G. McClellan (Eds.), *Serving Native American students* (pp. 95–98). San Francisco, CA: Jossey-Bass.

U.S. Department of Education, National Center for Education Statistics. (2011). *The Condition of Education 2011* (NCES 2011–033), Indicator 26.

Wright, B. (1985). Programming success: Special student services and the American Indian college student. *Journal of American Indian Education, 24*(1), 1–7.

Wright, B., & Tierney, W. G. (1991). American Indians in higher education: A history of cultural conflict. *Change, 23*(2), 11–19.

CHAPTER FOURTEEN

Leveraging THE Cultural Wealth IN Family AND Friend Networks

An Examination of Undocumented Latino/a College Students' Support Systems and Academic Achievement

AYANA ALLEN

Approximately 65,000 to 80,000 undocumented Latino/a students graduate from U.S. high schools every year, a quarter of whom matriculate to institutions of higher education (Perez, 2012). Although these students may encounter similar struggles and barriers as their fellow Latino/a students on college campuses (Baker & Robnett, 2012), undocumented students often encounter increased institutional and societal exclusion and rejection (Gonzales, 2012; Perez, Espinoza, Ramos, Coronado, & Cortes, 2009). In the midst of seemingly insurmountable obstacles including poverty, discrimination, lack of financial aid, emotional and psychological distress, academic achievement gaps, and personal challenges (Contreras, 2011; Perez, 2012; Perez, Cortes, Ramos, & Coronado, 2010), undocumented students are thriving as contributing members of their campus communities and society at large. In light of the looming remnants of the uninstated federal DREAM (Development, Relief, and Education for Alien Minors) Act and new immigration policies such as Deferred Action for Childhood Arrivals (DACA), there is a growing need for relevant, timely scholarship pertaining to undocumented Latino/a student experiences in postsecondary institutions. In this chapter, I glean from Yosso's (2005) discussion of cultural wealth as it relates to familial, social, and navigational capital as tools that undocumented Latino/a students can leverage to achieve academic success in postsecondary contexts. Additionally, in this chapter

I highlight the results from a qualitative research study that explored the roles of family, friends, and social networks in the social, emotional, and academic achievement of undocumented Latino/a college students.

THE ASSETS OF CULTURAL WEALTH AND FAMILIAL CAPITAL

Yosso (2005) contends that communities of color foster inter- and intra-community assets that are often negated, neglected, and ignored by traditionally hegemonic institutional structures in society. The institution of the "American college" represents the hallmark of individualistic and meritocratic values that often perpetuates deficit positionalities, consequently rejecting the cultural wealth of diverse communities. According to Yosso, *cultural wealth* is an array of knowledge, skills, abilities, and contacts possessed and utilized by communities of color to survive and resist macro and micro forms of oppression. The various forms of capital encapsulated in cultural wealth are aspirational capital, linguistic capital, familial capital, social capital, navigational capital, and resistant capital. For the sake of this discussion, familial capital will be utilized as a springboard to catapult the understanding of the role of families, friends, and communities in the success and achievement of undocumented Latino/a college students. *Familial capital* consists of the cultural knowledges nurtured among families that carry a sense of community history, memory, and cultural intuition (Yosso, 2005). Familial capital requires a commitment to community and the expansion of the concept of family to a broader understanding of kinship that is nurtured by extended familial ties and larger conceptions of community. Within the family structure, models of caring, coping, and education inform moral, emotional, educational, and occupational awareness (Yosso, 2005).

When social networks are viewed as families, marginalized students such as undocumented Latino/a college students defy cultural deficiency models that often blame families for the underachievement of students (Enriquez, 2011). Moreover, the prevalence of strong parental moral support for schooling has been "consigned to invisibility" and overlooked by many schools (Auerbach, 2006, p. 278). In contrast to these deficit frameworks, the family is the key institution for socialization and resource accumulation as well as the central referent, source of support, and obligation for individuals (Auerbach, 2006). In this vein, the role of family, friends, and even self are critical assets (purveyors of cultural wealth) that impact the persistence of undocumented college students. In as far as this discussion will address the role of family and friend networks, it is also important to examine the historical and contemporary landscape of undocumented student realities within institutions of higher education and within society at large.

UNDOCUMENTED LATINO/A STUDENTS, THE DREAM AND DACA

The plight of undocumented students has been well documented (Contreras, 2011; Perez, 2012; Perez et al., 2010; Schmid, 2013). Undocumented Latino/a students were granted the undeniable right to a K–12 education through the 1982 Supreme Court ruling in *Plyler v. Doe*, which grants undocumented children unobstructed access to public education (Contreras, 2011; Perez et al., 2010); however, equal access to an education stops when students graduate from high school. Perez and colleagues (2010) note, "Upon graduating and after extensive public educational investment, thousands of college-eligible undocumented students are unable to pursue higher education due to their legal status, federal law, and limited financial resources" (p. 36). The federal DREAM Act, which was first introduced in the U.S. Senate and House in 2001 and reintroduced in 2011 (Schmid, 2013), proposed legislation that strives to provide a pathway to legalization for undocumented immigrant students (Gonzales, 2010) as well as permanent residency (Schmid, 2013). In 2010, the bill was blocked in the Senate by six votes, which would have cut off a filibuster and brought it to the floor for a vote (Schmid, 2013). This lack of a comprehensive federal DREAM Act has left states to develop their own interpretations of the "educational rights of undocumented students and higher education" (Schmid, 2013, p. 697). On June 15, 2012, the Deferred Action for Childhood Arrivals (DACA) policy was passed through an executive order by President Barack Obama. DACA affords undocumented students who meet certain criteria temporary protection from deportation and grants students work permits and other benefits, such as access to drivers' licenses. DACA is only a temporary solution that does not provide a secure pathway to citizenship as the DREAM Act would, had it been voted into law.

NAVIGATING THE COLLEGE TERRAIN

The pathway to and through college is often complicated and strenuous for undocumented Latino/a students, and K–12 educational experiences greatly impact their higher educational trajectory. Gonzalez (2010) notes that students' positions within the school hierarchy structures impact vulnerable populations. According to Baker and Robnett (2012), Latino/a college students are less likely than any other racial and ethnic group to persist. Extant literature also documents a large discrepancy between the number of Latino/a students who initially enroll at postsecondary institutions and those who persist through to graduation. This discrepancy has been attributed to the myriad of stressors they face in college (Cano & Castillo, 2010; Llamas & Ramos-Sanchez, 2013) such as the lack of academic preparedness (Campos et al., 2009), social-emotional stress (Perez et al., 2010;

Llamas & Ramos-Sanchez, 2013; Torres & Solberg, 2001), and the lack of financial resources (Contreras, 2011; Gonzalez, 2010). Gonzales (2010) discusses the barriers faced by undocumented students in accessing affordable higher education, suggesting, "Given the profile of most immigrant families, the cost of college is prohibitive, if not restrictive for undocumented students" (p. 480). In the same vein, although in-state tuition is a possibility in 13 states throughout the nation (Schmid, 2013), there persists a strong anti-immigrant climate on college campuses as well as the looming fear of deportation for students and their families (Contreras, 2011). Even though these barriers to access, equity, and achievement exist, undocumented students leverage their respective communities and patch together resources provided by their social networks in order to "access social capital by a collective understanding of indirect reciprocity where resources and support are expected to be paid forward out of solidarity and commitment to community empowerment and social justice" (Enriquez, 2011, p. 477). Moreover, Yosso, Smith, Ceja, and Solorzano (2009) contend, "Latinos foster academic and social counter spaces in which they build culturally supportive community and develop skills to critically navigate between their worlds of school and home" (p. 660). Such leveraging of their own personal strengths and those of family, friends, and other social networks serve as mitigating factors and valuable sources of capital.

FAMILIAL CAPITAL THROUGH MORAL AND EMOTIONAL SUPPORT

The role of the family, and particularly parental roles in education, are often structured by social class and race/ethnicity while mediated by cultural belief systems and parent-child relationships (Auerbach, 2006). To say the least, parents are undeniable stakeholders in the educational trajectory of their children. In the case of undocumented students who have completed high school and are now seeking higher education, parents continue to play a vital role in student success. Auerbach (2006) examined Latino/a parents' moral support for their college-going children, which was perpetuated through "verbal encouragement, cautionary tales, and other 'consejos' (narrative advice)" (p. 278). Auerbach's findings indicate that moral capital is the greatest contribution that immigrant parents personally feel that they can make to their children's education. Although a very important characteristic, Auerbach discovered that moral support is not enough for first-generation college students to reach their college goals; instead, moral support serves as more of a mitigating factor for persistence if students have equitable access to advanced courses, individualized college counseling, and other resources. Likewise, Enriquez (2011) found that parents and families are the primary source of emotional support for students through their sympathy, encouragement, and motivation, as well as the catalyst for their persistence as they provide educational expectations and positive messaging about school.

Torres and Solberg (2001) investigated a model of self-efficacy, stress, social integration, and family support and examined the interconnectedness of these factors in predicting college persistence intentions. The authors state

> College students with high-perceived availability of family support build connections with faculty and other students and believe in their ability to complete their academic goals. In addition, for Latino students, one implication of growing up within a collectivist culture is the central role of family connections and harmony on their health. (p. 54)

Jimenez-Silva, Jimenez-Hernandez, Luevanos, Jimenez, and Jimenez (2009) provide autobiographical accounts of their experiences and recall the collective strength of their family support as all five siblings successfully navigated the college terrain. Beyond emotional and moral support, it has also been documented that family plays a critical role in the academic achievement of undocumented Latino/a students.

FAMILIAL CAPITAL AND ACADEMIC ACHIEVEMENT

Familial capital and support can also positively impact the academic achievement of undocumented Latino/a college students. Ong, Phinney, and Dennis (2006) explored the protective cultural resources that enable Latino/a college students to achieve positive outcomes in the face of socioeconomic inequalities. Through their work, they demonstrate that individual-and-family-level influences modify the effects of being from a low SES background in a positive direction. In particular, they highlighted the positive achievement outcomes that may ensue from protective profiles of family interdependence, parental support, and ethnic identity. The authors argue that the emergence of positive adaptation in the context of adversity eventuates from multiple influences that come in the form of both baseline resources (strong family interdependence and high ethnic identity) and intervening processes (i.e., consistent parental support): "Academic achievement is linked both to individual and family level influences. When present, these influences appear to be especially important to the academic success of Latino students who are low in SES" (Ong et al., p. 973). The results of their study demonstrate that family-level factors are positively related to academic achievement. Furthermore, over time their results suggest that persistent levels of parental support of education are accompanied by elevation in GPA performance, further implicating a robust relationship between parental support and college adjustment. Similarly, Torres and Solberg (2001) found that the availability of family support associates strongly with academic self-efficacy, which supports the ways in which family support is critical to the "developmental framework from which confident learners emerge" (p. 61). Parents' frames of reference become social capital that students can leverage for motivation and the push toward academic success (Enriquez, 2011). Beyond the support received within familial structures, friend and peer support is also critical to undocumented Latino/a student success.

PEER SUPPORT THROUGH SOCIAL AND NAVIGATIONAL CAPITAL

Strong peer networks and friendships are critical to the success of undocumented Latino/a college students because peers provide social capital and navigational capital (Enriquez, 2011; Mira, Morris, & Cardoza, 2003). Yosso (2005) defines *social capital* as networks of people and community resources and *navigational capital* as the skills of maneuvering through social institutions such as college campuses. Llamas and Ramos-Sanchez (2013) indicate that peer support is important to academic adjustment and success for college students as the Latino/a students in their study navigate intragroup marginalization versus acculturation. They assert that a lack of perceived support can negatively affect college adjustment but also influence poorer academic achievement and psychological wellness. In comparing the role of parents versus peers, Mira and colleagues (2003) compared the relative contribution of perceived social support from family and friends to psychological adjustment to determine whether family or friend support moderated the effects of such stresses. The authors suggest

> It is important to distinguish between support from family and friends because each does not often consist of the same type and amount of support, responsibilities, and obligations. College students may rely on or benefit from family and friend support to different extents and the provision of information, comfort, emotional support, and material aid provided by family and friends may also differ. (p. 237)

The findings indicate that there is more perceived support from family in the domain of pursuing higher education, and friends offer greater support through coping with the full burden of the challenges they face while navigating college.

METHOD

Herein lies the description and findings of a qualitiative research study (specifically a narrative analysis) that explored the lived experiences of undocumented Latino/a college students. The study examined various aspects of their collegiate experiences including academic, social, and emotional realities, and the ways in which they leveraged their multiple relationships among family members, friends, and others. For the purposes of this discussion, findings pertaining to family and friend relationships are highlighted to support the current discussion of the significance of family and friend networks for undocumented Latino/a college students.

Theoretical Framework

This research study was grounded in a Latino crital race theory (LatCrit) framework. LatCrit is a theory that elucidates Latino/as multidimensional identities through the intersectionality of racism, sexism, classism, and other forms of oppression that are unique to Latino/as. Moreover, LatCrit in education examines the ways in which the marginalization and oppression of Latino/a students is perpetuated through hegemonic educational structures and discourses (Delgado Bernal, 2002). Villenas, Deyhle, and Parker (1999) discuss the power of LatCrit, stressing, "It is useful in making clear how Latino students become recipients of the fury of an anti-immigrant, anti-Latino, xenophobic rhetoric that is gripping the nation and turning back the clock on the gains made for civil and human rights" (p. 35). LatCrit provides the lens through which to examine the unique experiences of undocumented Latino/a college students in this study.

Participants

This study sought the ideal candidate of an undocumented student of Latino/a descent who was currently enrolled at a two- or four-year institution of higher education (IHE) or a recent graduate of an IHE. Students were excluded from participation if they were American citizens or legal residents, not of Latino/a descent, and not enrolled at an institution of higher education. Potential participants were initially solicited through a detailed email that explained the research study and requirements of participation. This email was dispersed to alumni of three high schools located in the southern part of the United States. Interested students who self-identified as undocumented and who were enrolled in college were asked to recommend other potential participants who met the selection criteria, wherein snowball sampling ensued. Six students (4 females and 2 males) participated in this study, meeting the following criteria: (1) currently enrolled in a two-year or four-year institution of higher education or a recent graduate; (2) self-identified as undocumented status; and (3) of Latino/a descent. Three participants attended large public colleges, one attended a meduim public college, one attended a community college, and one participant attended an Ivy League college (see Table 14.1 for participant information).

Table 14.1. Participant Information.

Alias	Gender	Type of Institution	Level
Anita	Female	Large Public	Postgraduate
Leslie	Female	Community College	Sophomore
Juan	Male	Ivy League	Junior
Silas	Male	Large Public	Sophomore
Marianna	Female	Medium Public	Junior
Geneva	Female	Large Public	Sophomore

Data Collection and Analysis

Each student participated in a 1–1.5 hour face-to-face or phone audio–recorded interview. The interviews nurtured a storytelling atmosphere that was supported by the use of open-ended questions. Extensive observational notes were taken during each interview. I employed narrative analytic methods to excavate meaning and understanding as investigated through the storytelling framework of the interviews. I utilized a holistic-content perspective approach of analysis, which considers the entire narrative and focuses on its content to support emerging themes (Lieblich, Tuval-Mashiach, & Zibler, 1998). Each narrative was carefully analyzed in its entirety so as to discover a global impression of the told narrative. Within the global impression analysis, I highlighted various emerging themes with the purpose of making sense of experience, and the construction and communication of meaning (Chase, 1995). I further highlighted themes within each individual narrative as well as themes that emerged across all narratives. Reported data reflects universal themes across all narratives.

Trustworthiness and dependability

Trustworthiness and dependability were established through the triangulation of collected data. Triangulation is the use of multiple sources of data or data collection methods to confirm emerging findings (Merriam, 2009). Dependability in qualitative research represents whether findings in a given study are consistent with the data collected and presented. To triangulate the data I utilized data collected through the interviews, extensive observational and interview notes that I collected during the interviews, as well as my researcher journal/audit trail, which I utilized to capture my thoughts, ideas, and findings throughout the entire research process. I also employed member checking as a tool to triangulate data. Member checking entails sharing data and interpretations with participants to ascertain if findings are plausible. I collaborated with participants throughout the data analysis process and utilized their support for clarification and extended analysis of the data.

FINDINGS

The findings of this study strongly demonstrate that family and friend relationships are paramount to the success of undocumented Latino/a college students. The universal themes of family and friend support weaved in and out of all six narratives. Findings indicate that the relationships that the participants share with their family and friends are equally important although different in the scope, level, and type of support received. The emerging themes within the overarching theme of family support are (1) sacrifice, (2) encouragement, and (3) financial support. The major themes pertaining to friend networks and support are (1) encouragement, (2) academic motivation, and (3) navigational capital. These themes are consistent with the extant literature that highlights the intricate network of support that is needed and often received from family and friends for undocumented college students (Gonzales, 2010; Mira et al., 2003; Perez et al., 2009; Perez et al., 2010).

Family Support

Sacrifice

The theme of sacrifice was a consistent theme among all six narratives and was depicted in a myriad of ways in the findings. Sacrifice emerged early on in each narrative as participants began to tell stories of their families' selfless acts of sacrifice throughout their transitions to the United States. All but two of them arrived in the United States before the age of 10. The mere act of leaving their home countries to pursue an unknown future in the United States was an incredible sacrifice made on the parts of their parents. For example, Geneva came to the country as a fifth grader and her family made great sacrifices. For many years her father lived in the United States and worked to provide for his family back in Mexico until her parents made the decision that they would all reunite in the United States. Geneva and her sister were told that they would be entering the United States illegally and they were well aware of the risks and continued sacrifices of their families. Geneva stated, "I remember my dad working hard for pesos and sending us money from the United States, we were separated for many years. We had to sell our house in Mexico in order to come to the U.S." Silas came to the United States in the ninth grade knowing very little English. His family was an upper-middle-class family in

Mexico where Silas benefited from several luxuries that, as he stated, "typical Mexicans" did not experience. His family was economically influential in their town and he attended boarding schools. However, his mother sacrificed the privileged life that they lived in Mexico to come to the United States for greater opportunities for Silas and his brother. Silas stated:

> We sacrificed our sweet life in Mexico to come to the States. I was so insecure with a blurry future ahead. When I arrived in the U.S. it was the first time that I had been told no. My lack of citizenship held me back from so many opportunities. For once money didn't and couldn't buy me opportunity.

His journey was a little different from the other participants for the fact that he entered the country legally through a temporary tourist visa. The tourist visa granted him access to the United States but included very critical guidelines and restrictions, one of which that individuals were prohibited to attend school, work, or remain in the United States beyond their travel dates. Quickly thereafter, Silas enrolled in high school.

After successfully making the venture to the States, many struggles awaited several of the participants and there were consistent sacrifices made by their families almost daily. Anita came to the United States when she was nine years old and entered the fourth grade with very little English background. Her family made the journey to the United States for schooling opportunities for her and her siblings and work opportunities for her father. Within two years after coming to this country, Anita's father was deported, completely ripping her family apart. Thankfully her father returned with a visitor's permit and they were reunited. Anita noted:

> We always lived in fear and never felt quite normal, but my parents made so, so, so many sacrifices so that we could one day be successful and have a great life. I am a product of their sacrifices today.

Sacrifice was a common theme throughout the participants' current position as college students. Many noted that their parents continue to make sacrifices so that they can remain in college and earn their degrees. This sacrifice has inspired the participants to work hard and push toward their dreams. For example, Juan noted the continued sacrifices that his family has made in order for him to attend an Ivy League college in the northeast, where Juan received a full scholarship as an undocumented student. Juan expressed his parents' fear and hesitation in allowing him to go to college so far from home and their sacrifices in order for him to do so:

> When I first went to college, I had to drive across the country without my family because I couldn't fly due to my status and it was really expensive. I see my parents working all the time and it's their biggest sacrifice. They make it easy for me to focus on school and do well because that is the only duty that I have.

Marianna encountered a unique set of circumstances in her high school years when she became pregnant at 16 and became a mom her senior year of high school. Her family made and continues to make many sacrifices so that Marianna can attend college full-time as well as support her son. Marianna stated:

> My parents have made a lot of sacrifices for me, especially when I had my son. My mom takes care of my son when I go to school and my Dad works hard to support both of us, my sister and her kids, and my little brother. They have sacrificed and risked so much for us to have a better life. I would not be in college right now if it were not for my parents and their support.

In tandem with the sacrifices that their families have made for them, undocumented Latino/a college students have noted that family encouragement and motivation received has been a driving force in their success.

Encouragement

Another pervasive theme throughout the narratives was family encouragement, inspiration, and motivation. The struggles expressed by the participants as they attempted to navigate their transitions to the United States as children, and adjust to school and life in a foreign land were plagued with stories of hardship and the desire to give up. Some of these same sentiments trickled into their experiences in college. The encouragement and inspiration they received from their families were cited as critical to their abilities to persist through school. Also, encouragement served as a mitigating factor for feelings of insufficiency as cited by Leslie, feelings of isolation as cited by Anita, feelings of insecurity and uncertainty as cited by Silas, and feelings of not being smart enough as cited by Marianna and Juan as college students. Juan stated:

> Although they weren't able to help me with homework, they did motivate me a lot and always reminded me that education was my way out. So even though it was hard, they still motivated me to keep going and to chase my dreams.

Leslie was the one outlier of the group in terms of the encouragement she received from her family concerning her dream to attend college:

> My family was very supportive when I graduated from high school and they were just supportive in my decisions in general. When I told them that I wasn't going to continue to college after high school due to not getting any financial aid because I was undocumented, they were ok with that. After taking a year off, surprisingly when I told them I wanted to go to college, they weren't super supportive either which I was confused. They wanted me to save my money on other things. My mom especially, but I told her that the route to college was the best way to go.

Similar to family encouragement and motivation, financial support is another theme that emerged in this study.

Financial support

Financial support from families was one of the greatest assets in the family support overarching theme, particularly as it pertains to students' ability to persist in college with their families' financial support. All of the participants except for Leslie indicated that their families provided a significant amount of financial support for them. Furthermore, these five also indicated that their parents did not want them to work while in college but only focus on their studies. As indicated in the extant literature, the participants in this study also suffered from a lack of financial aid and assistance due to their undocumented status. All but Juan attended public schools in the southern part of the United States in one of the 13 states that grants in-state tuition to undocumented students. Silas's narrative describes the financial support that he received from his mother:

> My mother has spent her whole life saving for us to go to college. She pays my full tuition. I am unable to even get a work study job in the library to help out because of my status, but my mom continues to support me in whatever I need. We have to be very cautious with money because we have limited amounts, but my mom tells me to keep working hard and she will take care of the rest.

Juan chimed in with similar sentiments:

> Ever since I was little, my mom and dad would say our job is to work and your job is to get good grades. So the financial help from my parents has always been there and it was hard emotionally but they knew it was for a better future for me. When I started college they didn't want me to worry about work or bills or anything, it was very easy to focus on education.

Other stories of families working hard to provide for their children while in college were expressed throughout the other narratives.

Friend Support

Encouragement

Similar to family encouragement, the encouragement of friends was a pervasive theme in the narratives. Participants noted that childhood friends, high school friends, and college friends alike played critical roles in supporting them through college. For example, Anita immediately sought a friend network at her large public university and joined a sorority, which was a great support for her during this time because her parents got divorced. She admitted that many of her friends did not know that she was undocumented, yet they were her greatest source of encouragement on her college campus. It was through her friend relationships that she further internalized persistence, a "whatever it takes" mindset and the will to keep going.

Geneva discussed the encouragement that she received from her friends in various circles:

> My high school friends were all college oriented and I had great support from them. We were always pushing each other to go to college. I still talk to my friends from high school and they are an example to me. I also have friends from church and they are very spiritual and they tell me that God is by my side and I can do all things through Christ. Their support is both academically and spiritually and emotionally. My friends in college are always supportive.

Juan also leveraged the encouragement he received from his friends when he considered leaving his college to go back home. He noted that when he was down and depressed, his friends often reminded him that he was smart, that he belonged at their Ivy League college, and that he would make it. Leslie discussed her friend support in her pursuit of higher education as well. In light of the lack of support she received from her family in terms of her pursuit of college, her friends were very instrumental in her enrolling at a local community college:

> My friends have played a big role because they don't judge me because I didn't go to college right after high school. I have friends that are out of state in college and we keep in touch and they are always telling me how proud they are of me and it doesn't matter when I finish college but to keep going.

Academic motivation

Academic motivation was another theme highlighted in the narratives, specifically as the participants all discussed their difficult academic transition to college. Leslie noted:

> My high school friends and I would help each other out and push each other academically. We would sometimes compete with our grades and academics. We still hold each other accountable. One of my best friends transferred back home and I'm so glad she is back because we have study sessions together and support each other.

Anita was on academic probation for a few semesters until she found her way academically. Her friends were very supportive of one another and inspired each other to do well in their classes. Likewise, Geneva stated: "My friends and I are always trying to take classes together so that we can support each other. And we make study groups so we can study for tests and projects." The academic motivation and support that the students received from their friends was noted as a critical factor in their academic success. For instance, while Anita reflected on her undergraduate experience, she referenced the academic support of her college friends and some of the study habits she picked up from them as reasons by which she was doing so well in her graduate studies.

Navigational capital

Navigational capital, the skills of maneuvering through the social institution of college (Yosso, 2005) was another finding of friend support. Findings indicated that friends supported one another in helping to navigate the college campuses, what courses to take with which professors, who to speak with at financial aid, what clubs to join, and what dorms had the most Latino/as. Leslie stated: "My friends know what it is like to be in college, how hard it is." The shared lived experiences and helping each other through navigating college was cited as imperative to their success on campus. Silas stated:

> Information is powerful. You don't just have to be smart here to make it. You also have to know what to do, where to go, and who to talk to in order to survive. I have learned a lot about my college and how to do this whole thing from my friends. It is all about the system and working it.

Juan discussed his friend networks:

> My girlfriend has always been there and I made a really good friend at my college who is beyond smart and he has been helpful to me and helps me open my eyes and see things realistically. I'm very grateful for him and if I didn't have him I wouldn't be where I am. When it comes to motivating and encouraging me and navigating college support I get it from my friends.

DISCUSSION AND CONCLUSION

As demonstrated in this research study as well as through the extant literature, family and friends of undocumented Latino/a college students are valuable assets and capital in their lived experiences. Beyond the support that students receive within their intimate social networks, institutions of higher education must also play their part in ensuring the success of undocumented Latino/a students on their campuses. For example, colleges and universities should not advocate for Latino/a students to adapt to the school climate and culture; rather, institutions should provide culturally relevant curricula to allow students to feel validated and represented and culturally relevant mentoring to assist in helping students balance academic, financial, and familial responsibilities (Jimenez et al., 2009). Baker and Robnett (2012) assert:

> While support from family members is found to positively influence academic success of minority students prior to college, during college it may be more important for support to come from within the college environment in order to enhance students' adjustment to their new environment. Regular interaction with anyone outside of the college environment, such as family or employment obligations, may hinder academic success by focusing on the student's roles outside of school. (p. 326)

Cano and Castillo (2010) encourage universities to increase family support and "indirectly minimize the effect of White attitudinal marginalization" (p. 228) through the development of programs that promote parental involvement and educate parents about college experiences so that parents have a better understanding of the demands and benefits of higher education for their students. Furthermore, "institutions of higher education should provide the types of resources and outreach programs that tap into the strength of the Latino family" (Jimenez et al., 2009, p. 743). This once again highlights the importance of leveraging family capital as a component of cultural wealth (Yosso, 2005).

Institutions must also foster a myriad of opportunities for undocumented Latino/a students to get plugged in and connected on campus, such as involvement in student groups and the improvement of the efficacy of students' study groups (Baker & Robnett, 2012). Baker and Robnett (2012) found that programs that connect students with peers who are academically successful may improve the GPA and retention rates of underrepresented students, such as undocumented students. Moreover, they found that Latino/as who participated in student clubs are more likely to stay enrolled and feel connected to the college. Even still, there is an ongoing debate as to whether school success is a matter of agency or structure and whether students actively build such networks or if successful relationship building is facilitated through school (Gonzales, 2010). One thing is for sure, social support from within the college environment, as well as from close social networks such as family and friends, plays a large part in the retention and success of undocumented Latino/a college students: "College student programs and interventions targeted at promoting the academic success of Latino college students should strive to enhance both sources of support" (Mira et al., 2003, p. 247). Enriquez (2011) encourages us to expand the definition of family as well as reframe the origins of support networks so that nonfamilial individuals, such as peers, counselors, and institutions, who build a lifeline of support for undocumented college student success are enforced. This combination of on-campus social support, off-campus ties, and the perceived college environment (Baker & Robnett, 2012) is critical to undocumented Latino/a college student success. Furthermore, the cultural wealth and support gleaned from family and friends is instrumental to the success and academic achievement of undocumented Latino/a students.

REFERENCES

Auerbach, S. (2006). If the student is good, let him fly: Moral support for college among Latino immigrant parents. *Journal of Latinos in Education, 5*(4), 275–292.

Baker, C., & Robnett, B. (2012). Race, social support and college student retention: A case study. *Journal of College Student Development, 53*(2), 325–335.

Campos, C. M. T., Phinney, J. S., Perez-Brena, N., Kim, C., Ornelas, B., Nemanim, L., Kallemeyn, D. M. P., Mihecoby, A., & Ramirez, C. (2009). A mentor-based targeted intervention for high-risk Latino college freshman: A pilot study. *Journal of Hispanic Higher Education, 8*(2), 158–178.

Cano, M. A., & Castillo, L. G. (2010). The role of enculturation and acculturation on Latina college student distress. *Journal of Hispanic Higher Education, 9*(3), 221–231.

Chase, S. (1995). Taking narrative seriously: Consequences for method and theory in interview studies. In R. Josselson & A. Lieblich (Eds.), *Interpreting experience: The narrative study of lives* (pp. 1–26). Thousand Oaks, CA: Sage.

Contreras, F. (2011). *Achieving equity for Latino students: Expanding the pathway to higher education through public policy*. New York, NY: Teachers College Press.

Delgado Bernal, D. (2002). Critical race theory, Latino critical race theory, and critical race-gendered epistemologies: Recognizing students of color as holders and creators of knowledge. *Qualitative Inquiry, 8*(1), 105–126.

Enriquez, L. E. (2011). Because we feel pressure and we also feel the support: Examining the educational success of undocumented immigrant Latina/o students. *Harvard Educational Review, 81*(3), 476–499.

Gonzales, R. G. (2010). On the wrong side of the tracks: Understanding the effects of school structure and social capital in the educational pursuits of undocumented immigrant students. *Peabody Journal of Education, 85*, 469–485.

Jimenez-Silva, M., Jimenez-Hernandez, N., Luevanos, R., Jimenez, D., & Jimenez, A. (2009). Results not typical: One Latino family's experiences in higher education. *Harvard Educational Review, 79*(4), 730–744.

Lieblich, A., Tuval-Mashiach, R., & Zibler, T. (1998). *Narrative research: Reading, analysis, and interpretation*. Thousand Oaks, CA: Sage.

Llamas, J., & Ramos-Sanchez, L. (2013). Role of peer support on intragroup marginalization for Latino undergraduates. *Journal of Multicultural Counseling and Development, 41*, 158–168.

Merriam, S. B. (1998). *Qualitative research and case study applications in education*. San Francisco, CA: Jossey-Bass.

Mira, C. B., Morris, J. K., & Cardoza, D. (2003). Family or friends: Who plays a greater supportive role for Latino college students? *Cultural Diversity and Ethnic Minority Psychology, 9*(3), 236–250.

Ong, A. D., Phinney, J. S., & Dennis, J. (2006). Competence under challenge: Exploring the protective influence of parental support and ethnic identity in Latino college students. *Journal of Adolescence, 29*, 961–979.

Perez, W. (2012). *Americans by heart: Undocumented Latino students and the promise of higher education*. New York, NY: Teachers College Press.

Perez, W., Cortes, R. D., Ramos, K., & Coronado, H. (2010). Cursed and blessed: Examining the socioemotional and academic experiences of undocumented Latina and Latino college students. *New Directions for Student Services, 2010*(131), 35–51.

Perez, W., Espinoza, R., Ramos, K., Coronado, H. M., & Cortes, R. (2009). Academic resilience among undocumented Latino students. *Hispanic Journal of Behavioral Sciences, 31*(2), 149–181.

Rios-Aguilar, C., & Deli-Amen, R. (2012). Beyond getting in and fitting in: An examination of social networks and professional relevant social capital among Latina/o university students. *Journal of Hispanic Higher Education, 11*(2), 179–196.

Schmid, C. L. (2013). Undocumented childhood immigrants, the Dream Act and Deferred Action for Childhood Arrivals in the USA. *International Journal of Sociology and Social Policy, 33*(11–12), 693–707.

Torres, J. B., & Solberg, S. (2001). Role of self-efficacy, stress, social integration and family support in Latino college student persistence and health. *Journal of Vocational Behavior, 59*, 53–63.

Villenas, S., Deyhle, D., & Parker, L. (1999). Critical race theory and praxis: Chicano(a)/Latino(a) and Navajo struggles for dignity, educational equity, and social justice. In L. Parker, D. Deyhle, and S. Villenas (Eds.), *Race is … race isn't: Critical race theory and qualitative studies in education* (pp. 31–52). Boulder, CO: Westview.

Yosso, T. J. (2005). Whose culture has capital? A critical race theory discussion of community cultural wealth. *Race, Ethnicity, and Education, 8*(1), 69–91.

Yosso, T. J., Smith, W. A., Ceja, M., & Solorzano, D. G. (2009). Critical race theory, racial microaggressions, and campus racial climate for Latina/o undergraduates. *Harvard Educational Review, 79*(4), 659–690.

Afterword

The Case for Student Involvement and Desired Academic Outcomes for Today's Diverse College Populations

D. JASON DESOUSA

In light of lackluster national four- and six-year graduation rates in colleges and universities across the nation, a compelling question raised by Kuh, Kinzie, Schuh, Whitt, and associates (2005) remains timely, which is "Can institutions fashion policies, programs, and practices that encourage students to participate in educationally purposeful activities—so that a greater number of students [in this case diverse college populations] may achieve their potential?" (p. 10). The authors of this book address this timeless question and offer practical strategies to help higher education institutions craft engagement opportunities to support diverse students. As a 20-year higher education practitioner, many recommendations related to diverse college populations tend to be akin to "putting old wine in new glasses." *Student Involvement and Academic Outcomes: Implications for Diverse Populations*, however, provides a fresher, much-needed look at the conditions needed by college and university campuses to better promote the academic and personal success of students who have, generally, lagged behind other student subpopulations.

Important to note, the perspectives, viewpoints, and insights in these chapters undergird an important student engagement tenet proffered by Kuh and colleagues (2005): "What students *do* during college counts more in terms of what they learn and whether they will persist in college than who they are or even where they go to college" (p. 8). To optimize persistence to graduation from a student engagement model, however, great caution must be exercised not to exclude students who are not well understood or do not fit neatly into established student typologies, including African American and Latino males. In addition, even historically Black colleges and universities (HBCUs) may be excluding students who bring a less distinctive and understood set of characteristics and interests to such campuses. In other words, it could be that HBCUs (and perhaps other institutions) are surreptitiously marginalizing intra-diverse student populations. Yet, *Student Involvement and Academic Outcomes: Implications for Diverse Populations* provides a platform for deeper dialogue and debate to better engage an array of students and student groups regardless of institutional type.

Additionally, many of the authors of this book make an articulate case for institutions of higher education to rethink academic outcomes for diverse college populations. This is laudable given the profound competition for jobs as well as graduate and professional schools for which underrepresented students must compete. Thus, today's economic climate essentially mandates that colleges and universities, especially minority serving institutions (MSIs), develop the full potentialities (Bowen, 1977) of students. To their credit, most MSIs offer more than baccalaureate degrees to their students. These institutions devote copious human time and energy on skills that many of their students may not otherwise richly obtain (e.g., values clarification, character development, and leadership), making MSIs that promote unique and oftentimes unrecognized sets of talent development (Astin, 1993; Kuh, 1996; Kuh et al., 2005) practices. Still, today's MSIs should redouble their efforts to provide high-quality educational opportunities and experiences that overprepare graduates for the job market as well as graduate and professional schools. The recommendations offered in this book are an ideal starting point to achieve those outcomes.

Finally, if colleges and universities are committed to the academic and personal success of today's diverse college populations, fresher approaches are needed. Astin's (1993) student involvement theory or the concept of student engagement (Kuh et al., 2005), however, cannot be the sole linchpins. An important next step is getting diverse student populations interested and engaged in high impact practices (HIPs). In general, HIPs are organized around first-year seminars, service-learning, learning communities, study abroad, senior-culminating experiences, and diversity and global opportunities, and student-faculty interactions (Kuh, 2008). Students participating in HIPs typically persist to graduation at higher rates than their peers who do not and they academically outperform students not involved in HIPs, as measured by grade point averages (Brownell & Swaner, 2009). For first-year and senior students who participate in HIPs, Brownell and Swaner found that such students developed "deeper approaches" to student learning and development, which included "integrating ideas and diverse perspectives, discussing ideas with faculty and peers outside of class, analyzing and synthesizing ideas, applying theories, judging the value of information as well as one's own views, and trying to understand others' perspectives" (p. 26). HIPs particularly matter to diverse student populations because of the compensatory impact they tend to have on such students (Kuh, 2008). In particular, Brownell and Swaner found "substantial support for the value of these programs for students in general, and more specifically, for underserved students (underrepresented minority, low-income, and first-generation students)" (p. 26).

Implementing HIPs, however, could be a lofty proposition for many MSIs, as considerable resources are required to execute them. Most HIPs are Title III-supported, which are U.S. Department of Education–derived resources that help such institutions build institutional capacity for student retention, success, and development, among other important facets for such schools. Title III resources could be ideal to monetarily support HIPs, such as study abroad and other practices, expand the traditional campus boundaries to an array of outside historical, cultural, and educational venues. Yet, the U.S. Department of Education considers practices such as HIPs unallowable expenses—HIPs that could create opportunities for diverse college populations, particularly those that are in low-income tiers, to benefit from educationally purposeful practices that many other students enjoy. In the meantime, the recommendations that the authors of this book advance offer alternative opportunities for desired academic outcomes for today's diverse college populations.

D. Jason DeSousa
Fayetteville State University
Fayetteville, North Carolina

REFERENCES

Astin, A. W. (1993). *What matters in college: Four critical years revisited.* San Francisco, CA: Jossey-Bass.

Bowen, H. R. (1977). *Investment in learning: The individual and social value of American higher education.* San Francisco, CA: Jossey-Bass.

Brownell, J. E., & Swaner, L. E. (2009). High-impact practices: Applying the learning outcomes literature to the development of successful campus programs. *AAC&U, 11*(2), 26–30.

Kuh, G. D. (1996). Guiding principles for creating seamless learning environments for undergraduates. *Journal of College Student Development, 37*(2), 135–148.

Kuh, G. D. (2008). *High-impact educational practices: What they are, who has access to them, and why they matter.* Washington, DC: Association of American Colleges & Universities.

Kuh, G. D., Kinzie, J., Schuh, J., Whitt, E. J., & Associates. (2005). *Student success in college: Creating conditions that matter.* San Francisco, CA: Jossey-Bass.

Editor Biographies

Donald Mitchell Jr.'s PhD scholarship theoretically and empirically explores the effects of race, gender, and underrepresented identity intersections in higher education contexts, with a particular interest in historically Black fraternities and sororities and historically Black colleges and universities as microsystems and macrosystems of analysis.

He was awarded the Center for the Study of the College Fraternity's 2012 Richard McKaig Outstanding Doctoral Research Award for his dissertation, *Are They Truly Divine?: A Grounded Theory of the Influences of Black Greek-Lettered Organizations on the Persistence of African Americans at Predominantly White Institutions.* He also was awarded the Multicultural/Multiethnic Education Special Interest Group of the American Educational Research Association's 2014 Dr. Carlos J. Vallejo Memorial Award for Emerging Scholarship, the American College Personnel Association's Standing Committee for Men and Masculinities 2014 Outstanding Research Award (with Dr. Darris Means), and the Michigan College Personnel Association's 2013 John Zaugra Outstanding Research/Publication Award.

Mitchell is assistant professor of higher education at Grand Valley State University in Grand Rapids, Michigan. In addition, he currently serves as managing editor and editorial board member for the *Journal of African American Males in Education* and editorial board member for the *Journal of*

Diversity in Higher Education, the *Journal of Ethnographic & Qualitative Research,* and *Oracle: The Research Journal of the Association of Fraternity/Sorority Advisors.* He also is lead editor of *Intersectionality & Higher Education: Theory, Research, and Praxis* (with Charlana Simmons and Lindsay Greyerbiehl).

Mitchell earned a bachelor of science in chemistry from Shaw University, the first historically Black institution in the South; a master of science in educational leadership from Minnesota State University, Mankato; and a PhD in educational policy and administration with a concentration in higher education from the University of Minnesota–Twin Cities.

Krista M. Soria's PhD research interests primarily focus on the experiences of historically underrepresented and marginalized students in higher education, with an emphasis on first-generation and working-class students. She is also interested in exploring high-impact institutional practices to promote students' retention, academic achievement, sense of belonging, and development. Soria also investigates programmatic efforts to enhance college students' leadership development, civic responsibility, and engagement in social change.

Soria has a doctoral degree in educational policy and administration (higher education emphasis) from the University of Minnesota–Twin Cities; a master of education in adult education and a master of arts in English literature from the University of Alaska Anchorage; a master of science degree in academic advising from Kansas State University; and bachelor of arts degrees in English and psychology from Hamline University. She is currently pursuing a graduate certificate in multicultural teaching and learning at the University of Minnesota.

Soria has worked for more than a decade in higher education, serving as an admission advisor, TRiO education advisor, academic advisor, and adjunct faculty for the University of Minnesota, Hamline University, and the University of Alaska Anchorage. Soria currently works as a research analyst in institutional research and is an adjunct faculty with the leadership minor program at the University of Minnesota. She also serves as a publication reviewer for several higher education journals.

Elizabeth A. Daniele is a PhD student at Syracuse University. She is a fellow in the Department of Sociology and is also pursuing a certificate in the Program in Latin American and Caribbean Studies from Syracuse University's Maxwell School. Daniele's research interests include immigration and education. She is particularly interested in the movement of Mexican nationals throughout North America and in underrepresented minority populations who pursue postsecondary education.

Currently coediting *Gerontology: Changes, Challenges, and Solutions* (with Madonna Harrington Meyer), Daniele is also senior associate editor for *Annuals of the Next Generation*, a refereed journal published by the Center for African American Research and Policy. Daniele is president of the Sociology Graduate Student Association at Syracuse University and is a member of the Eastern Sociological Association.

Daniele holds a master's degree in higher education administration from University of Rochester's Warner School of Education, as well as a bachelor of arts degree in sociology from Smith College. She has professional experience as an academic advisor for two federally funded TRiO programs: the Ronald E. McNair Postbaccalaureate Achievement Program and Upward Bound, both of which serve low-income and first-generation college students. Daniele has co-presented multiple workshops regarding diversity in higher education, and although not a native speaker, she loves to hear and speak Spanish.

John A. Gipson's research explores student educational outcomes, diversity in higher education, and quantitative research methodology. He was awarded the National Academic Advising Association's 2014 Student Research Award for his thesis, *Understanding High-Achieving African American Students: A Quantitative Study at Grand Valley State University* and continued research, *A Comprehensive Investigation of High-Achieving African American Students*, partially funded by the National Association of Student Personnel Administrators (NASPA) Foundation. Gipson was also awarded the 2013 Outstanding Graduate Student Award from the Michigan Academic Advising Association and the 2013 Glenn A. Niemeyer Award for Outstanding Graduate Student by Grand Valley State University.

Gipson is recruitment specialist for the College of Health and Human Sciences at Purdue University in West Lafayette, Indiana. In addition, he serves on the advisory board of the newly established *College Student Affairs Leadership*, as associate editor of *Annuals of the Next Generation*, and as an ad hoc reviewer for the *Journal of Negro Education*. Previously, Gipson served as the national chair of the social and networking committee as well as the academic advising working group within NASPA's Student Affairs Partnering with Academic Affairs (SAPAA) Knowledge Community.

Gipson earned a bachelor of science in elementary education through the Lee Honors College at Western Michigan University and a master of education in higher education, emphasizing college student affairs leadership, from Grand Valley State University. He is currently pursuing a PhD in educational psychology with a specialization in quantitative research methods at Purdue University.

Author Biographies

Helen Alatorre is assistant dean of Students for Leadership at the University of Wyoming. She oversees student government and fraternity and sorority life efforts and collaborates on a wide range of leadership development initiatives on campus. She holds a BA in sociology from Cal State Fullerton and a MEd in counseling and personnel services from the University of Maryland. Previously, she worked at Loyola Marymount University as the director of Chicano Latino Student Services and as the associate director of Student Leadership and Development. Alatorre is a past chair for both the ACPA Latin@ Network and Standing Committee for Multicultural Affairs.

Ayana Allen, PhD is a postdoctoral fellow for the Urban Education Collaborative in the College of Education at the University of North Carolina at Charlotte. Her research focuses on urban education, postsecondary access and success for underrepresented students, and identity development within predominantly White educational contexts.

D. Jason DeSousa, EdD is assistant vice chancellor for student retention at Fayetteville State University. DeSousa has held positions such as vice president for enrollment management and student affairs, vice president for student affairs, and assistant vice president for academic affairs and university registrar. A past president of the National Association of Student Affairs Professionals

(NASAP), DeSousa served as one of 20 researchers on "Documenting Effective Educational Practices," which culminated in *Student Success in College: Creating Conditions that Matter*, of which he was an associate co-author. He has testified before the U.S. Senate's Health, Education, Labor, and Pensions Committee on innovation and best practices at minority serving institutions. DeSousa has been awarded nearly $2.5 million in external grants for student retention, collegiate men of color, and student leadership initiatives. He holds an EdD in higher education administration from Indiana University Bloomington, an MA in college student personnel from Bowling Green State University, and BS in sports administration from Morgan State University.

Mary J. Fischer, PhD is associate professor in the Department of Sociology at the University of Connecticut. Her research interests, broadly defined, concern processes of stratification, particularly by race and ethnicity, across diverse settings, including higher education and neighborhoods. She is co-author of *The Source of the River* and *Taming the River*, which focus on the background and experiences of students from different racial/ethnic groups as they navigate their college careers at 28 elite colleges and universities. Her current work examines how college finances, family support, and employment impact students' progression through school.

Marla A. Franco is a doctoral student and research assistant in the Department of Higher Education at Azusa Pacific University. She is also an assessment and research specialist for the Division of Student Affairs and Enrollment Management at the University of Arizona. She has 13 years of experience working in higher education, specializing in early academic outreach, academic support programs for underrepresented STEM majors, student leadership, and auxiliaries. Her research interests include examining contributors of success among Latino college students, as well as advocacy and policy implications for undocumented college students.

Jarrett T. Gupton, PhD is assistant professor of higher education at the University of Minnesota. He received his doctorate at the University of Southern California. His areas of scholarly interest are educational opportunity and equity. Much of his work focuses on low-income students and issues of access and equity in higher and postsecondary education. His scholarship highlights the ways in which social, cultural, and political structures constrain and enable educational equity and opportunity. His current research focuses on homeless students attending community college.

Frank Harris III, EdD is associate professor of postsecondary education and co-director of the Minority Male Community College Collaborative

(M2C3) at San Diego State University. His research is broadly focused on student development and student success in postsecondary education and explores questions related to the social construction of gender and race on college campuses, college men and masculinities, and racial/ethnic disparities in college student outcomes. He is currently engaged in a national study of productive masculinities and positive behaviors among college men. In his role as co-director of M2C3, he partners with community colleges across the United States to conduct research and design interventions to facilitate student achievement among men who have been historically marginalized in postsecondary education.

Angel C. Hernandez is director of California State University, Fullerton's TRiO Educational Talent Search Program, which is focused on assisting low-income and potential first-generation college students with preparing for college. He is also an adjunct counselor-instructor at Irvine Valley College. Hernandez has also worked at the University of Maryland as director of Student and Young Alumni Programs and Santiago Canyon College as outreach coordinator. Hernandez completed his bachelor's degree in sociology at California Polytechnic Pomona and his master's degree in college student personnel at the University of Maryland. He is involved in ACPA and currently serves as chair of ACPA's Latin@ Network.

Rashné Jehangir, PhD is associate professor in the Department of Post-Secondary Teaching and Learning in the College of Education and Human Development at the University of Minnesota–Twin Cities. Jehangir's research examines the experience of low-income, first-generation students in college. Her recent book, *Higher Education and First-Generation Students: Cultivating Community, Voice and Place for the New Majority*, focuses on how curricular and pedagogical interventions delivered in the first year impact students' longitudinal intrapersonal, interpersonal, and cognitive development. Two current research projects employ visual mediums, specifically photos and films shot with the iPad to explore how narrative pedagogy impacts students' learning and development outcomes in college.

Elizabeth A. John, EdD has been working in higher education for 13 years. She is director of First Year Experience at the University of Wisconsin–Whitewater and previously served as the assistant dean of students and director of student activities at Edgewood College. John received her EdD in educational leadership with an emphasis in higher education from Edgewood College and her MS in college student personnel from Western Illinois University. She has been actively involved with the American College Personnel Association

(ACPA) for many years and held several leadership positions within the Commission for Student Involvement, Multiracial Network, and the Mid-Level Community of Practice.

Young K. Kim, PhD is assistant professor in the Department of Higher Education at Azusa Pacific University. She received her PhD in higher education at the University of California, Los Angeles. Her research interests include college impact, college student development, conditional effects of college experience, and diversity and educational equity in higher education. Kim's work has been published in *Research in Higher Education*, the *Review of Higher Education*, the *Journal of Diversity in Higher Education*, the *Journal of the Professoriate*, *Journal of Excellence on College Teaching*, *Journal of Research on Christian Education*, and *Christian Higher Education*.

Georgianna L. Martin, PhD is assistant professor of higher education and student affairs administration at the University of Southern Mississippi. She is also the co-director of the Research Initiative on Social Justice in Education (RISE). Martin's research interests include the social class identity and college experiences for low-income students, the impact of college students' out-of-class experiences on learning outcomes, college student social responsibility, and social-political activism.

Melandie McGee is a doctoral student in higher education administration at the University of Southern Mississippi. McGee's research interests include college success for at-risk and underrepresented student populations, student activism at historically Black colleges and universities during the civil rights era, mentoring students of color, and student leadership and unethical hazing behavior among fraternities and sororities.

Robin Minthorn, PhD is an enrolled member of the Kiowa tribe of Oklahoma. She is assistant professor at the University of New Mexico in Educational Leadership and Native American Studies and teaches courses surrounding Indigenous leadership, leadership and organizations in educational settings, and conflict resolution. Her research interests include areas around Indigenous leadership in higher education, multigenerational leadership perspectives in tribal communities, and Native student participation in study abroad. Minthorn serves on the board of directors for the National Indian Education Association (NIEA), National Indian Youth Council (NIYC), and National Coalition for the Advancement of Natives in Higher Education (NCANHE).

Ricardo Montelongo, PhD is assistant professor of higher education administration at Sam Houston State University. He received his PhD in higher education from Indiana University. His research interests include educational outcomes associated with college student involvement, minority college student involvement, and factors influencing involvement in Latina/o college student organizations. He has 20 years' professional administrative experience in the areas of student success, undergraduate academic support, academic advising, Student Support Services/TRiO, institutional research, career development, and residence life. Montelongo is active in ACPA College Student Educators International and was co-chair of its Latin@ Network from 2011 to 2013.

Samuel D. Museus, PhD is associate professor of higher education at the University of Denver. His research agenda focuses on examining the factors that affect college access and persistence among underrepresented students in the K–16 pipeline. His current research is focused on the impact of campus environments on racial and ethnic minority college student access and success.

Mondrail Myrick is a doctoral student at Fayetteville State University, majoring in educational leadership. He has a master of arts in economics from Virginia State University, which includes coursework in statistics and mathematics. While attending graduate school, he served as a research assistant for Institutional Planning and Assessment at Johnson C. Smith University (JCSU) and has held research analyst positions at JCSU and Fayetteville State University. He has also held statistical, research, and technical consultant positions at other universities.

Amanda Suniti Niskode-Dossett, PhD has been actively involved as a leader with the American College Personnel Association's Multiracial Network and Standing Committee for Women, and served as the editor of *Developments*. Niskode-Dossett has presented and published on issues of gender and race, including a co-authored chapter in the monograph, *Biracial and Multiracial College Students: Theory, Research, and Best Practices in Student Affairs*. She earned her PhD in higher education from Indiana University and her MA in college student personnel from the University of Maryland. She currently works as a research associate for Imagining America's Undergraduate Civic Professionalism Collaboratory.

Angelica M. G. Palacios is a project associate with the Minority Male Community College Collaborative (M2C3). Palacios has worked in the field of education for the past seven years. Her work in education includes facilitating classroom discussions, research, consulting, and program assessment. Her recent research is focused on men of color and influencers of educational attainment among men. Currently, she is a doctoral student at San Diego State University, emphasizing community college leadership.

Joe Palencia is an advisor for the Student Support Services (SSS) TRiO program at Oakton Community College in Skokie, Illinois. He earned a MEd in higher education from Loyola University Chicago and a BA in communication and Latina/o studies from the University of Illinois at Urbana-Champaign. His current research interests include academic advising, the experiences of first-generation college students, and the retention of students of color, particular Latina/o students.

Ray Plaza, PhD is associate director in the Office of Multicultural Affairs at Bowling Green State University. He oversees retention, assessment and data management efforts, coordinates the annual Latino Issues Conference and Latino outreach efforts. He holds a BA in history and English and an MA in student personnel and counseling from the University of Florida. He is finishing his PhD in curriculum and instruction at Virginia Tech. Previously, he worked at Virginia Tech in Residence Life, Multicultural and Academic Affairs. Plaza is active in the ACPA Latin@ Network and the Commission on Global Dimensions in Student Development.

Robert D. Reason, PhD is professor of education in the Student Affairs and Higher Education programs at Iowa State University. He is also the director of Iowa State's Research Institute for Studies in Education (RISE). He studies how institutional policies, climates, and students' experiences interact to affect student learning. In collaboration with the Association of American Colleges and Universities (AAC&U), Reason currently directs the Personal and Social Responsibility Inventory (PSRI), which allows institutions to assess and improve students' civic learning.

Liz A. Rennick is a doctoral student and research–teaching assistant in the Department of Higher Education at Azusa Pacific University. Her research has been published in various academic journals and has been presented at the annual conferences for the Association for the Study of Higher Education and the American Educational Research Association. Her professional experience includes advising diverse student populations at several community colleges, most recently as interim director of student activities at MiraCosta College in Oceanside, California. Rennick holds an MEd in college student affairs from Azusa Pacific University and a BS in management information systems from Vanguard University.

Damaris Sanchez is the instructional support assistant for the associate dean and associate director in the Office of Academic Affairs at Columbia School of Social Work. She works alongside adjunct faculty and administrators to provide a supportive group system for the student body through academic advisement.

As well, she was an adjunct instructor at Baruch College to teach Freshmen Seminar. She received a bachelor of science in childhood/special education at NYU and graduated with a master of arts in higher and postsecondary education at Teachers College, Columbia University. As a first-generation, low-income, former HEOP student coming from a Puerto Rican single-parent household, she is motivated to offer guidance to a diverse population of students and staff. Sanchez is the historian-newsletter writer for ACPA Latin@ Network.

Stephen Santa-Ramirez is assistant director of multicultural affairs at the University of Texas at Arlington. He received his bachelor's degree in communication studies from West Chester University of Pennsylvania, and a master's in student affairs administration from Michigan State University. Over the last several years Santa-Ramirez has gained a strong interest in Latino/a student identity development and has been an active social justice advocate. He has also worked in Residential Education and Migrant Student Services.

Deronta Spencer is a doctoral student at the University of Connecticut. His research interests are race and education. His MA thesis focused on differences in parental involvement during college preparation between first- and non-first-generation students. His current work examines factors that affect the progression of students, particularly racial and ethnic minorities, through the education system.

Jennifer Trost is a doctoral candidate in organizational leadership, policy, and development at the University of Minnesota–Twin Cities. She works as a research analyst with the Minnesota Office of Higher Education. Her areas of research and professional interests are college readiness, access and equity in higher education, and K–12 to higher education transitions and partnerships. Trost's dissertation examines the opportunities for students of color to participate in dual enrollment programs that lead to acquisition of a baccalaureate degree.

J. Luke Wood, PhD is associate professor of community college leadership and director of the Doctoral Program Concentration in Community College Leadership at San Diego State University. Wood is also co-director of the Minority Male Community College Collaborative, chair of the Multicultural & Multiethnic Education special interest group of the American Educational Research Association, chair-elect for the Council on Ethnic Participation for the Association for the Study of Higher Education, and director of the Center for African American Research and Policy. He is also the founding editor of the *Journal of African American Males in Education*. Wood's research focuses on factors affecting the success of Black (and other minority) male students in the community college. In particular, his research examines contributors (e.g., social, psychological, academic, environmental, institutional) to positive outcomes (e.g., persistence, achievement, attainment, transfer, labor market outcomes) for these men. Wood has authored more than 80 publications, including 5 co-authored books, 5 edited books, and 40 peer-reviewed journal articles.

Varaxy Yi is a higher education doctoral student at the University of Denver. She is dedicated to research involving underrepresented communities and their educational attainment, aspirations, and experiences. Specifically, she is interested in the experiences of Southeast Asian American students as they navigate the postsecondary education system and factors that affect access, persistence, and degree completion for these communities. In addition, she is interested in examining factors affecting graduate students' experiences as they navigate the complexities of academic, personal, and professional life. Yi is also a 2003 Gates Millennium Scholar.

A BOOK SERIES FOR EQUITY SCHOLARS & ACTIVISTS

Virginia Stead, H.B.A., B.Ed., M.Ed., Ed.D., *General Editor*

Globalization increasingly challenges higher education researchers, administrators, faculty members, and graduate students to address urgent and complex issues of equitable policy design and implementation. This book series provides an inclusive platform for discourse about—though not limited to—diversity, social justice, administrative accountability, faculty accreditation, student recruitment, admissions, curriculum, pedagogy, online teaching and learning, completion rates, program evaluation, cross-cultural relationship-building, and community leadership at all levels of society. Ten broad themes lay the foundation for this series but potential editors and authors are invited to develop proposals that will broaden and deepen its power to transform higher education:

(1) Theoretical books that examine higher education policy implementation,
(2) Activist books that explore equity, diversity, and indigenous initiatives,
(3) Community-focused books that explore partnerships in higher education,
(4) Technological books that examine online programs in higher education,
(5) Financial books that focus on the economic challenges of higher education,
(6) Comparative books that contrast national perspectives on a common theme,
(7) Sector-specific books that examine higher education in the professions,
(8) Educator books that explore higher education curriculum and pedagogy,
(9) Implementation books for front line higher education administrators, and
(10) Historical books that trace changes in higher education theory, policy, and praxis.

Expressions of interest for authored or edited books will be considered on a first come basis. A Book Proposal Guideline is available on request. For individual or group inquiries please contact:

Dr. Virginia Stead, General Editor | *virginia.stead@alum.utoronto.ca*
Christopher S. Myers, Acquisitions Editor | *chrism@plang.com*

To order other books in this series, please contact our Customer Service Department at:

(800) 770-LANG (within the U.S.)
(212) 647-7706 (outside the U.S.)
(212) 647-7707 FAX

Or browse online by series at www.peterlang.com